THE BEST PUBS F(

THANK YOU

I am indebted to the many CAMRA members all over the country who suggested and vetted pubs for inclusion in this guide, as well as to staff at CAMRA HQ for their backup, and fellow Alma authors who let me trawl their regional guide manuscripts for any hidden gems. Thanks are also due to my husband without whose help and support this guide would never have been completed, and to my children without whom I might never have had the inclination to start.

THE BEST PUBS FOR Families

Jill Adam

Foreword by Nick Ross

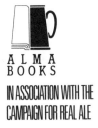

ALMA BOOKS

IN ASSOCIATION WITH THE
CAMPAIGN FOR REAL ALE

Author: **Jill Adam**

Design: **Opus**

*Cover photograph of Publican Schweppes Family Pub
of the Year, the Green Man at Brackley Hatch,
Northants:* **Roger Protz**

Cartography by: **Perrott Cartographics**

Typeset and printed by: **Cambridge University Press**

ISBN 1–85249–103–5

Published by **Alma Books Ltd.,** *a wholly-owned susidiary
of the Campaign for Real Ale Ltd., 34 Alma Road, St Albans,
Herts.*

© *Jill Adam/Alma Books Ltd* 1989/90

CONTENTS

PAGE

9 Introduction

17 England: County Listings

62 In-Car Entertainment

133 Pub Grub for Kids

217 Scotland

231 Wales

257 Maps

FOREWORD

I am no expert on pubs, but I have become quite expert at having children. It's been relatively easy – until I try to take them out to lunch. Is it that we British just don't like children very much? Or is it that we just make lousy entrepreneurs?

At any rate, precious few pubs are family affairs and only recently is a growing band of publicans responding to the opportunity. By catering for drinkers *en famille* pubs can tap a whole new source of revenue. And even at their worst, children are less troublesome than lager louts.

Some notes that might be useful to publicans thinking of running real public houses rather than drinking dens:

1. You are allowed to let children into the bar as long as you serve meals, but remember children come in all sizes from 0 to 18.

2. If space allows, set aside a room without a bar for families. Make sure it is comfortably furnished and provide a few simple amusements for children of all ages.

3. Be prepared, and ensure your staff are willing, to heat babies' bottles (about 50 seconds in a 650W microwave, but test the milk isn't hot on the back of your hand).

4. Provide somewhere to change a baby's nappy (and if you've never changed one ask someone who has: you need a flat, clean baby-size surface, ideally with a basin and paper towels nearby and a container for soiled nappies). Incidentally, some men have babies too – be *avant garde* and have baby-changing space in the gents as well.

5. While on the subject: for children of all ages your loo areas should be sparkling and hygienic, not the shameful bogs that are the norm in British boozers.

6. In the bar or restaurant have a few high chairs and keep them spotless, and buy some plastic booster seats – almost unheard of in this child-hating nation but ubiquitous in the USA.

7. Keep a few plastic plates, bowls and spoons for toddlers, and a good supply of paper napkins.

8. Remember under-five's eat almost nothing and rather than waste money parents will be tempted to give them titbits from their own meals. So have a toddler's menu (mini-portions) as well as one for older kids.

9. Have a range of non-alcoholic drinks for youngsters including milk, juices and proper ice-cream milkshakes, and …

10. …keep an enticing and profitable range of alcohol-free drinks for grown-ups too. Above all, dissuade drivers from drinking any for the road, or they're likely to kill their kids or someone else's. Dead customers are bad for business.

If you, like me, are sometimes looking for a pleasant pub where you can take the kids, please for all our sakes be terribly un-British and complain when there are no facilities for children or where the service is mediocre. Or cut the chances of having to complain by reading on…

Nick Ross is a broadcaster, real ale tippler, and father of three, under five.

INTRODUCTION

Just a few weeks before this guide went to press I managed to escape with my husband for a weekend on our own to the Cotswolds. The two greatest pleasures of that short trip were to be able to travel light, unencumbered by changing bags, toy bags and all the clobber that accompanies children on even a day's outing; the other was to visit some terrific pubs that normally, with the boys in tow, we would only be able to peer into and wistfully pass by.

It is still, unfortunately, rare to find decent pubs that willingly open their doors to families and provide proper amenities to make their visit comfortable and enjoyable. I am delighted that for this book, CAMRA members nationwide have come up with over 450 suitable hostelries, 200 more than the first edition. Even so, this is still a tiny proportion of the nation's public houses. My fellow Alma author, Susan Nowak, had a difficult task selecting entries for her "Good Pub Food" guide from the many hundreds recommended to her. I was in no such happy position.

Breweries and licensees still refuse to see families as a priority. I am all for pubs providing good wholesome food, but I do dislike them then being categorised as food pubs, as much as I would dislike the pubs in this guide to be shunned by the public at large as "kid's pubs". A pub is a pub. It exists to serve the whole community. Family pubs should not be in a minority and there should be no need for a guide such as this.

The pubs listed here really are, in our opinion, the best there is. It is true that a major criterion for selection is that they must serve real ale, in good condition, so that discounts quite a few possible entries. However we have not restricted ourselves to include only pubs with legal family rooms (ie a separate room without a bar) as this would be a slim volume indeed. In any case, the mere presence of a so-called family room does not necessarily indicate that families are welcome, but often just tolerated.

The pubs on offer here are all different. They all have their own individual character and appeal and by no means do they all offer the same level of amenities. The best really are superb, catering for customers from 0–100, the able and the less able-bodied. All the licensees here genuinely welcome families and do all they can to make their visit enjoyable. Only a few have all the requirements suggested by Nick Ross in our foreword, although most would like to be able to.

Many older pubs have problems inherent in their structure that make it impossible to provide indoor facilities (apart from mealtimes). Tiny single-bar pubs cannot provide a separate room without major renovation, but this does not prevent the licensees from providing terrific outdoor play areas, barbecues, etc. It is heartening to see that where old pubs are given a facelift these days, most are now giving thought to the needs of families at the planning stage.

Other pubs may set a room aside and make it comfortable for families to eat and drink, but not provide any amusements. This is a shame, but some publicans have told me that either they do not want to disturb other customers or that toys get broken too easily. If the family room is separate then the disturbance to customers is likely to be minimal, and in my experience of playgroups, toddler toys are not that fragile (especially the more robust makes, such as Fisher Price). In any case parents do not expect pubs to be like the Early Learning Centre, but a few simple amusements (even just pads of scrap paper and pens or crayons) show that a little extra effort has been made to cater for youngsters. The pubs listed here that do provide properly equipped rooms with toys and (brilliant idea) blackboard walls all get full marks.

One thing that all but a few enlightened publicans tend to forget is that we all started out the same – as babes in arms .... and in nappies. If small children are looked at askance in pubs, then babies are regarded with absolute horror. Several of the pubs listed here offer proper feeding/changing facilities (and a couple even offer free nappies), but this is still very unusual. However, if you need to breastfeed your baby, do ask bar staff as many will sympathetically find a suitable quiet corner; most pubs also have microwaves these days and it does not take much effort to pop a feeding bottle in, so again ask if it can be done.

As has been shown by Susan Nowak's experience, many pubs are now food-oriented. We also list in this guide pubs that have few amenities for families other than meals. These are mostly in big cities or popular tourist spots. In such places, pubs are generally very busy and do not want to make too much extra effort to attract families. Even so, many do provide children's portions, highchairs etc., so that families may eat in comfort. Personally, if I'm in a strange town at mealtimes with my children I would far rather go to a pub for good, wholesome food, than the dreaded burger bar. In any case, as Susan points out in her feature on page 133, if children want junk food the chances are the pub will oblige anyway, in which case we are all satisfied.

Whatever facilities the pubs in this guide offer, they are, I hope, listed accurately. It is quite clear whether a family room is available or not, and if there are any restrictions on the times when children are welcome. I would be pleased to hear of any discrepancies, or recommendations. A form for this purpose appears on page 269.

The licensees that wrote to me when I was compiling this guide often stated that "well-behaved children" are welcome (or in some cases children accompanied by well-behaved adults!). Some publicans refuse to admit children because they have had bad experiences in the past, or they truly believe that they cause too much discomfort to their other customers. This should not be the case. While we obviously want to go to the pub to have a drink and relax, the onus is on us as parents (for which read always guardian or other responsible adult too) to make sure that our children cause no more nuisance than they would in any other public place. One landlady (who happily still admits children) complained that a little girl caused £250 worth of damage to an antique longcase clock by swinging on the pendulum. When this was pointed out to her mother, she replied that she was "only playing hickory dickory dock'!

It makes sense that if children have been cooped up in a car for a long journey they will not want to go straight indoors and be told to sit still and be quiet. If the pub has a garden, allow them to let off steam a little first, then everyone will be more relaxed.

It is time that the British got used to the idea that children are people too, that they have their place in society (and in that epitome of British society, the pub). On the continent children are brought up to think of going out to bars and restaurants as part of the way of life, and are expected to and indeed, for the most part do, behave in a civilised fashion. Our children are no different, it is just attitudes that need to be changed.

HOW TO USE THIS GUIDE

Pub listings are arranged alphabetically by county in England and Wales (note that South, Mid and West Glamorgan are listed under the single heading of Glamorgan) and by region in Scotland. Greater London appears under L and Greater Manchester under M. The practical details for each pub are given in the left-hand column and symbols used to give the following information:

This symbol only appears where there is a separate family room without a bar. In other cases, children are often allowed into a bar area for meals, but details are given in individual descriptions.

A garden or where specified, other outdoor area for drinking. A play area is not provided unless specified in the description.

Food is available as specified. This always means full, adult meals. Pubs without the symbol often offer snacks. Details of children's menus/portions where applicable are given in the description. Prices, which were correct as we went to press, are given only as a guide.

Overnight accommodation is available. This has not been surveyed for the guide, nor are prices given. If family accommodation and/or cots are available, this is mentioned in the text.

Frequent live entertainment – normally live music but occasionally children's entertainers.

Only real ales are listed. For full details of beers and breweries, consult the "Good Beer Guide" or "Real Ale Almanack" by Roger Protz, both available from CAMRA.

WHAT IS REAL ALE?

The pubs listed here all serve real ale. Real ale is a definition accepted by the Concise Oxford Dictionary. It is also known as traditional draught beer or cask-conditioned beer. Real ale is brewed from malted barley, using pure water and hops and fermented by top-fermenting yeast. At the end of fermentation the beer is allowed to condition for a few days and is then racked into casks, often with the addition of priming sugar and a handful of dry hops for aroma. The beer then continues to "work" or ferment in the cask while a clearing agent called finings drags the yeasty deposits to the floor of the cask. The beer is neither filtered nor pasteurised and must not be served by any method using applied gas pressure.

Real ale can be served straight from the cask and many country pubs still use this method, while some special winter brews in town pubs are often dispensed from a cask on the bar. But most real ale is drawn – hence the word "draught" – by a suction pump from the pub cellar. The pump is operated either by a handpump, a tall lever on the bar, or by an electric pump. Electric pumps are rare in the south of England but are used widely in the Midlands and the North.

Real ale should be served at a temperature of 55–56 degrees F (12–13 degrees C). This is a cool temperature that brings out the best characteristics of a top-fermented beer. It is a higher temperature than those used for serving lager beers, but it is pure mythology that real is "warm".

PUB HOURS

In August 1988 the British Government made long-overdue changes to pub licensing laws, which had been severely restricted since the First World War. Pubs can now open Monday to Saturday from 11 am until 11 pm, but individual licensees can choose which hours they wish to open, to suit their trade. Sunday hours have only been slightly extended: the standard opening times are 12 noon to 3 pm and 7 pm to 10.30 pm. A year after the new law came into effect, when this guide was being compiled, publicans were still in the process of working out opening hours. Some have tried all day opening and found it not to be worthwhile, while others have instituted flexible afternoon closing (ie if the pub is full they stay open).

A surprisingly large number have stuck more or less to the traditional hours (old habits die hard), but many, particularly in tourist areas, at least stay open all day in the summer. The opening hours given in the pub listings were correct as we went to press. Licensees are however, at liberty to change their hours without notice. Some post their opening hours outside the pub, a practice which all should follow. It is frustrating waiting outside locked doors not knowing if the place will open at 5.30 or 6, even worse with impatient young children in tow.

Where there are restrictions on the times children are allowed into the pub, these have been given, although the majority of licensees make no restrictions at all. Many do say, however, that even though they make no official limits, they rather expect that children would be away to their beds long before evening closing time.

CHILDREN AND THE LAW

Now that the laws concerning opening hours have been revised it is about time something was done about the laws relating to children in pubs, which are confusing and unsatisfactory to say the least. Even many publicans do not strictly know what the law is, and many are so afraid of losing their licenses by serving under-age drinkers, that they react by banning children altogether from their premises. I am sure that liberalisation of these laws would have a favourable knock-on effect regarding publican's attitudes to allowing families into their pubs. In small out of the way villages and country inns where the law denying children access to bars seems to be particularly ludicrous, licensees often openly flaunt the existing regulations, by turning a blind eye to the presence of families in the pub.

In any case, for the moment the actual law is as follows. You cannot drink alcohol in a pub below the age of 18 years (although at 16, children accompanied by an adult may drink beer, wine or cider with a meal). You can go into a pub at 14 but you can only drink non-alcoholic products. Children of all ages can go into pubs that have a room, without a bar, set aside as a family room. Where a pub has a separate restaurant children are allowed in to eat with their parents, unless specified otherwise; in cases where food is only served in the bars, it is indicated in the description in the guide whether children may eat there. Children are allowed into any garden attached to a pub, but if the only access is via a bar, then parents are advised to ask staff for permission to take children through.

By the way, in case you thought you would try your toddler on a little tipple of Guinness, it is an offence for any child under five to be given any alcohol except in a medical emergency or on the advice of a doctor.

COMPTON MARTIN
Ring o' Bells

Tel. (0761) 221284
On A369 Bath-Weston-super
Mare road at the village centre
Open 11.30–2.30; 7–11

✗ lunchtime and evening

🍺 **Butcombe Bitter; Wadworth 6X; guest beer**

A complete pub in every way, the Ring o'Bells has a regulars' bar, snug, cosy, quiet lounge and a separate family room. Two hundred years-old, this free house is in a lovely setting, with the Mendip Hills forming a backdrop to the large garden. Nearby are Chew Valley Lake, popular for fishing, sailing and birdwatching and Blagdon Lake. The licensees do not treat children as second-class customers. The well-appointed family room has table skittles, a rocking horse and other toys, as well as highchairs. A children's menu is offered with prices starting at 95 pence. Outdoors youngsters can play in a former orchard, next to the car park, where there are swings and a slide.

CONGRESBURY
White Hart

Tel. (0934) 833303
Wrington Road (one mile east of
A370, Bristol-Weston-super-
Mare road)
Open 11.30–3; 6–11

✗ lunchtime and evening

🍺 **Adnams Broadside; Butcombe Bitter; Hall & Woodhouse Tanglefoot; Wadworth 6X**

This pretty pub is set in very large grounds, opposite a working farm and next door to a riding centre. It has a quiet, cosy beamed bar, warmed by real fires with a real "lived in" atmosphere. The family area is a large hexagonal conservatory where amusements include books, toys, ten-pence rides and sweet machines. The conservatory leads out into a huge garden which is home to guinea pigs and various birds in an aviary; climbing frames, a trampoline, swings and a slide are also provided. Weekend barbecues are held in fine weather, otherwise children may choose small portions from adult dishes, or from their own special menu. A highchair is available.

DUNDRY
Winford Arms

Tel. (0272) 392178
Bridgwater Road (A38 out of Bristol)
Open 11–2.30 ; 5 (7 Sat) - 11

☺

🏧

✘ lunchtime and evening

🍺 **Courage Best Bitter, Directors; John Smith Bitter**

A rural pub that is within easy reach of Bristol and Bristol Airport, the Winford Arms commands excellent views of the surrounding countryside and is also close to Cheddar Gorge. It has an authentic beamed lounge and a spacious family room with a selection of playthings, and toilets close at hand (although no facilities for babies are available). This room leads on to the garden where there are swings, a slide and roundabout. The usual children's pub fare of beefburgers, fishfingers, beans and chips is offered for around £1.50 a meal.

KINGSWOOD, BRISTOL
Highwayman

Tel. (0272) 671613
Hill Street (A420, half a mile east of Kingswood Shopping Centre)
Open 11–3.30 ; 7–11

☺

🏧

✘ lunchtime and evening

🍺 **Halls Harvest Bitter; Ind Coope Burton Ale**

Situated on the outskirts of Bristol, this pre-war traditional pub has a modern, but pleasant interior with a single, central bar, which seems to attract all age groups. Families are welcome in an enclosed patio area which has a perspex roof with two vines growing beneath it. Here there is seating for some 30 people and children can amuse themselves with the two video games and "Bambi" ride; there is also a two-pence fruit machine which should not break the bank for apprentice gamblers. Outdoors a floodlit skittle alley is available for hire for families and friends; as well as the more usual play equipment: slides, swings, seesaw and an enchanted tree. A tasty menu of English and foreign dishes is available at both sessions – small portions are available for young appetites or a choice from the children's menu. Highchairs are provided.

LONG ASHTON
Smythe Arms

Tel. (0272) 342245
Off A370 from Bristol
Open 11–2.30 (4.30 Sat) ; 6–11

☺

🏧

✘ lunchtime

🍺 **Courage Best Bitter, Directors**

The landlord of the Smythe Arms has won the Courage award for good cellarmanship, so you will be assured of a good pint, as well as a very reasonably priced lunch. It is a roomy, split-level pub which has been modernised to give a traditional feel, with new wooden beams and electric "gas" lamps, but it has a good atmosphere. Children are always welcome in the large, octagonal family room where there is a soft drinks bar. The garden, directly accessible from the family room, has a slide and climbing frames, one of which is designed as an adventure playground. The pub has changing/feeding facilities for babies (but no highchairs). Hungry youngsters may pick small portions of main dishes or something from their own menu.

NAILSEA
Blue Flame Inn

Tel. (0272) 856910
West End (on the moors between Nailsea and Clevedon

🍺 Draught Bass; Smiles Best Bitter, Exhibition, Bulmer Traditional Cider

This traditional free house is somewhat buried in the countryside: from Bristol take the A370, turn right through Chelvey, then left at the T-junction. You will then be rewarded by its pleasant rural setting and cosy atmosphere. The pub does not offer meals as such, but snacks, ranging from 80 pence to £2 are available at anytime. The cheery family room has a selection of books and toys, including board games for when you get caught out on a rainy day. In fine weather, children can enjoy the play equipment provided in the large garden.

TORMARTON
Compass Inn

Tel. (045 421) 242/577
Off A46 near Badminton
Open 11–11

✗ all day

🍺 Archers Village Bitter; Draught Bass; Wadworth 6X

Ideally situated for exploring the Cotswolds, this traditional stone inn offers many modern amenities without spoiling its special character. No particular room is set aside for families, but children are welcome in all four eating areas at any time the pub is open. There is a restaurant, but bar snacks are also available at most times with plenty of tasty things that appeal to young appetites; highchairs are provided. In the garden, families like to use the orangery or the tables out in the open. Overnight facilities include cots and breakfast.

WESTBURY-ON-TRYM
Prince of Wales

Tel. (0272) 623715
84 Stoke Lane (half a mile from
Westbury village roundabout)
Open 11–3; 6–11 (11–11 Sat)

Ⓟ

🅱

✗ 12–2

🍺 **Courage Bitter Ale, Best Bitter,**
Directors; John Smith Bitter

A delightful single-bar pub in a residential area, close to Bristol. An adjoining cottage has been tastefully converted to make a cosy, split-level, pine-clad family room. Care has been taken with the provision of toys and games; there is even a small library of children's books. This room can be hired for birthday parties and other occasions. The garden has a slide and climbing frame. Lunches are served daily, for around £2, but smaller portions are available for children. Visitors to the area may be interested to know that Blaise Castle grounds and the Rural Urban Life Museum at Henbury are both nearby.

© T. Bevan '88.

Blue Flame, Nailsea

WESTON-SUPER-MARE
Major From Glengarry

Tel. (0934) 29594
*Upper Church Road (half a mile
north of Britannia Pier, opp.
Knightstone Pier)*
Open 11.30–3; 6–11

⊚

🛏

✕

⚗ **Adnams Bitter; Butcombe
Bitter; Draught Bass;
Wadworth 6X, Farmers Glory;
Old Timer**

In this split-level, open-plan pub, the children's area has been cleverly incorporated into an area without a bar. The whole pub is large and comfortable; meals are served every day, including a Sunday roast. Children can choose from their own menu – their meals cost just £1.25. The roomy family area has a play space with a selection of toys and a tropical fish tank which always seems to be an endless source of fascination for young children. There is also some play equipment outside on the enclosed patio.

WORLE
Nut Tree

Tel. (0934) 510900
*Ebdon Road (off A370, three miles
north-east of Weston-Super-
Mare)*
*Open 11–2.30; 6–11 (11–11 Fri &
Sat)*

⊚

🛏

✕ lunchtime and evening

🍺

⚗ **Brain SA; Wadworth 6x;
Younger Scotch, IPA**

It seemed apt that the nursery rhyme of the same name kept going round my head as I wrote the entry for this pub as children are certainly well catered for here. This very old Somerset stone farmhouse is now a friendly Buccaneer Inn with a spacious open-plan layout. It offers unusual beers for the area and home-cooked meals including a carvery. Another notable feature is the large boules court. The family room seats 20 and is easily accessible from the bar. Amenities here include a toybox, blackboard and television. Special children's toilets have low doors, sinks and urinals. Small appetites are catered for by a special menu or portions of main dishes; prices from 95 pence. Outside there is an open patio.

BLETSOE
Falcon

Tel. (0234) 781222
*Rushden Road (A6 five miles
north of Bedford)
Open 11–3; 5.30–11*

✗ lunchtime and evening (not
Sun/Mon eve)

🍺 **Wells Eagle Bitter,
Bombardier**

This extensive seventeenth-century coaching inn lies on the bank of the river Ouse and possesses fishing rights. The proximity of the river means that children need to be supervised in the garden, but this does offer good equipment, including a garden room and a wendy house. Indoors there is a public bar with skittles and a smarter lounge where guests for the fairly pricey restaurant can enjoy an aperitif. For families, the cosy room between the bar and restaurant can hold around 20 people and here less expensive bar snacks can be eaten. A children's menu is available as are highchairs and baby feeding/changing facilities. Edward Fitzgerald, translator of the Rubaiyat of the Omar Khayyam, stayed here in 1833, and the pub is also steeped in the history of the St John family who resided at Bletsoe Castle and which is connected to the pub by a secret tunnel.

BROOM
Cock

Tel. (0767) 314411
*23 High Street (just off B658)
Open 12–2.30; 6–11*

✗ lunchtime and evening (not
Sun eve)

🍺 **Greene King IPA, Abbot Ale**

An old-style village local where beer is dispensed direct from the cellar. No particular room is set aside for families, but there are three bar-less rooms off a central corridor and so parents with children can choose which they like. One has a skittles table, the other two are rather delightful snugs. The enclosed garden has a pets corner. Another rather appealing feature is Miss Mouse's Kitchen, so named because the licensees specialise in cheese dishes. Here you do not just order a cheese salad, but salad with a choice of any of thirteen different cheeses, ranging from good old Cheddar, to Port Salut or Jarlsberg. Local places of interest include the Shuttleworth collection (aircraft and transport museum), Swiss Gardens and Southill Cricket Ground – all within two miles.

CLOPHILL
Stone Jug

Tel. (0525) 60526
10 Back Street (off A6, second right after Clophill roundabout, northbound)
Open 11–2.30 (3 Sat); 6–11

◎

🛏

✗ lunchtime

🍺 **Banks & Taylor Shefford Bitter; Courage Directors; John Smith Bitter; guest beer**

DEADMANS CROSS
White Horse

Tel. (023 066) 634
On A600 near Haynes, between Shefford and Bedford
Open 12–2.30; 6.30–11

◎

🛏

✗ lunchtime and evening (not Mon eve)

🍺 **Banks & Taylor Shefford Bitter, SOS, SOD**

HOUGHTON REGIS
Chequers

Tel. (0582) 865970
East End North
Open 11–11

◎

🛏

✗ lunchtime and Thu - Sat evenings

🍺 **Flowers Original Bitter; Wethered Bitter**

Situated in a back street, halfway along the "Greensand Ridge" walk, this small, popular free house is handy for Woburn Safari Park and Whipsnade Zoo. It has a single, sectioned bar where darts, dominoes and crib are played. The small family room has a stock of children's books and leads on to the patio. Baby changing/feeding facilities are provided and children's portions can be ordered from the lunchtime menu, which mainly consists of substantial snacks. The family room is occasionally booked, so it is worth checking in advance if making a special trip.

Built in 1732, this historic pub stands on the road to the Cardington home of Airship Industries who offer pleasure rides in airships throughout the summer – at a price. If your holiday budget won't stretch that far, the children will probably be just as pleased with a trip to the nearby Shuttleworth Collection, where over 30 aircraft are on display, or maybe just a ramble in the Chicksands woods. The pub has a restaurant (open Tuesday to Saturday), but bar meals are also served – children's meals can be provided on request. There is a cosy family room away from the bar, with easy access to the garden which is large enough to accommodate games of football and some swings. Barbecues are held in the summer. Ask the landlady for nursing/nappy changing facilities.

This large, community pub sets out to cater for the whole family, but children seem to be particularly favoured customers. The family room has a large, colourful playhouse with slide, tables with Lego and Duplo, a television and children's toilets. Their own set menu (the inevitable fish fingers, burgers or sausage and chips, a glass of squash and an ice cream) costs £1.50. Outside, the safe garden has an adventure playground with climbing frames, slides, swings and a rope ladder. What more could the little dears ask for!

LEIGHTON BUZZARD
Clay Pipe

Tel. (0525) 384387
Appenine Way, Clipstone (off Hockcliffe Road)
Open 11–3; 6–11

◎

🏠

🍺 Tetley Bitter

A friendly, welcoming pub on an estate on the outskirts of Leighton Buzzard. The comfortable family room is furnished in the same fashion as the pub's lounge, so feels very much part of the atmosphere. CD music is played in here, as in the rest of the pub, and there is a television. There is space to change babies in the ladies' toilet and a highchair is provided. No meals are served, but lunchtime snacks are available. Outside is a pleasant garden, and, on the other side of the car park a children's play area with swings. Leighton Buzzard has a popular narrow gauge railway which departs from Pages Park on a round-trip of over five miles. It is open every Sunday from Easter until the end of September, more often during the school summer holidays.

LUTON
Barn Owl

Tel. (0582) 29532
Leyhill Drive, Farley Hill (follow A5 towards Dunstable, turn right into Caddington, pub is two miles on)
Open 11–11 (11–5; 7–11 Sat)

◎

🏠

✗ lunchtime and evening

🍺 Flowers Original Bitter;
   Wethered Bitter

Another Whitbread pub where children are considered important customers, and the beer is reasonable too. Here the family room is a spacious, split-level conservatory at the side of the pub where amusements again include Lego, video games and a television. Children's toilets are provided and baby facilities due to be installed. The children's menu is exactly as at the Chequers above, but costs 25 pence more; highchairs are available. The conservatory opens on to a large, well-equipped garden with benches and plenty of toys. An added feature is the tuckshop selling drinks, crisps and ice-creams. Whipsnade Zoo is just ten minutes' drive away.

RISELEY
Fox & Hounds

Tel. (0234) 708240
High Street
Open 11–2.30; 6–11

@

🍴

✖ lunchtime and evening (not Sun eve)

🍺 **Wells Eagle Bitter, Bombardier**

Good rural footpaths run near this pub, so it is popular with walkers. Those that have really built up an appetite can try the unusual grill room which is a pick-your-own-steak operation – they come as big as you want! Those with smaller appetites may prefer to stick with the bar snacks and meals (very small appetites are also catered for). Children are welcome at any time in either the restaurant or the small family room which is decorated with appealing murals. There is a massive lawned garden at the rear of the pub with a slide, balls and other play equipment (including the licensees' son's own toys). This is an impressive sixteenth-century pub in a picturesque village.

STAGSDEN
Royal George

Tel. (023 02) 2801
High Street (A422)
Open 11–2.30; 6(7 winter)-11

🍴

✖ lunchtime Tue-Sat; evenings Thu-Fri

🍺 **Wells Eagle Bitter**

This really is a fairweather pub, but its garden makes it too good to leave out – in any case there is a "Kids' Kabin" in the garden if it should rain. It is a friendly place which offers good pub fare (including a children's menu) at reasonable prices. Ale is brought through to the lounge from the bar. The garden is completely enclosed – to keep in the chickens, goats and rabbits as much as the children. There are swings, slides and a tractor to play on and one very special feature, pony rides. If you can drag the offspring away, Stagsden Bird Gardens nearby is worth a visit.

BRACKNELL
Crown Wood

Tel. (0344) 489976
Opladen Way, Crown Wood (east of A322)
Open 11–11

@

⊛

✗ lunchtime Mon-Fri

⚑

⚐ **Marston Pedigree; Wethered Bitter**

A pub serving a housing estate that is definitely a notch or two above average. The Crown Wood is always very busy, especially with young people – and even very young people, as the family facilities here are excellent. The separate family room has plenty of toys and on Sunday lunchtimes performers come to entertain the children, it may be clowns one week and Punch and Judy the next. The garden has plenty of seating for mums and dads and there is an enclosed play area with safe, modern equipment. Lunches are served on weekdays (no particular provision for youngsters), and snacks (eg filled rolls) are available most other times.

CHARVIL
Lands End

Tel. (0734) 340700
Lands End Lane (One mile from A4, off A3032)
Open 11–2.30; 6–11

@

⊛

✗ lunchtime Mon-Sat

⚐ **Brakspear Bitter, Special, Old**

A busy, popular and friendly rural pub set among narrow lanes, by a ford. Indoors the family facilities are limited as the room is very small. Outdoors however, is a very large garden with slides, swings, climbing blocks and a "Herbie" tree. Children need supervision here because of the proximity of the river. Food – substantial snacks and salads – is available only at lunchtime.

ETON
Watermans
Arms

Tel. (0753) 861001
Brocas Street (in back streets, near Windsor Bridge)
Open 11–3; 6–11 (11–11 Sat)

@

⊛

✗ lunchtime and evening (not Sun eve)

⚐ **Courage Best Bitter, Directors; John Smith Bitter**

Not the easiest pub to find, this smart back street local is just a few steps from the river Thames; Windsor Castle is on the opposite bank. It has a single, largely unspoilt bar, where darts and shove ha'penny are played. A vine-clad conservatory acts as the family room and leads into the old courtyard which has been transformed into a paved garden area. Seating and a barbecue area are covered by a tiled roof. Meals are served at both sessions (except Sunday) until nine o'clock; children's portions are available on request.

LITTLEWICK GREEN
Seven Stars

Tel. (062882) 2967
Bath Road, Knowl Hill (on A4 between Maidenhead and Reading)
Open 11–11 (children welcome until 9 pm)

◎

🍴

✗ lunchtime and evening

🛏

🍺 **Brakspear Mild, Bitter, Special, Old**

Visitors to this smart, popular sixteenth-century coaching inn are always assured of a warm welcome – particularly in winter when blazing fires beckon. There is a large comfortable bar with a fairly basic but comfortable room off it for families to use so they do not feel ostracised from the rest of the pub. Pub games include petanque and a skittle alley. An attractive garden features a tree house and swings for children. Local tourist spots include Windsor Safari Park and the Courage Shire Horse Centre.

COURAGE SHIRE HORSE CENTRE

As many as 12 of Courage's "gentle giants" may be seen at any one time at their Shire Horse Centre in Maidenhead. A visit here is fascinating for all the family, as you cannot help being impressed by, and falling in love with these magnificent beasts.

This is a working stable as the horses are often used for shows and other appearances – even on television – so you may see a farrier making horseshoes or perhaps a cooper or wheelwright working at his trade.

There are also permanent displays of the brilliantly polished harnesses and brasses and some of the hundreds of rosettes and tropies won by the team. A children's playground and an area with small birds and animals also attract the youngsters. You can enjoy an audio visual performance telling the history of the shires and showing them preparing for a show. Guided tours are laid on.

A picnic area, tea rooms and a shop with a variety of inexpensive souvenirs will help make this an enjoyable family day out. The centre is open from 1st March until 31st October, 11 am - 5 pm (last admission 4 pm). The horses are fed at noon and rest until 1.15 pm, are fed again at 4 o'clock and then retire for the day. Admission prices are £2 for adults, £1.50 for children (four to 15) and senior citizens. Group bookings can be made. The Courage Shire Horse Centre is in Cherry Garden Lane, Maidenhead Thicket, Maidenhead, Berks. SL6 3QD. Tel. (0628) 824848.

LOWER BASILDON
Crown

Tel. (0491) 671262
*Reading Road (approx. five miles
from M4 jct 12)*
Open 11–3; 6–11

ⓒ

🅱

✗ lunchtime and evening (not
Sun eve)

🍺 **Courage Best Bitter, Directors;
John Smith Yorkshire Bitter**

This large detached house is set in a lovely stretch of countryside between Pangbourne and Goring, right next to the Child Beale Wildlife Trust. It has a quiet, comfortable lounge which contrasts with Basil's Games Bar and the bright family room which has recently been enlarged and furnished in keeping with the rest of the pub. A children's menu, of the usual burgers and chips variety is available, but small portions of the main dishes are also offered, including a Sunday roast for around £2.50. Enjoy beautiful views of the Chiltern Hills from the garden which is large enough to encompass a patio, lawns and barbecue area. The children's play equipment includes a slide, seesaw, swings and candy cottage (in fact a converted pig sty!); an "enchanted tree" is hung with a baby swing, slide and climbing rope. Facilities for baby changing/feeding are provided.

Crown, Lower Basildon

OLD WINDSOR
Oxford Blue

Tel. (0753) 861954
10 Crimp Hill (off A308)
Open 11–11

&

✗ lunchtime and evening

⋈

🍺 **Friary Meux Best; Ind Coope
Burton Ale; Tetley Bitter**

Nestling on the side of Crimp Hill, overlooking fields, the Oxford Blue is 300 years old and was first licensed to a retiring officer of the Oxford Blues by the reigning monarch. It has maintained its military connections over the years and the back bar is full of airline memorabilia. Children are allowed to eat in the restaurant, where the home-coooked fare represents good value, but the real attraction for them here is the garden which has swings, slides and a two-storey sheriff's office. Windsor Great Park, Windsor Castle and historic Runymede are all within 15 minutes' drive.

BLEDLOW
Lions of Bledlow

Tel. (08444) 3345
Church End (off B4009)
Open 11–2.30 (3 Sat); 6–11

◎

🍴

✗ lunchtime and evening

🍺 **Courage Directors; Morland Old Masters; Wadworth 6X; Wethered Bitter; Young Bitter; guest beer**

Set in the superb Chiltern countryside, this sixteenth-century pub benefits from some lovely views, and overlooks the village green which acts as an overspill area for the pub's customers in busy periods. Another local attraction is the charming Lyde water garden which is open to the public. Many good walks can be started from the pub, and the Ridgeway path is just half a mile to the south. It is a spacious old pub with original beams and tiled floor. The family room is furnished with chairs and tables and has a video game. While the garden has no play facilities as such, it is landscaped and shrubs provide hiding places for children's games. Children's portions of adult meals can be ordered at reduced prices. Incidentally, Bledlow takes its name from the early English meaning "bloody field", and it is thought that some fearful battle was fought here between the Danes and Saxons.

CLIFTON REYNES
Robin Hood

Tel. (0234) 711574
Three miles from A509
Open 12–2.30; 6.30–11

◎

🍴

✗ lunchtime and evening (not Mon eve)

🍺 **Greene King IPA, Abbot Ale**

It has to be said, unfortunately that most of the pubs featured here would not have been considered for inclusion in other counties with a better choice of family pubs. Few of them have really excellent facilities for children, and the Robin Hood is really the best of a poor bunch. This is a shame, when the pubs themselves are all worth visiting for their own merits. So come on Bucks publicans, buck up your ideas about families, your efforts will be appreciated by locals and visitors alike. The Robin Hood is a cosy little village pub, set in a quiet position in its own four acres of land. Traditional games played here include armchair skittles and shove-ha'penny. Families are welcome in the conservatory at the rear of the pub which overlooks the garden where there is some play equipment for youngsters. No particular concessions are made on the menu for children, but snacks and meals start at 60 pence, so you should find something your offspring will enjoy for a reasonable price.

FORTY GREEN
Royal Standard
of England

Tel. (0494) 673382
One mile from Beaconsfield (off B474 at Knotty Green garage)
Open 11–3; 5.30–11

©

🕮

✗ lunchtime and evening

🍺 **Brakspear Bitter, Special; Eldridge Pope Royal Oak; Marston Pedigree, Owd Rodger**

This free house is a rather special place, one of England's most famous pubs, and although difficult to find, many obviously do as it is often packed to the gills. You would be wise to avoid Sunday lunchtime if crowds bother you. A rambling, old world building, it is full of curios and curiosities. One bar, reputed to be 900 years old, is still lit just by candles; another feature is the varied array of stained glass windows. Charles II bestowed on the pub its unique name, when he was restored to the throne in 1660, as a recompense for hiding him in an upstairs room when he fled from the Battle of Worcester in 1651. One of the rooms is set aside for families to drink and eat; children's portions are served and there are facilities for feeding/changing babies. The menu includes an extensive range of salads, with cheeses, pies, meat and fish to go with them. There is an enclosed garden which has some play equipment.

NEW BRADWELL
New Inn

Tel. (0908) 312094
2 Bradwell Road (half mile off Newport road), Milton Keynes
Open 11–11 (11–4; 6.30–11 Sat)

🕮

✗ lunchtime and evening (not Sun eve)

👥

🍺 **Wells Eagle Bitter, Bombardier**

Sit and watch the waterborne activity as you sup in the front garden of this pub, set right on the Grand Union Canal. If you are worried about toddlers toddling off into the water, then go round the back, where the enclosed garden has swings and climbing frames for youngsters to enjoy, as well as a goat, rabbits and guinea pigs. Ample seating is provided out here for adults. Indoors family facilities are limited to the pool room and the upstairs restaurant which seats 70 and has highchairs for its smallest customers. A children's menu is available during all normal pub hours, except Sunday evening, but a dinner dance is held on Saturday nights.

NEWTON BLOSSOMVILLE
Old Mill Burnt Down

Tel. (023 064) 433
On River Ouse between A428 and A509
Open 12–3 (Sat/Sun only and maybe summer weekdays); 7–11

✖ lunchtime and evening (not Sun eve)

🍺 **Adnams Bitter; Marston Burton Best Bitter, Pedigree, Merrie Monk; Younger Scotch, No. 3**

The food at this pub is good enough to warrant an entry in CAMRA's "Good Pub Food" guide, and the menu includes all kinds of inventive dishes. Local produce is used as much as possible, and the butcher's Burlys Bangers are sure to go down well with the children, who can have half portions of most of the other dishes. Meals can be taken at the bar or in the separate restaurant. The family room here doubles as a games room and suitable amusements for the youngsters include skittles. At the time of writing, the licensees also had plans to convert an old barn into an outdoor play area, but check before making a special trip, to see if they have gone ahead with the scheme.

The Red Lion — Windover

TAPLOW
Dumbell

Tel. (0628) 21917
Bath Road (A4)
Open 10.30–2.30; 5.30–11

✕ lunchtime and evening (not Sun eve)

🍺 **Ind Coope Burton Ale; Tetley Bitter**

The Dumbell's title is an oddity as it relates to a bell without a clanger rather than weight-lifting. The bar is long and thin with a Victorian feel to the new wood decor. A wicker-furnished conservatory is open to families and very popular it is too, especially in the early evening and at weekends. The overspill can take advantage of the large garden where amusements include slides and swings. Children's portions are available on 90 percent of the menu. Places of interest nearby are Bolters Lock, Raymill Island with its gardens, aviary and putting greens and the grounds of Cleavdon Stately Home (now a hotel) which are sometimes open to the public.

WENDOVER
Red Lion Hotel

Tel. (0296) 622266
High Street (A413)
Open 11–11

✕ lunchtime and evening

🍺 **Fuller London Pride; Greene King Abbot Ale; Marston Pedigree; Morland Bitter**

Although the facilities for children are limited here, this free house is, however, ideal for families staying in the area. Cots are available and there is plenty to see and do in the vicinity, including Waddesdon Manor and Bekonscot Model Village which appeals to adults as well as children. Walkers will enjoy the Chiltern Hills and the nearby Ridgeway Path. The hotel, which has 20 bedrooms, does not have a family room as such, but children are welcome in restaurant (booking advised at weekends) or the more informal buttery. Highchairs and a limited children's menu are available. If you do decide to stay here you will be keeping auspicious company – Oliver Cromwell, Rupert Brooke and Robert Louis Stevenson have all partaken of this seventeenth-century inn's hospitality.

CAMBRIDGE
Free Press

Tel. (0223) 68337
Prospect Row, off Warkworth
Street (near Parker's Piece)
Open 12–3; 6–11

⚅

✗ lunchtime

🍺 **Greene King IPA, Abbot Ale**

The usual problem exists in Cambridge, as in all busy cities which also attract tourists: many of the pubs are already extremely well used so that publicans do not feel they have to worry about attracting extra customers in the form of families, or they are simply not prepared to try to cope with them. The Free Press is an exception. While it does not have a family room as such, many parents will welcome the opportunity of enjoying an inexpensive lunch here with their children, after a morning exploring some of the city's sights. Food here is very good, and families may eat in the right hand bar. Also unusual for a city pub, is the fact that it has a garden, with a small patio, where children just needing liquid sustenance are welcome. The pub's unusual name comes from the time when the temperance movement launched a paper, called the Free Press, campaigning against the evils of drink. This was back in the 1830s when the pub was just getting established. The pub, as you see lived to tell the tale, the paper lasted no longer than the first issue.

Old Spring

Tel. (0223) 357228
Fenny Path, off Chesterton Road
Open 11–3; 5.30–11; all day Sat

☺

⚅

✗ lunchtime and evening

🍺 **Greene King IPA, Abbot Ale,**
Rayment BBA

Good family rooms have obvious virtues, but it is also pleasant for parents of (it must be said) well-behaved children to be able to mingle with the rest of the customers and not be socially ostracised by the mere fact of having produced offspring. Here families are welcome in the conservatory, which leads off the main bar, and is also the area where most meals are taken. Food includes hot dishes, a salad bar and ploughman's. Small portions are provided and some highchairs should have been acquired by now. The leafy conservatory has been refurbished recently, along with the rest of the pub in Victorian style, but it has been done well with bare floorboards and assorted furniture. Beyond the conservatory is a patio area for summer drinking.

ELY
Prince Albert

Tel. (0353) 663494
62 Silver Street
Open 11–2.30; 6.30–11

🛇

✗ lunchtime (not Mon)

🍺 **Greene King XX, IPA, Abbot Ale**

Like the Free Press in Cambridge, indoor facilities at the Prince Albert are limited to families taking meals. However, in a city that is popular with tourists, and with few good pubs at all, let alone ones that accept children, this will come as a welcome to anyone footsore and crick-necked from cathedral gazing. An added attraction here though is the excellent garden, where children take great delight in the mini-zoo with its variety of animals and birds. Some play equipment is also provided outdoors. The pub itself is a friendly place with open-plan bar and real fires.

ELSWORTH
George & Dragon

Tel. (09547) 236
41 Boxworth Road (between A45/A604)
Open 11–2.30; 7 (6.30 Sat)-11

◎

🛇

✗ lunchtime and evening

🍺 **Tolly Cobbold Bitter, Paine's XXX, Original**

The delightful village of Elsworth, easily reached via either the A45 or the A604, is the setting for this well-kept pub of traditional character. Oak beams, copper implements and a large inglenook provide a rustic atmosphere in the large bar. There is a separate area for non-smokers, and the family room at the back of the pub is furnished with cane seats, pine tables and plants. This room leads on to the garden which has swings, a slide and three Fisher Price tricycles for small children. In the spacious grill room, meat and fish are displayed for customers to make their choice to be cooked over a charcoal grill. Children are offered meals with chips, or salad for around £1.25. Wimpole Hall and Woodgreen Animal Shelter nearby both make good venues for family days out.

Royal Oak, Hail Weston

HAIL WESTON
Royal Oak

Tel. (0480) 72527
High Street (off A45)
Open 11–2.30 (3 Sat); 6–11

◎

🕭

✗ lunchtime and evening (not
Sun/Mon eve)

🛡

🍺 **Wells Eagle Bitter,
Bombardier; Mansfield Riding
Traditional Bitter**

An ideal pub for active children, the Royal Oak's large garden has swings, seesaw, an adventure play unit, slide, climbing frames and swing-ball. If this little lot does not take up all their surplus energy, then take them round the nine-hole putting course. The garden is safe, enclosed and dogs are strictly forbidden. A patio area provides seating for parents to observe their offspring at play. This sounds like the introduction to a pub recommended for sunny days only, but in fact this fine seventeenth-century village hostelry caters well for families inside too. There are two suitable areas: a small, but very pleasant snug, and a comfortable games room where further amusements include bar billiards, darts, cards, shove-ha'penny, dice and dominoes. At the food bar, prices start at around 80 pence for soup or a sandwich and a children's menu is available. The landlord is a professional folk singer and performs at the pub once a month. The Royal Oak was renovated not long ago, happily retaining all its original features. Its thatched roof, hanging baskets and window boxes give it a very appealing appearance.

HILDERSHAM
Pear Tree

Tel. (0223) 891680
Half a mile from the A604
Open 11.45 (11 Sat)-2.30; 6–11

🕭

✗

🍺 **Greene King XX Mild, IPA,
Abbot Ale**

In contrast to the Royal Oak, above, this really is a fairweather pub, but is included as a special effort is made to cater for children, even though the single bar layout does not allow for a family room. However, the Barn Bar in the garden which is used for functions, is also open for families in cold or wet weather. A traditional village pub situated on a Roman Road Circular Walk, the Pear Tree has an unusual timbered bar with hanging tables and ancient bric-a-brac. It is becoming very popular for its food which is served during all the pub's opening hours. Vegetarian dishes are always available and a special children's menu, including ice-cream, costs £2.25. The beer garden features an inflatable castle for youngsters to bounce around on in fine weather, as well as some rabbits and an aviary.

HOLYWELL
Old Ferryboat
Inn

Tel: (0480) 63227
Off A604, near St Ives
Open 11–3; 6–11

◎

🕭

✗ lunchtime and evening

🛏

🍺 **Adnams Bitter; Draught Bass;
Greene King IPA, Abbot Ale;
guest beer**

Listed in the Guinness Book of Records as one of England's oldest pubs, the Ferryboat is a partly thatched inn set right on the River Ouse, making it very popular with waterborne visitors in summer. As befits its age, the interior of the pub is beamed with inglenook fireplaces and also, somehow fitting too, is the fact that it has a gravestone to mark the resting place of "Juliet" who is now said to haunt the pub. It could hardly fail to have a ghost being as ancient as it is! The family area, down some steps from the main bar, is in a bay window overlooking the garden. It seats around 30 people at chairs and tables. Children may eat here – either portions of the adult menu or burgers, sausages, etc. The lovely garden is safe enough for youngsters, although there is a bank which eventually leads down to the river. The holy well, from which the village takes its name, can still be visited in the churchyard.

FOREST, GUERNSEY
Deerhound Inn Hotel

Tel. (0481) 38585
Le Bourg
Open 11.30–2; 6–11.45

◎

🏠

✗ lunchtime and evening

🛏

🍺

🍺 **Guernsey Bitter**

Despite being right by the airport, this free house at the top of Petit Bot valley remains a pleasant, cosy and characterful inn, where families are made very welcome. The family room is equipped with games: cards, chess, dominoes, Trivial Pursuits (junior as well as the adult version) and an electronic game with the sound mercifully turned down. Children may eat here or in the restaurant (where diners are often entertained by a classical guitarist). Half portions are offered on the bar menu which also features a children's section and vegetarian dishes. Highchairs are provided, and a cot is available for overnight guests. The garden has a swing and climbing frame.

GROUVILLE, JERSEY
Pembroke

Tel. (0534) 55756
Grouville Coast Road
Open 9 am–11 pm

◎

🏠

✗ 12–2; 9–11 (not Sun)

🍺 **Draught Bass**

Situated next to the Royal Jersey Golf Club and five minutes' walk from the beach, the Pembroke comprises a public bar, lounge and small children's room. Some toys and a rocking horse are provided indoors and the room leads on to the garden which has no play equipment but is safe for children. Sandwiches and meals, including a children's menu are served every day except Sunday.
The pub is a mile from Mont Orgueil Castle.

HERM
Mermaid Tavern

Tel. (0481) 710710
Open 11–11 (not Sun)

◎

🏠

✗ 12–2

🍺 **Guernsey Bitter**

The only pub on a tiny island which is famous for the fact that no cars are allowed here. Everything is within walking distance of the pub – the harbour, gift shop, campsite and hotel. It is a typical old-world "boatmen's" pub as can be seen by the many prints, photographs and artefacts of lcoal interest. A small, non-smoking area is licensed for family lunches (snacks are available all day) and there is a separate, unlicensed family room which has some play equipment. A children's menu, highchairs and facilities for dealing with babies are all provided. There is a large enclosed courtyard which is used for barbecues in summer, and a separate restaurant.

ST. ANDREWS, GUERNSEY
Last Post

Tel. (0481) 36353
St Andrews Road
Open 10.30 am-11 pm (not Sun)

☺

🏠

✖ 12–2; 7–9

♔

🍺 **Randall Best Bitter**

At the heart of this lovely island, the Last Post is a busy country pub with a large bar and comfortable lounge. The family room is set away from the bar and has its own WC and highchairs. A children's menu is served, except on Sundays when the whole pub is closed. There is a beer garden as well as a safe children's play area with sandpit, seesaw, swings and a climbing frame. Places to visit nearby include the Little Chapel, the German Underground Hospital and the Rose Centre. There are two independent breweries that serve the Channel Islands, the Guernsey Brewery and Randalls; they are both based on Guernsey.

ST LAWRENCE, JERSEY
British Union Hotel

Tel. (0534) 61070
Open 10 am-11 pm

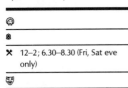

✗ 12–2; 6.30–8.30 (Fri, Sat eve only)

◙ Guernsey LBA Mild, Bitter

Licensees Steve and Sarah Skinner have four children of their own and their very firm ideas about family facilities have been incorporated into the new interior design of their pub. There is not one, but two family rooms. The first is just off the lounge, so feels very much part of the pub. Here, the toy cupboard can keep youngsters occupied for hours and games lie scattered around the room, but are never left idle for long. The other family room is set off the enclosed garden area at the rear of the pub and contains the more usual modern pub amusements, such as pool, darts and video games. Baby changing amenities are available, as are highchairs. The pub offers a varied selection of good fresh food, including a children's menu. Close to the centre of Jersey, the pub is less than six miles from any point in the island. Not surprisingly, it is very popular and can get very busy.

COTEBROOK
Alvanley Arms Inn

Tel. (08292) 200
On A49 near Tarporley
Open 11.30–3; 5.30–11

◎

🛏

✗ lunchtime and evening

🛏

🍺 **Robinson Best Mild, Best Bitter, Old Tom**

This is an attractive Georgian hotel close to Oulton Park race track and Delamere Forest. There is a heavy accent on food here – most of which is home-cooked – served both in the bar and the Cobbles Restaurant. A children's menu is available and highchairs provided. The pub has many rooms, and one without a bar is set aside for families. Overnight accommodation includes a cot. The open garden has a children's play area.

DUNHAM MASSEY
Axe & Cleaver

Tel. (061) 928 3391
School Lane (off A56 near Altrincham)
Open 11–2.30; 7–11.30 (all day summer)

◎

🛏

✗ lunchtime and evening

🍺 **Ruddles County; Webster Yorkshire Bitter; Wilson's Original Bitter**

Situated on National Trust land, close to Dunham Massey Park and within walking distance of the Bridgewater Canal, the Axe and Cleaver is a Grade I listed building. Families are welcome in the conservatory at any time. In the evenings a children's menu is served whilst at lunchtime, half portions of adult meals are available for around £1.50. The safe garden has a large play area with swings, slides and other equipment.

GREAT BUDWORTH
Cock O' Budworth

Tel. (0606) 891287
Warrington Road (four miles from A559, off A556)
Open 11–3; 6–11

◎

🛏

✗ lunchtime and evening

😀

🍺 **Greenalls Bitter**

Beware – this pub is haunted. That should set the little ones' spines tingling. I doubt though, that they will actually encounter Barnaby, the resident ghost of this sixteenth-century hostelry! Children are made more welcome than phantoms these days. The conservatory is a no-smoking area so very pleasant for families to eat and drink. A video machine has been installed to amuse children, but in summer they generally prefer to be out in the attractive garden playing on the swings, seesaw and boat. Football goalposts are provided for budding Bryan Robsons. Children are allowed in the conservatory until 9 pm, but there are no restrictions in the restaurant where they may choose from their own menu, or portions of most main dishes. Highchairs are provided. The pub is situated at the edge of a picturesque village and is convenient for the Anderton Boat Lift, Marbury Country Park and Arley Hall and Gardens.

HEATLEY
Railway

Tel. (0925) 752742
Mill Lane (one and a half miles from the centre of Lymm)
Open 12–11

ⓒ

⊗

⛉

⚐ **Boddingtons Mild, Bitter**

As I sat down to write this entry, my husband called upstairs to tell me that Boddingtons had just sold out to Whitbreads, so there will now be two minutes' silence. I shall carry on with the details in front of me, but the takeover will inevitably mean that some pubs will be affected, so be warned; they will still sell "Boddies" bitter – but at a price. The Railway is popular with locals and with visitors to the Lymm area (Styal Mill etc.). It is a multi-roomed establishment and the room given over to families has no particular facilities, although you can eat there (snacks and light meals only). The large garden is the real attraction here and has good play equipment. There is a children's toilet outside, too.

HUXLEY
Farmers Arms

Tel. (082924) 342
East of Waverton, off A41
(OS 616505)
Open 12–3; 6–11

ⓒ

⊗

✘ lunchtime and evening

⚐ **Greenalls Bitter, Thomas
Greenall's Original Bitter**

This charming old whitewashed pub is buried in the depths of the Cheshire countryside and has remained totally unspoilt. It is less than a mile from the Shropshire Union canal. Once you have found your way there you may well be hungry; the reasonably priced bar menu caters for children as well as vegetarian tastes.

The comfortable family room is just off the main bar, decorated with horse brasses and with a real pub atmosphere. Out in the garden, there are plenty of seats and six items of play equipment, including seesaws, swings and climbing frame.

MALPAS
Red Lion

Tel. (0948) 860368
1 Old Hall Street
Open 11–11

◎

⌗

✗ evening

⋈

🍺 Draught Bass

An historic hotel, the Red Lion boasts royal connections. King James I stayed there in 1624 and a reminder of his visit is the King's Chair in the bar. Customers must pay a penny to sit in this impressively large yew chair – the penalty for not doing so is to buy a drink for all present company. Other unusual features of this welcoming hostelry are its own sauna and solarium and the landlord's own malt whisky on sale at the bar. There is a family room without a bar and a half acre garden for children to enjoy.

MOULDSWORTH
Goshawk

Tel. (09284) 302
On B5393 near station
Open 11.30–11 (children
admitted until 8.30 pm)

◎

⌗

✗ lunchtime and evening

🍺 **Greenalls Mild, Bitter, Thomas
Greenall's Original Bitter**

Set in its own nine-acre site in the lovely surroundings of Delamere Forest Country Park, it is little wonder that the Goshawk attracts many ramblers. It is particularly good if you wish to eat here as a family; there is a large dining area where the children's menu includes a choice of six meals all priced at £1.60. A separate family lounge is open until 8.30 pm. The garden is wonderful for youngsters too. The adventure playground has a wooden fort, rope pulley and other wooden apparatus; more suitable equipment is supplied for younger children too. There is a bowling green for hire and plenty of tables and seating outdoors for adults. The area offers much to see and do for visitors; nearby attractions include windsurfing, Mouldsworth Motor Museum (Sundays only), Northwich Salt Museum and Ellesemere Port Boat Museum.

NANTWICH
Bowling Green Inn

Tel. (0270) 629051
Monks Walk (town centre, behind St Mary's church)
Open 11–11

◎

🛏

✕ lunchtime and evening (not Mon eve)

🍺 **Ruddles Best Bitter, County; Webster Yorkshire Bitter**

This traditional old pub, parts of which date back to the fifteenth century, is set right at the heart of the historic town of Nantwich. It is popular for its large beer garden, which can seat a hundred people. This is totally enclosed, away from the road and as it also has swings it attracts a lot of families. The spacious family room has french windows opening on to the garden. Highchairs are provided here and children may choose from their own menu or portions of main dishes (prices range from 85 pence up to around £7). At time of writing the licensees were proposing to buy further play equipment for the pub. Local tourist attractions include Stapely Water Gardens, Bridgemere Garden World and Bridgemere Wildlife Park.

RUNCORN
Windmill

Windmill Hill
Open 11.30–3; 5–11 (all day Fri, Sat) – children until 9 pm

◎

🛏

✕ lunchtime and evening

🍺 **Hydes Anvil Light, Bitter**

A new pub only opened in late 1988 to serve the nearby residential area and, as I am encouraged to note is becoming the norm, as a new pub it was designed in the first place to cater for the family trade. It has a small, cosy bar, an unusual large circular lounge and a separate family room (open until 9 pm). However, although designed to be used by children, no particular amusements have so far been provided to entertain them, which is a shame. The garden has no special features either, but maybe equipment will be provided in time. A children's menu is offered though, with reasonable prices. Nearby is Norton Priory, an excavated medieval priory with museum and gardens.

TIMBERSBROOK
Coach & Horses Inn

Tel. (0260) 273019
Dane-in-Shaw (off A527 from Congleton)
Open 11–3; 6–11

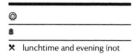

✗ lunchtime and evening (not Mon eve)

🍺 **Robinson Best Mild, Best Bitter**

Popular with walkers, this country inn lies at the end of the Pennine chain with splendid views over the Cheshire plain towards Wales on one side and over the Lancashire hills to the other. Indeed customers say that the gents' toilet must have the finest views in the country! There is no family room as such but children are made genuinely welcome in the lounge where food is served (small portions available). As with so many family pubs, though, the real attraction is the garden. This one has a large "Herbie" Tree ("Herbie" badges are given out to small customers), as well as rocking animals and swings. The National Trust beauty spot of Boseley Cloud is within a mile.

EGGLESCLIFFE
Pot & Glass

Tel. (0642) 780145
Church Road (Yarm turning off A66 or A19)
Open 12–3; 5.30–11 (children until 8 pm)

☺

🛏

✗ lunchtime

🍺 **Draught Bass**

This charming pub which boasts a long and interesting history stands opposite the fifteenth-century church in a village near Stockton. The unusual bar fronts were ornately carved from old furniture by a former licensee. There is a comfortable family room (occasionally used for functions, so check if making a special trip). Children's portions are available from the lunchtime bar menu. Evening meals maybe provided on request, but children are expected to be out of the pub by 8 o'clock.

GUISBOROUGH
Voyager

Tel. (0287) 34774
The Avenue, Hutton Meadows (A174)
Open 11–3; 6–11 (children until 8 pm)

🛏

✗ lunchtime and evening

🍺 **Cameron Traditional Bitter, Strongarm, Strongarm Premium**

A modern estate pub, but close to good walking country in the Cleveland Hills, the Voyager is on the main route to Whitby and the coast. Other places of interest in the locality include Guisborough Priory and a variety of museums. The design of the pub, while well laid out on different levels, is a single bar which does not allow for a family room as such, although children are welcome in the restaurant area where a special menu is provided for them. Adults can choose from a varied selection of good value dishes. The real attraction for youngsters here though, is the large, enclosed garden with its excellent play area where the equipment includes a slide, climbing frame and tree house. The pub has a WC for the disabled.

MOORSHOLM
Toad Hall Arms

Tel. (0287) 60155
High Street (off A171)
Open 12–2; 7–11

☺

🛏

✗ lunchtime and evening

🍷

🍺 **Tetley Bitter; Whitby's Own Ammonite**

Conjuring up visions of Ratty, Mole and the irrepressible Toad himself, the family room at the Toad Hall Arms would be just the place to settle down for a good read of Kenneth Grahame's superb book with the children; especially as it is a quiet pub and no particular amusements are provided for little ones. Quoits and dominoes however, number among the traditional games on offer. The family room in fact doubles as a dining area, but you are not obliged to eat, although the the food is excellent value here.

Another reason to visit is because it is one of the very few outlets where the tiny, independent Whitby's Own brewery's products can be sampled. Family-run, the Toad Hall attracts locals, tourists and customers from outlying areas. In rural surroundings, it enjoys splendid views of the moors and coast; the garden is safe for children to play in.

STOCKTON ON TEES
Elm Tree

Tel. (0642) 677942
Elm Tree Avenue, Elm Tree Farm Estate (off A1027)
Open 11.30–3 (4 Thu, Fri, 4.30 Sat); 6–11

◎

🏠

✗ lunchtime and evening (not Tue eve)

🍺 **John Smith Bitter, Magnet**

A modern estate pub, just five years old and decorated in Art Deco style, the Elm Tree was designed to cater for the needs of all its customers. Access is provided for wheelchairs; good-value, home-cooked meals are provided for the hungry; and a well-furnished conservatory is open for families to enjoy. Some indoor amusements are provided and the garden is safe for children to amuse themselves in. A children's menu, for around £1, or portions from the main dishes can be ordered; look out too for the daily lunchtime specials.

YARM
Ketton Ox

Tel. (0642) 788311
100 High Street
Open 11–2.30; 5.30 11 (all day Sat)

🏠

✗ Lunchtime and some evenings

🍺 **Vaux Samson, Double Maxim**

Built as a coaching inn during the eighteenth century when Yarm was an important port, this listed building is centrally situated in the High Street. In its heyday, the pub had cock-fighting pits to draw the crowds. Now customers are happy to come for the more mundane pleasures of a good pint and a reasonably-priced meal. It is the restaurant in fact which doubles as a family room; children's portions and a separate menu for them are on offer. Summer visitors can take advantage of the enclosed garden. There is a pleasant riverside walk nearby and another local family attraction is the Preston Park Museum.

CAMBORNE
Old Shire Inn

Tel. (0209) 712691
Pendarves Road (B3303, Helston road)
Open 10.30–3; 5.30–11

◎

🛏

✗ lunchtime and evening

⊨

🍺 **Shire Bitter (Plympton Pride);**
Tetley Bitter

This former lodge is set in delightful parkland outside the village and makes an ideal base for touring the area. The bar is comfortable with open fires in winter. Children are welcome in the separate family room or outside on a verandah which has tables and seating for 12. Meals, with children's portions, can be served in the family room. The garden is enclosed and has a play area.

GOLANT
Fisherman's Arms

Tel. (0726) 832453
Fore Street
Open 11–11 (11–3; 6–11 winter)

◎

🛏

✗ lunchtime and evening

🍺 **Courage Best Bitter, Directors;**
St Austell Tinners Bitter

On the bank of the river Fowey, in the tiny, secluded village of Golant, the Fisherman's is popular with anglers and yachtspeople. It has a pleasant, peaceful atmosphere unsullied by electronic machines or jukebox. The family room is small, but there is plenty of seating for summer visitors both in the garden which has a play area, and on the terrace which offers lovely views across the river and upstream to Lostwithiel. Small portions at reduced prices can be offered on most of the items of the menu. There are several beaches within a ten minutes' drive from here – but beware, the pub is occasionally cut off by river at high tide.

GUNWALLOE
Halzephron

Tel. (0326) 240406
Off A3083
Open 11.30–2.30; 7–11

◎

🛏

✗ lunchtime and evening

🍺 **Cornish Original; Wadworth**
6X

A typical Cornish smugglers' inn, the Halzephron stands on the west coast of the Lizard from which the pub takes its name; it means "hell's headland" in old Cornish. This is National Trust property with magnificent sea views across Mount's Bay to Lands End. The pub has retained many features of its disreputable past – a wall between the two bars contains a vertical shaft to a tunnel which in years gone by led to the beach. The family area is an alcove adjoining the Revenuers Bar; a children's menu is served. Outside, the enclosed garden has a play area.

NANCENOY
Trengilly Wartha Inn

Tel. (0326) 40332
*Off Gweek-Constantine road
(follow signs)*
Open 11–3; 6–11

✖ lunchtime and evening

🛏

🍷

🍴 range varies

This unusually-named pub enjoys a particularly beautiful, if somewhat remote situation, in its own extensive grounds in a peaceful, wooded valley near the Helford river. The free house has had a change of ownership since our first edition and the four regular draught beers have been replaced with a changing selection – normally half from national brewers and half from (mostly local) independents, such as St Austell, Golden Hill and Cotleigh. Families are welcome in the conservatory-style room at the front of the building; highchairs and a children's menu are provided. There is some play equipment in the small garden. Cots are provided in the overnight accommodation. Places of interest to take children locally include Flambards Theme Park and the Gweek seal sanctuary.

PORTMELLON
Rising Sun Inn

Tel. (0726) 843235
Portmellon Cove, Mevagissey
*Open 11.30–3; 6–11 (closed
October to Easter)*

☺

✖ lunchtime and evening

🍴 St Austell Hicks Special;
     Wadworth 6X

Writing about this pub stirs up some ancient memories from the time when, as a student, I spent my summer holidays working as a waitress in Mevagissey. It was beginning to be a very popular holiday resort then, but the place is often seething nowadays. However, the Rising Sun is half a mile from "Meva" itself, right on the beach, and so is obviously ideal for families. There is a modern public bar and a spacious lounge, but the best views are to be had from one of the family rooms upstairs which has a balcony overlooking the beach. Both these large rooms are excellent: one is used for games with video machines, pool table and table football; the other has a children's bar serving "kiddie cocktails", soft drinks, chocolate and crisps. A children's menu is also available. The pub operates on a six-month licence and so is closed all winter.

PROBUS
Hawkins Arms

Tel. (0726) 882208
On A390 St Austell-Truro road
Open 11–2.30 (3.30 summer);
5.30–11 (children summer only)

ⓐ

⊞

✗ lunchtime and evening

ᵬ

ᵭ **St Austell Tinners Bitter, HSD**

As the family room reverts to being a restaurant in winter, the Hawkins is strictly speaking another summertime pub. A traditional Cornish hostelry that has managed to retain its original character, it is close to Truro in a village renowned for having the highest church tower in Cornwall. The village also boasts two beautiful gardens. The pub's own garden has a play area which includes an assault course for youngsters to try. Tables and chairs are provided for an outdoor eating area. Meals, including small portions and a children's menu, can also either be taken in bar or the first-floor family room where there are games and video machines.

ST BREWARD
Old Inn

Tel. (0208) 850711
Four miles across Bodmin Moor
from A30
Open 11.30–3; 6–11

ⓐ

⊞

✗ lunchtime and evening

😋

ᵭ **Ruddles County; Ushers Best Bitter**

At the top of the village, high on Bodmin Moor, this large friendly inn certainly is old. It has slate floors, granite walls and a large, welcoming fireplace. It enjoys a good local trade, but "expands" to cope with the influx of summer tourists. The large family room at the back of the pub has a pool table, fruit machine, juke box, video machine and a piano, as well as plenty of seating. The meals are standard pub fare, but a children's menu is offered. A restaurant was being built as we went to press. The garden has splendid views over the moor (except when there is low cloud!).

ST JUST IN
PENWITH
Star Inn

Tel. (0736) 788767
Open 11–11 (11–3; 6–11 winter)

ⓐ

⊞

ᵭ **St Austell Tinners Bitter, Hicks Special; Cornish Scrumpy Cider**

The oldest pub in St Just, the Star has managed to retain its traditional atmosphere despite increasing demands from an ever-growing tourist trade. Even more admirable, in the face of visiting *emmets*, is that the licensees steadfastly refuse to cook chips as they feel fried food and real ale do not mix. However, they have never had any complaints about the food from their younger customers who usually find something from the range of snacks available, and they are always happy to heat bottles for the tiny ones.

Babies can be changed in the ladies' toilet. A cosy pub with open fires in winter, the family room is the "Snuggery" (here the fire is guarded), which has a playbox, books, games and a television. The Star is convenient for the lovely beach at Sennen and other smaller coves; and plenty of coastal walks can be enjoyed locally.

STRATTON
Tree Inn

Tel. (0288) 352038
Fore Street (off A3072)

@

✖ lunchtime and evening

⋈

🍺

🍺 **Draught Bass; St Austell Tinners Bitter**

Do not take your children here if they are of a sensitive disposition. The Tree Inn was the home of the last of the Cornish giants – Anthony Payne was reputedly 7' 4" tall and there is a lifesize portrait of him in the courtyard. Payne was the manservant of Beville Grenville whose family used to live at the inn when it was a manor house. Beville led the royalists to victory at the Battle of Stamford Hill in 1643 and the Sealed Knot Society re-enacts the event every year. It is worth seeing as their regalia is splendid and the atmosphere electric. The Grenville Room is now a large, bright family room with plenty of tables and comfortable seating. Children are also welcome in the separate games room. There is a thirteenth-century Galleon restaurant, complete with ships' timbers; or bar meals are available with children's portions and highchairs readily provided. Babies' needs at feeding time are also dealt with very happily. The pub's four bars are set around the courtyard.

TRAVEL PURSUITS

A game that used to keep me occupied for hours in the car as a child was making my own maps. With a pad of paper on a firm base, I used to let my pen doodle at will (according to the movement of the car), to form an "island". Of course cars these days have rather better suspension, so a bit of help from the artist is permissible. Once the outline was done I used to spend time making up placenames and positioning them on the "island". This can be done by jumbling up letters of places you pass through, or by giving the island a name that provides a theme: "Zoo Island" gives rise to places like Zebratown or Hippoville. It never did me any good though, I was always hopeless at geography!

TREBARWITH
Mill House Inn

Tel. (0840) 770200
Three miles south of Tintagel, off
A3263
Open 11–3.30; 6–11

⊚	
⊛	
✖	lunchtime and evening
⋈	
⍟	
⍟	**Flowers IPA, Original**

Tim Webb, in his excellent guide, "The Best Pubs in Devon and Cornwall", describes the Mill House as "a trifle posher than most". This sixteenth-century inn is set in more than seven acres of its own wooded valley with a trout stream running by. Pretty and secluded terraced gardens lead down to a brilliant playground with wooden climing frame, tyre swings, seesaw and slides designed as an elephant and dinosaur. Indoors, the clean 42–seater family room is adjacent to the main bar; it has a one-armed bandit and pool table. Baby changing/feeding facilities are provided and children's portions can be ordered from the excellent menu. Tim points out that even if you were not intending to eat here, you will be sorely tempted by the aroma of herbs and good food that comes wafting by.

AMBLESIDE
Golden Rule

Tel. (0966) 33363
Smithy Brow
Open 11–11

◎

🅱

🍺 **Hartley Mild, XB**

The Golden Rule from which this pub takes its name is a brass measuring rod from an infamous P1 fighter which now has pride of place behind the bar. At the bottom of the Kirkstone Pass road, this old (1640) pub is popular with visitors, walkers and locals alike, and attracts quite a crowd from the Charlotte Mason college nearby. Although not easily seen from the main road, this unspoilt, beamed pub has an attractive white-painted exterior bedecked with colourful window boxes. Two of the pub's three rooms are available for families to use; no particular amusements are provided, just a warm welcome. Snacks are available at lunch and suppertime and children can be catered for. There is an enclosed yard and garden at the rear of the pub where families can stretch their legs in warm weather. Places of interest in the vicinity include the old mills on Stock Ghyll and the ancient farmhouse at How Head.

CARTMELL FELL
Masons Arms

Tel. (04488) 486
Strawberry Bank (between Bowland Bridge and Windermere)
Open 11.30–3; 6–11 (children until 9.30 pm)

◎

🅱

✗ lunchtime and evening

🍴

🍺 **Bateman XB; Thwaites Bitter; Yates Bitter; guest beer**

The Masons is not the easiest pub to find, but that's not so uncommon around these wilder parts of the country. When you do find it you will be delighted with its excellent views of Whitbarrow Scar and Witherslach woods and further to the Winster valley. You will also appreciate its old world charm of slate floors and beamed ceilings in the tiny rooms. The family room is attached to the main bar (this room has a wood floor) and children are welcome here until 9.30 pm. Space hardly allows for any amusements, but children are catered for on the menu. When you have eaten, you can walk off any excess on one of the many pathways that are nearby. The pub also offers self-catering accommodation in a converted barn.

HALE
Kings Arms Hotel

Tel. (05395) 63203
On A6 near Milnthorpe, two miles from M6 jct 35
Open 11–3; 6–11 (children until 8.30)

◎

⊛

✗ lunchtime and evening

⊲ **Mitchells Bitter**

Not, in fact, an hotel, this pub provides a convenient, and pleasant stop for refreshment on the busy A6. The traffic may be whizzing by outside, but the atmosphere inside is calm and unhurried. The large ground-floor lounge has a huge collection of plates, prints and photographs. The family room is the upstairs lounge where children are welcome until 8.30 in the evening. Children's dishes are available on the menu where prices range from around £1 for Cumberland sausage to £5.25 for a mixed grill. The beer garden is safe for children to play in and has a bowling green.

HEVERSHAM
Blue Bell

Tel. (04482) 2018
Princes Way (A6, one mile from Milnthorpe)
Open 11–3; 6–11

◎

⊛

✗

ⱶ

⊲ **Samuel Smith OBB, Museum Ale**

My colleague Mike Dunn visited this pub (as well as many others listed in this county) while he was researching his "Best Pubs in Lakeland". He was surprised to find that in such a well-conceived conversion from a former vicarage to a three-star country inn that the family room was a somewhat neglected feature. However, at least a small room is available and the service is friendly. Highchairs, and children's portions are provided from an excellent selection of bar food. The hotel has 24 bedrooms and cots are available. Situated at the gateway to the Lakes and the Dales, it is also convenient for visitors to Levens Hall and Sizergh Castle.

KESWICK
George Hotel

Tel. (07687) 72076
St Johns Street
Open 11–11 (no children Fri/Sat eve)

◎

✗ lunchtime and evening

ⱶ

⊲ **Theakston Best Bitter; Yates Bitter**

This historic inn, close to the Moot Hall, is the oldest in Keswick and it shows. The quarry-tiled floors and all the other original features have been carefully maintained. It is perhaps not the ideal family pub as amenities are a bit limited, but it is really the only one in this busy tourist town that caters at all for children. The family "room" is an area segregated away from the main bar and as such is just as attractive, with old prints covering the walls. A children's menu or portions are served either from the bar or in the separate restaraunt. Family accommodation (including cots) is available. Among its famous customers, the George can boast that Wordsworth, Coleridge and Shelley used to come here to drink.

LOWESWATER
Kirkstile Inn

Tel. (090085) 219
Open 11–11

◎
🕭
✕
⋈
🍺 **Jennings Bitter**

The Kirkstile Inn has provided food and shelter for travellers for some 400 years and continues to offer warm hospitality. Food is served practically all day, including breakfast and afternoon tea. The beer's not bad either. Set close to Loweswater itself amid some beautiful countryside, the inn would make a good base for touring – there are three family bedrooms and two cots available. For residents and casual visitors alike the small family room in the pub offers a pool table, video game, jukebox and darts. In summer the large garden comes into use with tables set out on the lawn. Children's portions and their own menu are provided as are highchairs.

NEAR SAWREY
Tower Bank Arms

Tel. (09666) 334
On B5285 (west shore of Windermere)
Open 11–3; 5.30–11

◎

🅱

✘ lunchtime and evening

⋈

🍺 Matthew Brown Mild;
Theakston Best Bitter, XB;
Younger Scotch, No. 3

This pub is listed more for its position than its brilliant family amenities. It is the pub that sits right next to Beatrix Potter's house and which featured in the "Tale of Jemima Puddleduck" and so is popular with "children" of all ages. Both the pub and the house, Hill Top Farm, are now owned by the National Trust, and despite that organisation's efforts to stem the tide, it is still the most visited house in the Lake District, so do go out of season if possible. Happily, the pub has managed to remain virtually unchanged since the author's time. Families are welcome to use the family room at lunchtime, but in the evening only the dining room is open to children. Half portions are served and there is a highchair. The overflow can use the garden in summer.

SILECROFT
Miners Arms

Tel. (0657) 2325
Off A595, Millom-Whitehaven road
Open 11–2.30; 7–11

◎

🅱

✘ lunchtime and evening

⋈

🍺 Matthew Brown Mild;
Theakston Bitter; Younger
Scotch, No. 3

Silecroft, at the south-western end of the National Park, has some unusual and interesting features, such as a horse-ginn (where a horse or mule was used to turn rollers to grind grain), Arrow Hill, part of an ancient natural dam which used to keep back a vast lake, and Swinside stone circle. You might be in need of some refreshment after that tour, so repair to the Miner's Arms which has a comfortable lounge and public bar, and a bright, airy family room. A fairly extensive menu is offered and children's portions are served. The family room has double doors opening on to the garden which is safe for youngsters, but no play equipment is provided. However, there is a lovely beach just half a mile away.

TALKIN
Hare & Hounds Inn

Tel. (06977) 3456
Off B6413 (M6 Jct 42 for Brampton)
Open 12–2.30 ; 7–11

◎

☒

✗ lunchtime and evening

⋈

🍺 **Hartley XB ; Theakston Best Bitter, XB, Old Peculier**

Not far from Carlisle, this excellent country inn set at the heart of the Cumbrian Fells, was once used as a stop-over by monks on their way from Armathwaite to Lanercost Priory. The monks have now been replaced by tourists who receive an equally warm welcome in this traditional pub, full of old beams, antiques and stone fireplaces. There are some playthings in the family room and a very reasonably-priced children's menu is served here. If you wish to eat in the evening, then it is advisable to book a table. The garden also has some play equipment and cots are available for overnight stays. The pub is half a mile from the beauty spot of Talkin Tarn, said to be the site of a submerged town, but these days perhaps rather too popular for its leisure facilities including windsurfing and boating. Other local attractions include Hadrian's Wall, Brampton golf course and the RSPB Bird Reserve.

THRELKELD
Salutation Inn

Tel. (07687) 83614
Off A66, four miles east of
Keswick
Open 11–3; 5.30–11

✗ lunchtime and evening

🍺 **Matthew Brown Mild, Bitter;**
Theakston Best Bitter, XB, Old
Peculier

According to Mike Dunn (see Heversham above), this pub has possibly the best family room in the Lake District. Situated on the first floor and recently refurbished, it is very large and equipped with pool table, jukebox, darts, dominoes, shove-ha'penny and a colour television. This is rather unexpected because from the outside, the Salutation appears to be a simple, village local, although is does have a separate eating area which is popular with tourists as the food is very good. Half portions are offered for youngsters, or items such as fishfingers can be prepared if preferred. The licensees are proud that this is one of the last traditional lakeland pubs left, with lots of polished wood and absolutely no plastic tat. Nestling beneath Blencathra, the garden has a safe play area for children.

BRAILSFORD
Rose & Crown

Tel. (0335) 60242
Main Road (A52)
Open 11–3; 7–11

🍴
✗ lunchtime and evening
🍺 **Draught Bass**

Ironically, the Rose and Crown, which dates from the eighteenth century, used to be a Temperance House. From a family point of view, it is basically a fairweather pub, although children are allowed indoors if having a meal – the dining rooms are separate from the bar. It may well be worth visiting then, as the pub enjoys a good reputation for its food and does cater for youngsters on the menu. Baby changing facilities are available in the ladies' toilets. The large, enclosed garden is very appealing to children, with slides, swings and a home-built wooden activity centre.

BROADHOLME
Fisherman's Rest

Tel. (0773) 825518
Broadholme Lane, Belper (just off A6)
Open 11.30–3; 6–11

☺
🍴
✗ lunchtime
🍺 **Marston Pedigree**

This stone-built cottage pub recently underwent alterations to provide a kitchen, WC for the disabled, baby changing facilities and a children's room. Happily, the renovations did nothing to spoil the pub's charm and pleasant atmosphere. It is an unfortunate fact that the reason why many of our finest pubs do not provide family facilities is because the old buildings were not designed to enable them easily to be created, so it is good to see them incorporated when old places are updated. Here the family room is attractive with interesting black and white pictures on the walls. Highchairs are provided as are a menu and small portions for children at lunchtime. The garden has two play areas – one designed with the under-sixes in mind with swings and seesaws – the other with equipment for older children: slides, swings and climbing frame.

DERBY
Brunswick Inn

Tel. (0332) 290677
1 Railway Terrace
Open 11–11

@

✗ lunchtime

♥

♫ **Draught Bass; Bateman Mild;
Hook Norton Old Hookey;
Marston Pedigree; Taylor
Landlord; Ward Kirby Ale;
Westons Scrumpy; guest beer**

The proud boast of the Brunswick Inn is that it is the oldest (1842) purpose-built railway pub in the world. Brick-built, at the end of a row of restored terraced houses, it has retained its stone-flagged floor, although the smoke room is now a non-smoking room! The carpeted family parlour is at the front of the pub. Here some toys and usually balloons, too are provided. The video which is showing in the bar is also scanned to this room. Lunchtime meals are served from 11.30–2.30 – children's portions are available – and snacks are available all day, everyday. There is no garden as such, but some outside seating is provided for sunny days.

Maypole

Tel. (0332) 44560
*Brook Street (off Ashbourne road,
off A38 ring road)*
Open 11–3; 6–11

@

♥

♫ **Home Mild, Bitter**

This bustling back-street pub has more the atmosphere of a social club than an ordinary local. Regular activities include a weekly tote and meat raffle, singalong music sessions at the weekends and there are keen darts, dominoes and crib teams. It is warm, friendly and welcoming to allcomers. The family room has a pool table and plenty of room for children to run about and play – some toys are provided. No meals are served but rolls and sandwiches are available.

HARDWICK
Hardwick Inn

Tel. (0246) 850245
Hardwick Park
Open 11.30–3; 6.30–11

@

⊞

✗ lunchtime and evening (not
Sun eve)

♫ **Theakston XB; Younger
Scotch, IPA**

Situated at the south gate of the Hardwick Hall Estate, this delightful stone inn was built in 1607. It is surrounded by lawned gardens and is a fitting neighbour to Hardwick Hall which is an Elizabethan mansion. There are two children's rooms, situated to the left of the main door as you enter. No particular amusements are provided for children indoors or out, so it is sensible to bring something for them. The inn has a popular carvery restaurant where the food is good value and plentiful, but bar meals and a children's menu are also served.

SHARDLOW
Dog & Duck

Tel. (0332) 792224
2 Aston Lane (A6)
Open 11–11

@

🍴

✗ lunchtime

🍺 **Marston Mercian Mild or Merrie Monk, Pedigree**

This much extended, cruck-built pub is situated on the main road, but has a safe, enclosed garden. If you visit in good weather, you are likely to have a hard time getting away as there is so much to keep the little ones occupied: swings, sandpit, bouncing castle; apart from all the animals to attract their attention including a goat, donkey and pony. It is just as well that the pub has adopted all day opening hours. Inside there are four main rooms featuring original beams and panelling. The glass-roofed, heated verandah is very popular with families, as is the children's shop at the back of the pub. Meals are served at lunchtimes (other times by arrangement) and snacks are available "until they are sold out".

WETTON
Olde Royal Oak Inn

Tel. (033 527) 287
Nine miles north west of Ashbourne
Open 11.30–2.30; 7–11

@

🍴

✗ lunchtime and evening

🍺 **Ruddles Best Bitter, County; Theakston XB**

The Royal Oak has nothing like the amenities for families that the Dog and Duck offers, but it is included because it is welcoming to children and enjoys such a lovely setting. A seventeenth-century free house, it stands above the picturesque Manifold Valley and close to Thors Cave in the Peak District Park. The oldest part of the pub has heavy black beams and stone fireplace with welcoming log fire. The family room is a carpeted lounge which looks out on to the garden. There are benches and tables in the garden itself which is part paved and part lawn. Children's portions are available on some items on the menu.

IN-CAR ENTERTAINMENT

Keeping children happy and comfortable on long car journeys can be exhausting for parents, especially if the only adult in the car is the driver. I am extremely lucky as my children do not go out in the car on a day-to-day basis as many do, so for them it is still a treat and I am quite amazed at their capacity to sit happily for up to three hours at a stretch. However, I remember clearly my own mother having to spend all her time narrating stories and thinking up simple games to stop us squabbling in the back as kids.

We are fortunate in that we now have better resources for in-car entertainment. For families, personal stereos are one of the best inventions ever. Teenagers can happily listen to their kind of music without constant exhortations to "turn it down", and now that they can be bought relatively cheaply, they are also suitable for much younger children. I bought one for my son at the tender age of two and he will sit happily listening to story tape after story tape. For the educationally minded, tapes are now available for children to practise their times tables and even learn foreign languages, and many children surprisingly are happy to use them – maybe it doesn't seem like learning to them.

In this electronic age there are plenty of small hand-held games on the market that are ideal for travelling. You may need a few of these space-invader type amusements though, as older children can get quickly bored with them. Many of the more established games also come in travel sets on magnetic boards such as chess, backgammon, scrabble and so on. These small games are also ideal to take into those pubs that provide family areas, but no amusements.

It is not, however, necessary to spend a lot of

money to keep children occupied. Some of the more "old-fashioned" games and toys are still popular. Adults and older children can pass away several miles engaged in word games, such as those favoured by the radio's "I'm sorry I haven't a clue". Taking turns to relate a story; having to make up stories starting each word with the next letter of the alphabet; thinking up suitably silly guests to be invited to the publican's (or whatever) ball. Younger children can be introduced at a surprisingly early age to "I spy" and toddlers are often happy to look at picture books on their own or be read to, but this does necessitate an adult sitting in the back too. My local newsagent sells "magic screens" for just 25 pence and these drawing toys, which have been around for years, keep my under-fives happy for quite a while. Puzzle books are relatively cheap too and can provide hours of amusement for all ages.

If all else fails, resort to food and drink. Some parents do not like their offspring to eat in the car; the mess and potential travel sickness can sometimes be more trouble than its worth. However, I always travel with emergency rations of fairly plain, but satisfying goodies: rich tea biscuits, apples, raw carrots, watered down fruit juice (not squash, this *does* make them sick); for babies, just a bottle of slightly flavoured or plain water will often keep them happy until they doze off again. Of course you may be unlucky enough to have one of those fractious babies that just does not like cars, but other books have been written about them!

When you have all really had enough just flick through the pages of this guide, pull off and have a rest and refreshment at a welcoming pub.

BLACKAWTON
Normandy Arms

Tel. (080 421) 316
Chapel Street (one mile from B3207)
Open 11.30–2.30; 6.30-11 (12–2; 7–11 winter)

◎

⊗

✗ lunchtime (not winter) and evening

⋈

⊞ **Draught Bass; Blackawton Bitter, Forty-four; Ruddles County**

The Normandy Arms could almost be considered the perfect pub (if there is such a thing). It is certainly perfect for families who are treated with as much care and consideration as the other customers. It is professionally run and well situated for tourists – Dartmouth and the South Hams beaches are no more than five miles away and the Woodland Adventure Park and campsite have recently been opened near the village. The family room is upstairs, with plenty of tables and chairs and a toy cupboard full of toys. A highchair is provided and children may choose from their own menu or off the main list. Food is home-made, imaginative and highly recommended. It sounds the sort of place you could be tempted to stay awhile and cots are provided for overnight guests, but you do need to book ahead in the summer.

BLACKMOOR GATE
Old Station House Inn

Tel. (059 83) 274
Six miles south west of Lynton at A39/399/B3226 jct
Open 11–11 (11–3; 6.30–11 winter)

◎

⊗

✗ lunchtime and evening

⋈

⊞ **Courage Best Bitter, Directors; Exmoor Ale; guest beer**

In his "Best Pubs in Devon and Cornwall", which is a must for serious pub-going holidaymakers, Tim Webb describes the Old Station House as a "pub for children who have discerning beer drinkers as parents." I think he makes no understatement. The adults have the smaller of the pub's two rooms, whilst the huge modern bar concentrates entirely on families with all sorts of games and amusements, including a miniature pool table and space invader machines, and a long children's menu. In Tim's book, the food does not rate as well as the beer, which he says is one of the landlord's passions. Outside, the large garden has an extremely good play area, where safety is one of the main considerations, so parents are able to relax and enjoy the excellent ale in the knowledge that their little ones are unlikely to came to much harm.

BOWD
Bowd Inn

Tel. (0395) 513328
Bowd Cross (A3052, three miles from Sidmouth)
Open 11–11 (11–2.30; 5.30–11 winter)

⊚

🏠

✕ lunchtime and evening

🍺 **Cornish Royal Wessex;
Marston Pedigree**

Another inn that caters extremely well for families, but is perhaps kinder to unencumbered adults than the Old Station Inn. Originally a barn, dating from 1631, it now has a lovely old bar – all heavy beams and brass – which is the preserve of the grown-ups. Senior citizens are also well considered; they can enjoy half-price buck's fizz until 12.30 on Sundays, so why not take granny and grandad along too? Children are welcome in a bright family room which maintains, nevertheless, a good pub atmosphere. It opens out on to a patio area, leading to a large garden which has a playground with swings, roundabout and a playhouse. There is a standard pub food menu which caters for both adults and children (for half price), highlighted by a home-made pie of the day and a few special dishes. Highchairs are provided. Curry evenings are a special feature on Fridays and Saturdays in winter.

Normandy Arms, Blackawton

CLAYHIDON
Merry Harriers

Tel. (0823 42) 270
Forches Corner (three miles east of Clayhidon)
Open 11.30–2.30; 6–11

◎

🛏

✗ lunchtime

🍴

🍺 **Cotleigh Tawny Bitter, Harrier; Exmoor Ale; Marston Pedigree; Wadworth 6X**

The sign on the pub simply says The Harriers, but I guess the place is fairly merry. Well at least, you are likely to be merry when you eventually find it, because it is not easy. Situated right on the border with Somerset it is really in the middle of nowhere; the most straightforward direction is to take the road over the Blackdown Hills from Taunton (five miles). Local attractions include Buckland Wood (opposite) and a Bird Garden, two miles away. The family room is a conservatory with wicker furniture, overlooking the large garden. This is attractively set out and has a play area with a Tudor play house, swings and an aviary. Freshly prepared meals can be taken in the bar or restaurant; children and vegetarians are catered for and there is a highchair. An unusual feature at the pub is an uphill skittle alley!

DALWOOD
Tuckers Arms

Tel. (040 488) 342
Off A35, four miles from Axminster
Open 11–2.30; 6.30–11

◎

🛏

✗ lunchtime and evening

🍺 **Courage Best Bitter, Directors; Theakston Best Bitter; Wadworth 6X; Young Special**

Another pub rather off the beaten track, two to three miles from the main road but well worth finding. The owners are slowly modernising this attractive thatched inn, but making every effort to keep its original features intact. They have also extended it to provide overnight accommodation. The skittle alley is the latest room to be done – this has been redecorated and refurbished as a dining room, and children may eat here (the skittles are still available too). The food is recommended; the menu includes freshly made daily "specials" and fish dishes. Children's favourites such as fishfingers can be provided, but the owners here find (rather refreshingly) that most youngsters prefer to eat the same as their parents. A second room is also available for families not wishing to eat. At the time of writing the garden was suffering the effects of being part of the building site, but it is hoped that it will be cleared up and play equipment provided in the not-too-distant future. There are several beaches within a 13 mile radius and Seaton, with its popular tramway, is also close by.

EXETER
Double Locks

Tel. (0392) 56947
Canal Bank (on towpath, through Marsh Barton trading estate)
Open 11–11

☺

🍴

✘ all day

♕

🍺 **Eldridge Pope Royal Oak; Exmoor Ale; Greene King Abbot Ale; Marston Pedigree, Owd Rodger; Wadworth 6X; Gray Farm Cider**

One of the reasons that this delightful pub does not get packed to the gills is its inaccessibility – it is approached via a single track road, but many people prefer the half-mile walk along the towpath to get there. Despite these difficulties, it *is* extremely popular. It comes particularly recommended by Susan Nowak, author of CAMRA's "Good Pub Food", who says it not only offers good food ("lovely icecreams"), but is wonderful for children. There are two bar-less rooms inside where families can drink and eat if they wish – adult dishes can easily be split and extra plates are provided on request. An assortment of games are provided, eg cards, backgammon, bar billiards. Outside there is seating and plenty to see on the Exeter Ship Canal, although young children need some supervision here; but there is also an enclosed play area, with plenty of room to run around and interesting equipment such as hanging tyres and climbing ropes. When the pub does get very crowded in the summer, there is an overspill bar in the outside barn. Barbecues are held regularly on summer weekends. Camping is permitted in the grounds of the pub. The Exeter Maritime Museum is close by and popular with families.

GALMPTON
Manor Inn

Tel. (0803) 842346
2 Stoke Gabriel Road (off A3022)
Open 11–3; 5.30–11

☺

✘ lunchtime and evening (not Sun eve)

⋈

🍺 **Ansells Best Bitter; Plympton Dartmouth Best Bitter, Strong; Tetley Bitter**

This is a traditional, family-run inn, set in an old-world village, close to the beautiful Galmpton creek on the River Dart estuary. Nearby, the Greenway Ferry takes passengers (not cars) across the river to Dittisham, passing Greenway House, the former home of Agatha Christie. Other local attractions include a steam railway, horse riding, golf course and a sandy beach (one mile distant). The family room has potted palms and an open fireplace. A highchair and "Kiddy's Korner" menu are offered, and there is a separate restaurant too. Outside is a patio, but no garden. The pub has some self-catering flats, suitable for families; cots can be provided.

HAYTOR
Rock Inn

Tel. (03646) 305
Off B3344
Open 11–2.30; 6.30–11

⊚

⦿

✕ lunchtime and evening

◪

⬗ Draught Bass; Eldridge Pope
Dorset IPA, Royal Oak

Situated just inside the Dartmoor National Park, nestling under its highest outcrop (Hay Tor), this lovely old inn is popular with walkers, and provides overnight accommodation (including cots). It has no less than four bars, a restaurant and a large lounge where families are welcome to drink and/or enjoy a bar meal from a varied menu. The pub's garden is across the road, but is enclosed and safe for children.

PRINCETOWN
Plume of
Feathers

Tel. (082289) 240
Open 11–11 (11–3; 6–11 winter)

⊚

⦿

✕ lunchtime and evening

⬚

⬗ Draught Bass; St Austell
Tinners Ale, Hicks Special

Princetown is Dartmoor's principal village and the Plume of Feathers caters well for vistors to this National Park, particularly walkers. It has a campsite and a new "Alpine bunkhouse" with two dormitories offering accommodation for 20 people as well as cooking facilities. As for the pub itself, it is the oldest (1785) building in the village and retains many of its original features: exposed beams, granite walls and open fires. There is a family room with some games and a large garden with picnic area and children's playground. An extensive range of bar food includes a menu for younger appetites. All kinds of outdoor activities are available within easy reach of the pub, including sailing, riding, canoeing and climbing. It is also close to Dartmoor prison, which was originally built to house French and American prisoners of war.

TIVERTON
Country House

Tel. (0884) 256473
St Andrews Street
Open 11–11.30

⊚

⦿

✕ lunchtime and evening

⬗ Draught Bass; Wadworth 6X;
guest beer

Convenient for Tiverton's museum, this pub is, despite its name, in the town centre. Popular with families, it was nearly excluded from CAMRA's "Best Pubs in Devon and Cornwall" because of the author's abhorrence of canned *muzak*. That aside, it does cater very well for children (who probably like the music anyway). The large back room is set aside for families and is well equipped with toys and has a fishtank to provide another source of interest for the little ones. Outdoors the large garden is enclosed to prevent youngsters from toddling off into the River Exe. Here there is a small playground with a climbing frame and slides, and a menagerie of domestic animals is an added attraction. There is a full food menu for children – much the same as the adults' but with added baked beans! A highchair is provided and staff will always try to find a quiet corner for feeding the baby.

WELCOMBE
Old Smithy Inn

Tel. (028 883) 305
Off A39, Bideford-Bude road
Open 11.30–2.30; 6–11

⊚

🏠

✗ lunchtime and evening

⋈

🍺 **Butcombe Bitter; Marston
Pedigree**

This ancient pub, dating back to the thirteenth century, with thatched roof and oak beams, is set in an area of outstanding, if somewhat windswept, natural beauty. It is at the north-western tip of the county between Bideford and Bude. The bars have retained to a large extent the old character of the pub, while the family room is in a more modern annexe. The seasonal family trade is important to the continuing survival of this house, and good amenities are provided. A pool table and video games are to be found in the family room, while the large attractive garden is safe for young children who can enjoy meeting the farmyard animals living there. A wide range of dishes for small appetites is available on the substantial bar menu; there may also be a separate restaurant by the time you read this. Cots can be provided for families staying overnight.

Manor Inn, Galmpton

WILMINGTON
White Hart Inn

Tel. (0404 83) 226
*On A35, Honiton to Axminster
road*
Open 11–2.30; 6.30–11

✕ lunchtime and evening

🍺 **Draught Bass**

As the White Hart has managed to retain its several original small rooms – quite an achievement for one of the big brewer's pubs – it enables families to have a choice of two, either the "snuggery" lounge with easy chairs (but unfortunately, nothing in particular to amuse the children), or the dining room for those wishing to have a meal. A children's menu, or half portions of adult meals are provided, and the promised highchairs should have been purchased by the time this guide goes to press. Facilities for nursing mothers are available. The pub has two gardens, one of which is enclosed and therefore favoured by families. There is also a skittle alley. Dating back to the sixteenth century, this attractive pub makes a useful break from the busy A35.

ANSTY
Fox

Tel. (0258) 880328
Near Dorchester, four miles north of A354 (OS766033)
Open 11–3; 6–11

Ⓨ

🗨

✗ lunchtime and evening

☕

ⓒ **Hall & Woodhouse Badger Best Bitter; Tetley Bitter; Wadworth 6X**

The aptly named Toby Bar in this pub houses what is reputed to be one of the largest collections of Toby jugs in the country – almost 800 of them! While youngsters may not be too interested in such things, they are bound to enjoy the skittle alley and other games to be found in the large, purpose-built children's room and the garden play area. The brick and flint building dates from 1771 and was the original Woodhouse brewery and family home. Now it is a multi-roomed country free house, which caters well for the disabled as well as families. A good range of meals is on offer including salads, hot and cold carvery and a children's menu; baby feeding and changing facilities are also provided.

CERNE ABBAS
New Inn

Tel. (03003) 274
14 Long Street (off A352 Dorchester-Sherborne road)
Open 11–11 (may close winter afternoons)

Ⓨ

🗨

✗ lunchtime and evening

☕

ⓒ **Eldridge Pope Best Bitter, Dorset Original IPA, Royal Oak**

Cerne Abbas is an idyllic village whose peaceful surroundings and atmosphere are a tonic to city and town dwellers; the New Inn is in the main street. An added attraction on summer week-ends are the Morrismen who often perform in the village. Children are welcome in a family room which is separate from the bars, and also to the part of the bar where food is served. It is definitely worth going at mealtimes, especially for the cold "help-yourself-buffet" (£4.50); good sandwiches and snacks are also available. The garden is fully enclosed and safe for children. The Cerne Giant carved in the hillside, can be seen from here, but is not close enough for younger members of the family to observe his most obvious feature!

CHARMINSTER
New Inn

Tel. (0305) 64694
High Street
Open 12–2.30; 7–11 (maybe longer summer)

◎

🐕

✕

🍺 **Draught Bass; Charrington IPA**

There appears to be a plethora of New Inns in Dorset – this one is a Bass house. It is a fairly small pub on the main road to Cerne Abbas and Sherborne and close to Dorset. So while it benefits from being set in beautiful countryside, it is also handy for sightseers. Families are welcome in a large conservatory which opens onto the garden. Here there are slides and swings as well as chickens and geese; a stream runs along at the foot of the property so care must be taken with small children. Children's food (including vegetarian dishes) is always available and they are welcome in the pub at any time.

DORCHESTER
Stationmasters House

Tel. (0305) 65551
Weymouth Avenue (A354, near Dorchester South station)
Open 11–3; 5.30–11 (11–11 Wed)

◎

🐕

✕

🍺 **Eldrige Pope Dorset Original IPA, Royal Oak**

A brand new pub which only opened in July 1989, in the shadow of the expanding Eldridge Pope brewery, who thankfully had the good sense to include a purpose-built family room. This room in fact overlooks the station and railways are the theme of the pub, even down to the imaginative menu – try the Devon Belle, succulent ham in cider and apple sauce, or Copper Capped Chimneys (crème caramel). The special children's menu is designed along the same lines (pardon the pun). Food may be taken out to the small grassed area and terrace outside. The whole pub is very pleasant and tastefully designed, but avoid going on market day (Wednesday) when it gets very crowded. Dorchester is a very interesting place to visit – one notable former resident was Judge Jeffreys who held his infamous Bloody Assizes here after the Monmouth Rebellion.

EASTON, PORTLAND
New Inn

Tel. (0305) 821232
Open 11–2.30; 7–11 (maybe longer, especially summer)

☺

🍴

✘ lunchtime and evening (not Sun eve)

🍺 **Cornish JD Dry Hop Bitter, Wessex Stud**

Three miles from Chesil beach and Portland Bill, the New Inn makes an ideal watering hole after a brisk clifftop walk. And if you have built up an appetite, you can fill up at very reasonable prices – Sunday lunch for £2 for example, while children's meals (including vegetarian dishes) start from just 40 pence. The family room has a video jukebox and opens on to the garden which is full of playthings.

HIGHCLIFFE
Hinton Oak

Tel. (0425) 271040
Lymington Road (near Christchurch)
Open 11–2.30; 5.30 (6 winter)-11 (maybe open longer in summer)

☺

🍴

✘ lunchtime and evening

🍷

🍺 **Draught Bass; Charrington IPA**

The clean, comfortable conservatory which serves as the family room is possibly the nicest area of this large, modernised pub. Ideally situated for holidaymakers, it is five minutes' walk from the beach, within easy reach of Christchurch and New Milton, while a short drive takes you to the heart of the New Forest. The licensees make every effort to welcome and please everybody: WCs and facilities are provided for the disabled; there are separate toilets for children, highchairs and a baby changing room. All tastes are catered for too, with vegetarian dishes and a daily specials board; a three-course children's menu is offered at £1.75. Outside the open garden is safe for youngsters to roam around in and enjoy the play area.

KINGSTON
Scott Arms

Tel. (0929) 480 270
On B3069, south of Corfe Castle
Open 11–2.30; 6–11

☺

🍴

✘ lunchtime and evening

⋈

🍺 **Cornish Wessex Stud**

This creeper-clad, eighteenth-century hilltop pub enjoys panoramic views of Corfe Castle, Poole harbour and the distant Purbeck hills. In winter blazing log fires warm the bars and also the comfortable family room which features an inglenook.
In fine weather, children can enjoy the garden. Good, home-cooked bar meals are served – favourite dishes with customers are steak and kidney pudding and Dorset apple cake. Extra

plates are given for children so there is no restriction on choice. A notable feature of the pub is the photographic record of cinema and TV films which have been made locally; another is the lady ghost who closes doors – would-be overnighters take heed (the pub offers comfortable accommodation with two cots available). Kingston is just two miles from the sea and other attractions include the Abbotsbury swannery and sub-tropical gardens nearby.

LYME REGIS
Pilot Boat Inn

Tel. (02974) 3157
Broad Street (at foot of A3052 hill into town)
Open 11–11 (may close winter afternoons)

⊞

✕

🍺 **Palmer Bridport Bitter, IPA, Tally-Ho**

Set in the very centre of the small seaside town of Lyme Regis, this is a bright airy pub, improved of late from the dark low beamed bar it once was. Plans for sea defences may take away what beach there is, but it is a most pleasant spot. The Duke of Monmouth landed here in 1487 to begin the ill-fated Monmouth Rebellion. Children are welcome in the large family bar, where they and their parents may choose from the very enterprising (and long) menu which has a natural emphasis on local seafood. Children's portions are available.

OSMINGTON MILLS
Smugglers

Tel. (0305) 833125
One mile off A353
Open 11–11 (11–2.30; 6–11 winter)

◎

⊞

✕

⋈

🍺 **Courage Best Bitter, Directors; Ringwood Old Thumper or 4X**

The coastal path runs through the garden of this pub, so it is popular with walkers, but please note – no boots allowed indoors. It is a large, rambling free house (beware of low beams, both real and plastic), which can get very busy in summer. Children are welcome in a large room to the left of the bar which feels very much a part of the pub. In summer though, the garden is popular for its large play area. Food, including vegetarian dishes, is available most of the day, but only at lunchtime in winter. There is a children's menu or small portions from around £2. Six rooms are let for those who have walked far enough for the day.

RAMPISHAM
Tigers Head

Tel. (093583) 244
*One mile off Dorchester-
Crewkerne road*
Open 11–3; 6.30–11

✕ lunchtime and evening

⏾ **Draught Bass; Butcombe
Bitter; Greene King Abbot Ale;
Palmer IPA; Wadworth 6X**

A completely unspoilt pub, set in a very pretty garden at the heart of some of the most delightful countryside right by the river Frome. For unspoilt, read devoid of background music or fruit machines, just quiet, comfortable surroundings. The room set aside for families is also comfortable, carpeted and furnished with tables, chairs and a large sofa. Books, boxed games and jigsaws are provided, but space does not allow for larger toys. Meals, including fresh fish and a children's menu, are served at both sessions. Family accommodation (with cots) is available. Local attractions include the famous conservation centre at Kingcombe, and the coast which is just 12 miles away.

Langton Arms, Tarrant Monkton

STUDLAND
Bankes Arms

Tel. (092944) 225
*Well signposted from village,
near Swanage
Open 10.30–11 (10.30–3; 7–11
winter)*

@

🏠

✗ lunchtime and evening

🛏

🍺 Flowers Original; Whitbread
Pompey Royal, Winter Royal

At the time of writing this fifteenth-century coaching inn was awaiting an extensive modernisation from its owners, the National Trust. Hopefully, all the improvements will be good ones. Indeed, at present the family room is somewhat basic, but the pub is worth including for other reasons. A former smugglers' haunt, the inn is a stone's throw from a safe beach and is at the start of a coastal footpath walk. Meals are available at both sessions, as well as cream teas, but all at "tourist" prices. The garden has a play area. Most of the six en-suite bedrooms have sea views.

TARRANT MONKTON
Langton Arms

Tel. (025889) 225
*One mile from A354 at Tarrant
Hinton
Open 11.30–2.30; 6–11*

🏠

✗ lunchtime and evening

🛏

🍺 Draught Bass; Wadworth 6X;
guest beer

This traditional thatched pub is situated in a charming village near Blandford Forum and surrounded by some of the most spectacular scenery in England, which has changed little since Thomas Hardy immortalised the area at the turn of the century. There are two pleasant bars with real fires where a selection of home-made meals are available; small portions and a menu are offered for children and highchairs are provided. Youngsters are welcome here but mostly families prefer to use the huge skittle alley where there is plenty of space to run around, or go out into the garden. The pub has family accommodation (including cots) and is ideally situated for touring, being close to Salisbury, Wimborne Minster and the stately home of Kingston Lacy.

BLACKHOUSE
Charlaw Inn

Tel. (0207) 232085
Between Durham and Chester-le-Street
Open 11–3; 6–11

◎

🕭

✗ lunchtime and evening

🍺 **McEwan 80/-; Younger No. 3**

This large country pub is convenient for Durham City and also the fascinating Beamish Museum. This is an absolute must for families, with its reconstructed miners' cottages, shops, mine workings, old vehicles and other displays showing how people used to live. The Charlaw, which has a lively bar and pleasant lounge, welcomes families in the conservatory and restaurant. A children's menu is available as are feeding/changing facilities for babies. The enclosed garden is safe for children and has a play area with varied equipment.

DARLINGTON
Arts Centre

Tel. (0325) 483271
Vane Terrace (west of centre)
Open 12–2; 6–10.30 (11 Thu-Sat); closed Sun

✗ 12–2

🎭

🍺 **McEwan 80/-; Theakston XB; Younger Scotch, No. 3**

Although obviously not a pub, the Arts Centre deserves inclusion because, apart from anything else, there appears to be no decent pubs in the town where you can take children. Here entertainment is laid on too. There is no family room as such. The children's centre is used mostly by regular playgroups, but can be hired for parties. Otherwise children are allowed in any of the areas away from the bar, ie the large foyer/bistro, garden bar and ballroom. There is a children's menu, and although meals are only served at lunchtime, snacks are available 10–3 and 5.30–9. Highchairs are provided and while no special feeding facilites for babies are available, staff will always try to find a quiet space if asked. Regular children's workshops are held at the centre as well as visits by puppet or children's theatre companies.

LOW CONISCLIFFE
Baydale Beck

Tel. (0325) 469637
On A67
Open 11–3; 5–11 (11–11 Thu, Fri and summer)

✖ lunchtime daily and evening Thu-Sat

🍺 John Smith Bitter

The Beck, from which this pub takes its name, flows alongside the pub into a particularly scenic stretch of the Tees. Another attraction is the historic Tees cottage pumping station nearby, which is now a working museum. This two-bar pub is just outside Darlington at the western side of the town. It can get pretty busy as there are not many pubs around here. The conservatory is very popular with families, who come just for a drink or for a meal (children's menu provided); bar snacks are also served. There is some play equipment in the garden.

METAL BRIDGE
Wild Boar

Tel. (0740) 654268
One mile east of Thinford (A167)
Open 11.30–3; 6–11

✖ lunchtime and evening

🍺 Draught Bass; Bass Special Bitter

Recently refurbished, this Victorian country pub is very much food-oriented. Indeed family facilities inside the pub are really only provided for mealtimes. It is worth eating here though as the food is very good and a children's menu is served. If you do not wish to have a meal, then go on a fine day and enjoy the large, secure beer garden and play area. It would make a useful lunch spot on the way to or from Durham City (seven miles), the Beamish Museum (15 miles) or the vast shopping extravaganza at the Metro Centre (18 miles).

NEASHAM
Fox & Hounds

Tel. (0325) 720350
24 Teesway
Open 11–3; 6–11

✖ lunchtime and evening

🍺 Vaux Samson, Ward Sheffield Best Bitter

Backing on to the Tees, along a particularly attractive stretch of the river, the Fox and Hounds is a pleasant and popular village pub. It has a busy, friendly bar, the haunt of dominoes players, while the spacious lounge is predominantly used by diners. The family room is quite small, but should have been extended by the time you read this, into a new conservatory. Games and video machines are provided indoors, while the large garden has a good adventure playground and swings. Children's portions are offered from main dishes (average adult price is around £3).

WOLSINGHAM
Bay Horse Hotel

Tel. (0388) 527220
59 Upper Town (B6296 Tow Low road)
Open 11.30–3; 5.30–11

✗ lunchtime and evening

⌐ **Tetley Bitter**

Facilities for children are a bit limited here, but the Bay Horse is listed as it can accommodate families overnight and has a good reputation for food and will cater for children at mealtimes. Situated in a picturesque part of the town, it is a cosy two-roomed pub, decorated in traditional country style, and always kept neat and clean. There is no separate dining area, but children are always made welcome if eating with adults; meals are served from midday until two and from seven until ten o'clock.

CASTLE HEDINGHAM
Bell Inn

Tel. (0787) 60350
10 St James Street (B1058)
Open 11–2.30; 6.15–11

ⓐ

🛉

✖ lunchtime and evening (not Mon eve)

🍺 **Greene King IPA, Abbot Ale**

An excellent old pub with a friendly atmosphere, situated in a timeless north Essex village. It has real fires and a separate public bar with cribbage and dominoes. The real attraction for visiting families (and steam buffs), however, is the nearby Colne Valley Railway. The village also boasts a Norman castle. Families are welcome to eat in the saloon bar which oozes character with its beams, polished wood floor and open fire, or if you prefer, there is a separate small room without a bar. Summer visitors can also enjoy the garden. Good value food is served daily, ranging from ploughman's for around £1.80, to steaks for £5.50.

GESTINGTHORPE
Pheasant

Tel. (0787) 61196
*Audley End (off B1058
Hedingham-Sudbury road)*
Open 11–3; 6–11

ⓐ

🛉

✖ lunchtime and evening

🍺 **Adnams Bitter; Greene King IPA, Abbot Ale; Mauldon Pheasant Bitter; Nethergate Bitter, Old Growler**

This traditional country free house with beams and log fires in both bars, offers an interesting selection of real ales. There is an intimate dining room (serving a chip-less menu) or bar snacks and meals are available; children's portions can be ordered. The family room is just off the saloon bar so benefits from the pub atmosphere. Soft drinks cocktails make a nice change for youngsters from the usual coke and lemonade choice. Baby changing facilities are provided. The licensees' private garden has play equipment and can be opened to customers on request.

GREAT CLACTON
Robin Hood

Tel. (0255) 421519
211 London Road (A133)
Open 11–2.30; 6–11

ⓐ

🛉

✖ lunchtime and evening

🍺 **Draught Bass; Charrington IPA**

Although there is an emphasis on food here, with an extensive and varied menu, the pub is not given over entirely to catering for diners. An attractive, multi-roomed building with plenty of exposed beams, the pub was originally several medieval cottages. Pool is played in an extension at the rear. The clean, tidy family room is quite large, furnished with tables and bench seats and overlooks the garden. Baby changing facilities are provided. Outside are some swings and a safe play area. The pub is on the main road into Clacton, so handy for daytrippers.

LANGHAM
Shepherd & Dog

Tel. (0206) 272711
Moor Road (off A12, near Colchester)
Open 11–3; 6.30–11

⊕
⊞
🍺 Adnams Bitter; Courage Directors; Greene King Abbot Ale; John Smith Bitter

This is a popular pub with just one bar, but lots of cosy corners. It is frequented on some Saturday afternoons by teams and supporters from the soccer club at the new village hall nearby. A restaurant was opened during 1989, but closed due to lack of demand, although the owners may try again later. For the moment upmarket bar snacks are available (vegetarian if requested) and may be eaten in either the bar or the family room which is in fact the former restaurant. Children need to bring their own entertainment to the pub (eg books or games). There are some tables on the grass outside where traffic is light, but small children do need supervision. Constable fans should know that Old Langham church, near Stratford St Mary lock on the river Stour, features in some of Constable's work.

RAYLEIGH
Paul Pry

Tel. (0268) 742859
14 High Road (A129 towards Rayleigh Weir)
Open 10–2.30; 6–11

⊕
⊞
✗ lunchtime and evening
🍺 Ruddles Best Bitter, County; Webster's Yorkshire Bitter

The unusual name of this pub comes from a popular early nineteenth-century play about a chap who had so little to occupy him, that he was always prying into other people's business. This little snippet of information comes from "A Dictionary of Pub Names" (available from CAMRA) which is a wonderful resource for car games to keep restless passengers amused on long journeys. But back to the pub in question, which is a very old building that has been tastefully enlarged and modernised – although the Robbers' Roost bar somewhat lowers the tone! There is a reasonably sized family room with tables and chairs, video games and fruit machines. This has direct access to the ladies/children's toilets where babies can be changed, and to the garden. At mealtimes, children may choose from their own menu, or take small portions of adult dishes which range in price up to around £6. Outside, the large, well-equipped garden has a play area and Rayleigh Mount and windmill are within walking distance.

RICKLING GREEN
Cricketers' Arms

Tel. (079988) 322
Open 11–3; 6–11

◎

⊞

✖ lunchtime and evening

ⱨ

ⵂ Greene King Rayment BBA,
Abbot Ale, guest beer

Rickling Green has been a cricket green for over three hundred years and two teams still play every weekend throughout the summer. The highest score in English cricket was made here in 1882! In addition the green makes a large, safe play area for children of all ages and the pub's family room – the Pavilion – was in fact the cricket pavilion until recently. This can seat over 20 people and is in the oldest part of the pub (late sixteenth century) as its heavy beams attest. The Pavilion is next to the saloon bar; there is also a public bar and restaurant all offering a warm, cosy atmosphere. Children may have small portions of adult meals; bar meals cost from £2, the restaurant is rather more pricey. The licensees are also happy to provide simple sausage and chip type meals if required. Highchairs are available. The pub has a good reputation locally for its food and drink; Wednesday is fish and chip night.

SHOEBURYNESS
Parsons Barn

Tel. (0702) 297373
Frobisher Way (next to the Asda store)
Open 12–3; 6–11

◎

⊞

✖ lunchtime and evening (not Sun eve)

ⵂ Adnams Bitter, Broadside;
Greene King IPA, Abbot Ale;
Ruddles Best Bitter; Webster's
Yorkshire Bitter

Although we at CAMRA bewail the big brewers' tactics on many issues, it has to be said that they do often make an effort to cater well for families, and the facilities are not always tacky and plastic. This Chef and Brewer operation is in a converted barn where the stone floor and many original timbers have been retained. Families are welcome in a separate room with space invader machines (not my personal favourite, but many kids love them), which leads on to an enclosed garden. This features an adventure playground, aviary and mini-zoo. Baby changing amenities are provided in the ladies' toilet. Children are offered portions of adult dishes at approximately half price – from £1. The pub is a few minutes' drive from the seafront which has all the usual amusements and a safe beach. Also nearby are Foulness Island (birds) and Southend Airport (bigger birds).

SOUTHEND-ON-SEA
Liberty Belle

Tel. (0702) 466936
10–12 Marine Parade
Open 10–11

☺

🛏

🍴

🍺 **Courage Best Bitter, Directors;
John Smith Bitter**

A seafront pub with an appropriately nautical theme, the Liberty Belle sits opposite Southend's famous pier and is handy for the amusement arcades and cafes. The abundance of local food outlets means that the pub does not offer much in the way of solid sustenance, just snacks. There are two family rooms; videos are shown in the "summer" one, while the "winter" one is simply furnished with tables and chairs. Two pool tables are available for adult entertainment. The garden has a play castle and fibre tree with swing and slide. A friendly atmosphere pervades the pub which caters for a good local trade as well as the heavy influx of summer trippers.

WEST TILBURY
Kings Head

Tel. (03752) 3081
The Green (half a mile south of East Tilbury-Chadwell St. Mary road)
Open 11–2.30; 5.30–11

🛏

✖ lunchtime and evening

🍺 **Charrington IPA**

Although called the Kings Head, this pub's greatest claim to fame is that it was visited by Elizabeth I during the Armada Review. A listed building on the village green, this is very much a fair weather pub as no indoor facilities are provided. It is, however, handy for Tilbury Fort and Coalhouse Fort and has a large garden and play area for children. A good variety of home cooked meals is served at both sessions, with vegetarian dishes available on request. Altogether a very pleasant place to stop awhile.

UPMINSTER
Thatched House

St. Marys Lane, Cranham
Open 11–3 (3.30 Thu, Fri; 4 Sat); 5.30 (6 Sat) - 11

☺

🛏

✖ lunchtime

🍺 **Draught Bass; Charrington IPA; Tolly Cobbold Original**

Situated just on the outskirts of Upminster, this really is a country house, with a large open field to the rear where the horses are tame enough to be approached by children. The usual type of bar food – scampi and chips, steak and kidney pie, etc. – is available at lunchtime; small portions are offered for children. The small family room should have been refurbished by the time this guide goes to press, but check that it is finished.

WORMINGFORD
Crown Inn

Tel. (0787) 227405
*Main Road (B1508, at north-west
end of village)*
Open 11.30–3; 6–11

🐾

✗ lunchtime and evening (not
   Sun eve)

🍺 **Greene King IPA, Abbot Ale**

On the south side of the Stour valley, the tiny village of Wormingford has one church and two pubs. The church is featured in Constable's work and some of the artist's family lie buried in its graveyard. Just uphill from the church is the lovely seventeenth-century, half-timbered Crown Inn. This is a pleasant, quiet pub, lit by real fires in both bars. Darts and pool are played in the public bar. Children are welcome in a comfortable room between the lounge and restaurant, so families feel very much part of the pub. Meals and bar snacks may be eaten here; these are mostly prepared from fresh produce and vegetarian dishes are an option. The large garden is very well equipped with seven tables, and a huge DIY barbecue. While parents sweat and curse over the hot coals, their offspring can amuse themselves in the safe play area or watch the goat, geese and ornamental pheasants.

BLEDINGTON
Kings Head

Tel. (060871) 365
The Green (B4450)
Open 10.30–2.30; 6–11

@

🍴 lunchtime and evening

🛏

🍺 **Hook Norton Best Bitter;
Tetley Bitter; Wadworth 6X**

In the heart of the Cotswolds, this fifteenth-century inn is set on the village green which comes complete with brook and ducks (all of whom are known to the locals by name) – sounds just like "Ambridge" doesn't it? The old-time country feel is continued in the pub with its beams, antique pews, and inglenooks. All that is missing is Sid Perks behind the bar. Families are welcome in the garden room, just off the lounge bar which leads out into the garden. There is a restaurant as well as an extensive bar menu which caters for children with small portions and also offers "potty potatoes" specially for youngsters. The traditional pub game of Aunt Sally can be played in the garden which is enclosed and safe for children. At the front of the inn, the green has swings and a seesaw. With overnight accommodation (including cots) available, the Kings Head would make a good base for touring the Cotswolds, it is conveniently situated for most of the main tourist spots eg Bourton on the Water with its model village, motor museum and game park, Burford and Stratford on Avon.

BROCKHAMPTON
Craven Arms

Tel. (0242) 820410
*Open 11–2.30 (3 Sun); 6–11
(children lunchtimes only)*

🍴 lunchtime and evening

🍺 **Butcombe Bitter; Hook
Norton Best Bitter; Wadworth
6X**

At the heart of a Cotswolds village, the Craven Arms is a sixteenth-century inn and restaurant where the emphasis is on food – indeed it has earned a place in CAMRA's "Good Pub Food" guide. Children are welcome at lunchtime in the dining room, but it is necessary to book on Sundays when there is a carvery. Children's portions are offered from the home-cooked fare on the extremely tempting menu which changes often; highchairs are available. The garden is enclosed and has some play equipment.

BROCKWEIR
Brockweir
Country Inn

Tel. (02918) 689548
Open 11–2.30 (3.30 Sat); 7–11
(maybe longer summer)

◎

🍴 lunchtime and evening

🍺 **Boddingtons Bitter; Flowers Original; Hook Norton Best Bitter;**

Facilities for families are a bit limited here, but is included mainly for its spectacular setting and tourist appeal. It is a picturesque seventeenth-century inn situated in the beautiful Wye valley, just 50 yards from the river. Tintern Abbey is a mile away and other local attractions include salmon fishing, riding and walks along Offa's Dyke. There is a campsite nearby. Stone walls and open fires are attractive features of the pub, as are the oak beams which came from a ship built at Brockweir many years ago. Families are welcome in a room which can seat 20 and, which leads directly off the bar, with no door to separate them from the rest of the pub. The safe, enclosed garden is also popular. Straightforward pub fare is offered, but it is all home-made, well presented and in generous portions.

Highwayman Inn, Elkstone

ELKSTONE
Highwayman Inn

Tel. (028 582) 221
On A417 between Cirencester and Birdlip village
Open 11–2.30; 6–11

🍴 lunchtime and evening

🍺 Arkells John Arkell Bitter, Best, Kingsdown Ale

An original Cotswold stone inn, full of beams, open fires and antique furniture. Hungry drinkers may choose from an extensive bar menu or eat in Turpin's Restaurant which is open in the evenings from Tuesday to Saturday; children's portions or special dishes are available. On Sundays the restaurant serves as an additional family area, although the pub already has two other rooms set aside for children. Baby changing facilities are provided in the ladies' toilet. Outside is an enclosed garden and a play area with swings and a slide.

GRANGE COURT
Junction Inn

Tel. (045276) 307
Off A48 at Westbury-on-Severn.
OS725160
Open 11.30–2.30; 6 (6.30 winter)-11; all day Sat

🍴 lunchtime (not Sun) and evening

🍺 Burton Bridge XL; Donnington Mild, SBA; Hook Norton Best Bitter; guest beer

As its name implies, the Junction has railway connections, with much memorabilia displayed in the bars. The menu continues the theme with "Stokers' Standby" being the speciality dish. Home-made curries are served every Friday (shades of "A Passage to India" I suppose). Apprentice stokers are offered their own menu or small portions; do little boys still want to be engine drivers I wonder, now that the romance of the steam age has passed? Ask staff for a room to feed or change babies, they will happily oblige. The family room doubles as the skittle alley which has tables and chairs and is due to be updated to provide other amusements. The enclosed garden has a playhouse, slide and sandpit and there is also a large field where children can let off steam (sorry!) and play ball games. The pub may stay open during the afternoons in summer if it is busy. Situated in the Forest of Dean, it is convenient for a vist to the Dean Heritage Centre, popular with families for its good walks, adventure play area, museum and animals.

KINGSCOTE
Hunters Hall
Inn

Tel. (0453) 8600393
On A4135 between Tetbury and Dursley
Open 11–3; 6.30 (6 Fri, Sat)-11

@

&

✗ lunchtime and evening

⋈

🍺 **Draught Bass; Butcombe Bitter; Hook Norton Best Bitter; Smiles Best Bitter; Uley Old Spot**

Children are well catered for at this old stone coaching inn. Even families wishing to stay are provided for – two bedrooms with cots and their own cooking facilities. Passing visitors, however, can enjoy the large family area where there is food service. Children's dishes of the fishfingers and chips variety are available, or parents may prefer to order portions of the adult dishes. Highchairs and baby feeding changing amenities are provided. Outside, youngsters are in their element in the extensive play area, which for the peace of other customers is set apart from the main garden where summer barbecues are held. Here they can be let loose on the mini assault course, swings, slides and play barrel fort. When they have had enough of that you can take them off to one of the local tourist attractions – Slimbridge Wildfowl Trust, Berkeley Castle, Westonbirt Arboretum or Gloucester National Waterways Museum.

LITTLE
WASHBOURNE
Hobnails Inn

Tel. (0242 602) 237
On A438, six miles from Tewkesbury
Open 11–2.30; 6–11

@

&

✗ lunchtime and evening

🍺 **Flowers Original, IPA**

At the foot of the Cotswolds, where the wide valley sweeps down to the river Severn, lies the charming Hobnails Inn, which has been run by the same family since 1743, although it was built nearly three centuries earlier. The pub has a good reputation for food, but children have their own "puppy" menu, which they may take home as a souvenir. All puppy meals are served in "Hot Dog Rolls" and include such delights as Puppy Dog in a Kennel – sausage and baked beans or more imaginatively, Puppy Hot Chicken which comes in a creamy sauce. For very young puppy customers baby soup and soldiers or Heinz dinners and clown face ice cream can be provided. Three highchairs are available. Families are welcome in the dining room if they wish to eat, or in a separate function room (check availability). The public bar has darts, skittles and shove-ha'penny, while children's play equipment is in the garden. There is a campsite nearby.

MINCHINHAMPTON COMMON
Old Lodge Inn

Tel. (045 383) 2047
*On the top road across the
common – Stroud-Cirencester
road (take road to Nailsworth at
Tom Long's Post, then follow signs
up private road)
Open at 12 noon and 6 pm;
closing time varies*

⊙

🏕

✗

🍺 **Ind Coope Burton Ale; Tetley
Bitter; Theakston Best Bitter;
Wadworth 6X**

Built in the sixteenth century as a hunting lodge for Henry VIII, the pub later became the original home of the Minchinhampton Golf Club in 1889. It lies alongside the golf course, amidst 600 acres of National Trust land with magnificent views overlooking the Cotswolds in what has become known as the "Royal Triangle". The area is popular for airborne activity – kites and remote-controlled aircraft, as well as balloonists can often be observed from the pub garden. The family room has natural stone walls and can seat around 24 adults; doors open directly on to the lawned garden where there are swings. The spacious building also encompasses a lounge bar, Tom Long bar, candlelit restaurant and skittle alley. Tom Long, incidentally, was a local highwayman who was hanged at Tom Long's post near the pub. The Old Lodge is popular for food – you need to book Sunday lunch. Children's portions or their own menu are provided, as are highchairs and baby facilities.

Old Lodge Inn

BEAUWORTH
Milburys

Tel. (096 279) 248
Off A272 to Petersfield, through village
Open 10.30–2.30; 6–11 (9.30–3; 7–10.30 Sun)

✗ lunchtime and evening

🍺 **Courage Best Bitter, Directors; Gales HSB; John Smith Bitter**

Children (and adults) are fascinated by the unusual feature of this pub's family room: a 300–foot well with a 24–foot treadmill, reckoned to be 250 years old; youngsters are particularly keen to drop ice cubes down through the safety grid! This friendly free house, which boasts the best views in Hampshire, is set in the "middle of nowhere" in beautiful countryside half a mile outside the village. The owners not only welcome children but dogs and horses too if accompanied by well-behaved adults. The family room is actually the converted stable, but I trust that horses are now excluded from their former home. The garden has some play equipment; the quiet bars are lit by real fires. The lunch and evening menus offer small portions or children's dishes. Most of the dishes are prepared on the premises and daily specials are chalked on the blackboard. The pub opens at 9.30 on Sunday mornings for brunch. Highchairs are provided.

CHANDLER'S FORD
Cleveland Bay

Tel. (0703) 269814
1 Pilgrims Close, Knightswood Road (off Templars Way)
Open 11–11

✗ lunchtime and evening

🍺 **Hall & Woodhouse Tanglefoot; Wadworth IPA, 6X, Farmers Glory, Old Timer**

Opened just a couple of years ago, this pub was built to serve a new housing development at the edge of Chandler's Ford. It has a large bar with flagstone floor and bare red brick walls. Although none of the five distinct areas of the bar is given over specifically to families, the pub was designed to, and indeed does successfully cater to their needs. Meals are inexpensive and good value for money, with a choice from the adult or children's menu; two highchairs are provided. Food may be taken out to the large garden which is set with tables and chairs and has a brook running through it. Some play equipment should have been purchased by the time you read this.

DAMERHAM
Compasses Inn

Tel. (072 53) 231
On B3078, six miles from M27
Open 10.30–2.30; 6–11

ⓐ

🛏

✗ lunchtime and evening

🛏

🏆

🍺 Ind Coope Burton Ale;
Wadworth 6X

Ideally situated for visitors to the area, within easy reach of the New Forest and the coast, the Compasses offers free accommodation for the under-fives. It lies practically on the village green with cricket pitch and trout lakes nearby for idling away summer days. Indeed summer is best for visiting this pub for its large garden with swings and play area. Inside families are welcome in the dining room, where half portions and a children's menu are served. The pub has two bars, warmed by real fires in winter when games such as darts, pool and shut-the-box are popular.

DUMMER
Sun Inn

Tel. (0256) 75234
Winchester Road (four miles
from Basingstoke on A30)
Open 12–2.30; 5.30–11

ⓐ

🛏

✗ lunchtime and evening

🍺 Courage Best Bitter, Directors

This popular old-world roadhouse is set back off the A30 in attractive rural surroundings. Early evening visitors can take advantage of the "happy hour". There is an extensive menu of mostly standard pub fare; the "Kiddies Corner" offers the usual sausages, burger or fishfingers, all served with chips. But I should not gripe – my own offspring think its a great treat to be offered such delights and tuck in readily. The small children's room has a blackboard and space invader machine, whilst an extensive play area in the garden offers swings, climbing frame, seesaw, swingboats and a trampoline.

HANNINGTON
Vine Inn

Tel. (0635) 298525
A mile and a half off the A339
Open 12–2.30; 6.30–11

ⓐ

🛏

✗ lunchtime and evening

🍺 Gales HSB; Hall &
Woodhouse Badger Best
Bitter, Tanglefoot; Marston
Pedigree; Ringwood Old
Thumper, Ruddles Best Bitter,
County; Wadworth 6X, IPA

It seems rather appropriate that Old Thumper should be served in a pub so close to Watership Down (or was he in "Bambi"?). In any case, the Vine is situated in a small village near the location of Richard Adams' famous bunny novel and also a popular walk along the Kingsclere Downs. Although off the beaten track, this is a very busy pub with many of its customers being attracted by its restaurant's good reputation. Snacks are always available if you do not want a full meal and a children's menu is served. The family room holds 30 people and has a video machine. The garden covers an acre, with an area set aside for play equipment.

HAYLING ISLAND
Rose in June

Tel. (0705) 463208
2 Selsmore Road (near seafront)
Open 11–3; 5–11

ⓐ

🅱

✗ lunchtime and evening

🍺 **Gales HSB; Ruddles Best
Bitter; Webster's Yorkshire
Bitter**

This is a very pleasant old four-bar pub, close to the beach and other facilities. A small area where families are welcome gives out on to the garden which boasts slides, swings, a climbing frame and an aviary. Meals are available at any time, with a children's menu to choose from.

HOLBURY
Old Mill Inn

Tel. (0703) 891137
*Lime Kiln Lane (off A326 near
Hardley Industrial Estate)*
Open 11–11 (11–3; 6–11 winter)

ⓐ

🅱

✗

♟️

🍺 **Harvey Sussex Bitter;
Ringwood Fortyniner, Old
Thumper; Ruddles County;
Webster's Yorkshire Bitter;
Young Special**

Originally a barn and adjoining thatched cottage dating back to the fourteenth century, this large, rambling pub has many rooms, each with its own individual character. The family room is next to the main bar and can seat 24. It has table football, pool and a video game, suitable for older children. At lunchtimes, when the pub fills up with customers hungry for its home-made food, an overspill family room is available in an unopened bar. Highchairs, small portions and a children's menu for £1.75 are offered. Children are welcome (and actively encouraged) except Monday evenings when the family room is closed. Not surprisingly, the garden is favoured by youngsters; its huge range of equipment includes two trampolines, a "dizzy disc", climbing frame and adventure house. Local places of interest are Beaulieu House and Motor Museum, Buckler's Hard, Exbury Gardens and the New Forest.

KINGS WORTHY
Cart & Horses

Tel. (0962) 882360
London Road (A33)
Open 11–3; 5.30–11 (all day on
Bank Holidays)

ⓐ

🅑

✗ lunchtime and evening

🅓 **Marston Burton Best Bitter,
Pedigree, Owd Rodger**

Another large rambling pub, this time a road-house on the A33 which aims to cater for all needs. The public bar provides a quiet retreat from the rest of the pub, and indeed, the world in general. A busy restaurant offers a good selection of food, including home-cooked daily specials. The family room doubles as the skittle alley and is, unfortunately, in an adjoining building, but ideal if you like skittles! Perhaps best for children though is the very large garden and playground.

OLD NETLEY
Plough

Tel. (042 121) 2743
Portsmouth Road, Bursledon
(A3035)
Open 11–3; 6–11 (all day Fri &
Sat)

ⓐ

🅑

✗ lunchtime (not Sun)

🅓 **Ruddles Best Bitter, County;
Webster's Yorkshire Bitter**

This two-bar pub lies to the east of Southampton near the area immortalised in TV's "Howards Way". Pleasing to the eye, the pub has been a winner of the Phoenix Brewery's Floral Awards for its hanging baskets. Reasonably-priced, standard bar fare includes a children's meal for around £1.30. Families are welcome in a room off the lounge bar where there are two space invader-type machines and separate toilets (with facilities for mother and baby). Various domestic animals can be observed in the large garden which also has a trampoline, swings and a seesaw (and flowers!).

PORTSMOUTH
Thatched House

Tel. (0705) 821527
Locksway Road, Milton, Southsea
Open 11–2.30 (3 Sat); 6–11

ⓐ

🅑

✗ lunchtime and evenings

🅓 **Friary Meux Best; Ind Coope
Burton Ale; King & Barnes
Sussex Bitter; Tetley Bitter**

A thoroughly modernised old pub which enjoys extensive 'views over Langstone Harbour. It stands close to the old sea lock that once joined the harbour with the now defunct Portsea Canal. Families appreciate the fact that it is also not too far from the beach and other attractions of the resort of Southsea. There is a large family room with half-glazed walls, so you still feel part of the pub. Indoor amusements include video games designed for children, and there is more play equipment in the extensive outdoor area. Highchairs and a children's menu are offered, but meals here tend to be a little pricey.

UPPER CLATFORD
Crook & Shears

Tel. (0264) 61543
At the village centre, two miles south of Andover
Open 11–2.30; 6–11

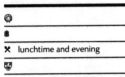

✕ lunchtime and evening

🍺 Flowers Original; Whitbread Strong Country Bitter, Pompey Royal (or guest beer)

Families are not the only members of the community that are thoughtfully considered here as this pub is the regular meeting place of the local disabled group. It is also a popular choice for walkers, cyclists and anglers. A charming thatched house in the delightful Test Valley, it is everything a village local should be: friendly public bar, cosy lounge, comfortable dining room and a skittle alley for hire (this serves as the family room in winter). There are baby changing facilities and even a cot and baby alarm for tiny customers (although the pub has no overnight accommodation). Most of the meals and snacks are home-made; children may choose from their own menu. In summer families make a beeline for the spacious courtyard – note the 200 year-old wisteria – and enclosed garden which has a good play area.

BRETFORTON
Fleece

Tel. (0386) 831173
The Cross (off B4035)
Open 10–3; 6–11 (maybe longer summer)

✕ lunchtime and evening

🍺 **Hook Norton Best Bitter;**
M & B Brew XI; guest beer

Bretforton is a delightful Cotswold village and the lovely timber-framed Fleece Inn is one of its showpieces. Originally a medieval farmhouse, it was converted to an inn in 1848 and the interior remains much as it was in the nineteenth century. Now owned by the National Trust, no outside signs are allowed. The pub's two main rooms have no bar – service is from a central point – so families are able to enjoy the premises to the full. Traditional games, such as Evesham quoits, are played and the garden has some children's play equipment. The good value meals are prepared using local produce as much as possible, eg home-cured ham and Gloucester sausages; children's portions are available.

GRIMLEY
Camp House Inn

Tel. (0905) 640288
*One and a half miles off A443,
Camp Lane*
Open 11–3; 6–11

⊚

☷

✗ lunchtime and evening (not
   Sun)

🍺 **Flowers Original, IPA;
    Wadworth 6X; Whitbread
    West Country Pale Ale**

This unspoilt riverside inn has been a recent winner in Whitbread's regional Best Garden competition. On the bank of the Severn, the pub provides moorings for boats and so is particularly popular on summer weekends, when barbecues are held. The garden has a covered area for when it gets cool and there is also a safe play area for children. Families are welcome to use the room provided inside the pub, but most prefer to watch the riverside activity. Excellent, home-made bar meals are served at very reasonable prices. The pub has its own caravan park and being situated close to Worcester, it is a useful base for tourists.

LEOMINSTER
Royal Oak Hotel

Tel. (0568) 2610
South Street (A44/A49 jct)
Open 10–2.30; 6–10.30

✗ all day

🛏

🍺 **Hook Norton Best Bitter;
    Wadworth 6X; Wood Special**

This pub does not have the most brilliant family facilities, but it is convenient for visitors to this ancient market town, especially if you wish to eat, and have a decent glass of beer at the same time. Food is served virtually all day, from breakfast through until 9.30 pm. An extensive children's menu is available in a separate area of the lounge bar where families are welcome. Highchairs are provided and there is a video machine, but no other amusements. Overnight accommodation includes cots. Leominster is an attractive town in itself, surrounded by some breathtaking countryside, and also makes a useful stopover en route for Wales.

LONGDON
Plough

Tel. (068 481) 324
On B4211, near Tewkesbury
Open 11–2.30; 7–11

✗ lunchtime and evening

🍺 **Marston Burton Best Bitter,
    Pedigree; Tetley Bitter;
    Wadworth 6X**

An unusual feature of this pub, which is full of bric-a-brac, is its collection of gas masks. It is a very popular hostelry, convenient for Malvern and Tewkesbury, and gets particularly busy on summer weekends. Customers then spill out into the garden, which is not huge, but does have a slide, and more play equipment, including a sandpit, is planned for 1990. Families are welcome, but the only room without a bar is the skittle alley, a game that can be enjoyed by all ages. Standard pub fare is served and beefburgers and chips, etc are offered in junior portions.

PEMBRIDGE
New Inn Hotel

Tel. (05447) 427
On A44, Leominster-Kington road
Open 11–3; 6–11

◎

✗ lunchtime and evening;

⋈

⊞ **Flowers Original, IPA;**
Marston Pedigree

This is an imposing fourteenth-century inn set in a square of buildings of the traditional local black and white design. A cobbled drinking area in front of the pub overlooks the town's old Wool Market. Inside the bar has flagged floors, antique settles and log fires. Originally a courthouse, the cellar was used as the jail and the restaurant has been converted from the former stables. It is believed that the Treaty for England's Crown was signed at the inn's Court Room as the pub is less than six miles away from Mortimers Cross, site of the decisive battle of the Wars of the Roses. Families are welcome in a small room off the main bar which has books, toys and a television. The pub is popular locally for its food – there is a varied menu, including vegetarian dishes, and children's portions are offered. A highchair and baby changing/feeding facilities are provided. A cot can be provided for overnight guests. Local places of interest include Offas Dyke and Ludlow Castle.

SPETCHLEY
Berkeley Knot
Inn

Tel. (090565) 293
Evesham Road, Sneachill (B4084)
Open 11–3; 6–11

⊠

✗ lunchtime and evening

⊞ **Draught Bass; M & B Brew XI**

This really is a fairweather pub, as it has no indoor room for families, so do not go on a rainy day, unless you wish to eat in the restaurant (children's portions are served). Internally, the pub's many small rooms have been knocked together to make a large lounge and restaurant – good home-made food is a major feature here. It is a country inn, set in three acres of ground with two patios. Food is served to both patios during the summer. Children however, are far more interested in the field where they can run around and enjoy the playground. If you can drag them away, then Spetchley Gardens and the historic city of Worcester are both a short drive away.

WORCESTER
Kings Head

Tel. (0905) 26204
Sidbury
Open 11–11

✕ 12–2 (not Sun)

⋈

⊕ **Banks's Mild, Bitter**

The King's Head is another of those pubs, scattered throughout this book, which warrants a mention, simply because of its situation. It is remarkably difficult to find pubs that have good facilities for children in busy tourist towns. Presumably, because they have so much trade anyway that they do not need to bother to attract any more. Very centrally situated, near the cathedral, canal and museums, this is a pleasant old pub where families are able to sit out in the courtyard in fine weather, or ask to use the skittle alley if wet. Snacks and meals start at 60 pence. As I say, it would not normally deserve inclusion, but if it's a choice between this and McDonalds I know which I would plump for.

YARPOLE
Bell Inn

Tel. (056 885) 359
Green Lane (half a mile off B4362)
Open 11.30–2.30 ; 6.30–11

⊛

✕ lunchtime and evening

⊕ **Wood Special Bitter**

A classic black and white village inn where the adjacent former cider mill has been converted and incorporated into the pub to provide an additional lounge-cum-family area. A children's menu is provided, but the food is slightly on the pricey side for the area. There is an enclosed garden which has safe play area with a climbing frame and swings for children. The Bell is not far from the market town of Leominster and the Welsh border.

CHORLEYWOOD
Old Shepherd

Tel. (09278) 2740
*Chorleywood Bottom at the corner
of the common
Open 11–3; 5.30–11*

✗ lunchtime & evening (not
Wed eve)

🍺 **Benskins Best Bitter; Ind
Coope Burton Ale; Tetley
Bitter**

A pub for Thomas the Tank Engine fans! Licensee Mike Farrant is an addict, so not only is the children's room decorated along this theme, but the main bar too. I expect he's disappointed the pub's not called the Railway Tavern (it is close to the station). This is a small, friendly place where you are recommended to bring your appetite if you intend to eat (although children's portions are served too) – try the home-cooked specials. The family room has a couple of tables and chairs, a rocking horse and some other games (not all TT jigsaws). There is a large garden which the licensees have managed to tidy up since they moved in a couple of years ago and play equipment is planned, but not yet acquired.

Sportsman Toby
Hotel

Tel. (09278) 5155
*Station Approach
Open 11–3; 5.30–11*

✗ lunchtime and evening

ᴍ

🍺 **Draught Bass; Charrington
IPA**

This upmarket hotel near the common and golf course caters well for families, including those staying overnight (cot available). The Huntsman Bar has bar billiards and darts and there is a larger saloon upstairs. Childen are welcome in the separate family room and the well-equipped garden which has a slide, swings, wendy house and climbing frames. Barbecues are held occasionally in summer; otherwise children can choose from their own menu in the Toby Grill or small portions from the adult menu. Under-fives are welcome to have an extra plate to share their parents' meal. Highchairs are provided.

TRAVEL PURSUITS

Some of the traditional games that have been passed down for years through the generations, are still hugely enjoyable (which is why they have endured) and although they may strike us parents as being rather jaded, to children who have not encountered them before they are fresh and new. One such simple game that is ideal for travelling is cats cradle – and all you need is a length of string. The problem is of course trying to remember how those rather complicated hand movements worked. I can only recall the most basic ones. However my local library came up with a book on the subject, so I am now practising hard.

CROXLEY GREEN
Artichoke Ale House

Tel. (0923) 772565
The Green (off M25 at Rickmansworth)
Open 11–3; 5.30–11 (all day summer)

☺

🛏

✗ all day (not Sun eve)

🍺 **Ruddles Best Bitter, County; Webster's Yorkshire Bitter**

The Artichoke looks like the archetypal village inn; flower-bedecked and standing on a large village green where folk bands and clog dancers occasionally perform. It makes a wonderful escape from the urban sprawl of Watford, just 15 minutes' drive away. It is a popular Chef and Brewer establishment where food, to suit all appetites, is available any time the pub is open (no hot meals are served during the afternoon). The small children's area leads off the single bar and has junior tables and chairs, but parents would be well advised to bring a few small toys with them. There is an enclosed garden with a slide, playhouse and ride machine.

HERTFORD
Woolpack

Tel. (0992) 583766
Millbridge (just off town centre)
Open 11–2.30; 5.30–11

☺

🛏

✗ lunchtime

🍺 **McMullen Original AK, Country Best Bitter**

Hertford is an attractive old market town, bulging with antique shops and home of the family brewers McMullen. The Woolpack is a very traditional style inn, with ivy-covered exterior and hanging baskets. Inside, the theme is continued with country furniture, sawdust on the floor, open fire and even gas lighting. The children's playroom has games machines. The pub is set right by the river and in summer it is very pleasant to sit out on the patio and watch the activity on the water.

HITCHIN
Sailor Boy

Tel. (0462) 59727
Woolgrave Road (off A505, Letchworth side of town)
Open 11–11

☺

🛏

✗ lunchtime (not Sun)

🍺 **Flowers IPA; Wethered Bitter**

This is a very popular, modern pub on the outskirts of town. The large main room is divided with partitions and very pleasantly decorated and furnished – pine is much in evidence. Families are welcome in the conservatory attached to the main lounge area. On Sundays at 12.30 children's videos are shown, which leaves parents free to enjoy their drinks and relax. There is some play equipment in the garden.

KINGS LANGLEY
Langleys
Steakhouse

Tel. (09277) 63150
Hempstead Road (A41 road to Hemel Hempstead)
Open 11–11

✕ lunchtime and evening

⊲ **Theakston Best Bitter; Younger Scotch, IPA**

More of an eating establishment than a pub, Langley's does however have a separate bar. This is decorated in thirties style to match the restaurant. I would not choose to come here for an evening drink *sans enfants*, but the family facilities are good. For a start, it is set in over three acres of wooded garden which includes a safe play area with wooden benches, swings and other equipment. Indoors the large, comfortable family lounge has games machines and rides for children and videos are shown at the weekends. Children may choose dishes from their own or the snack bar menu. Highchairs and baby changing/feeding facilities are provided.

MARSWORTH
Red Lion

Tel. (0296) 668366
90 Vicarage Road (off B489)
Open 11–3; 6–11 (children welcome until 9)

✕ lunchtime and evening (not Sun)

⊲ **Draught Bass; Halls ABC Bitter; Wadworth 6X**

A true waterways pub, this Grade II listed building was built at the same time as the Grand Union Canal on which it stands (by Bridge 130). It is set at the foot of an attractive flight of locks and adjoining canal reservoirs – one of which is a bird sanctuary. This unspoilt pub has quarry tiled floors and exposed beams. The family/games area used to be a private cottage adjoining the pub, and earlier this century housed a family of eight – some of them must have slept in cupboards! The family room leads into the garden, which is safe for children. Morris dancers sometimes perform here and the pub is also a venue for two travelling theatre companies (phone for details of performances).

PATCHETTS GREEN
Three Compasses

Tel. (0923) 856197
Near Aldenham, close to the A41
Open 11–3; 5.30 (6 Sat) - 11

☺

🛏

✗ lunchtime and evening

🍺 **Benskins Best Bitter; Ind Coope Burton Ale; Tetley Bitter**

This deceptively large pub enjoys a pleasant rural setting, yet is not far from the busy towns of Watford and St Albans, which I am ashamed to say, being my own home as well as the hometown of CAMRA, cannot provide a single decent family pub. It is a good job most Albanians have cars these days, to take them out to the Three Compasses, combined with a visit to the nearby, unspoilt Aldenham Country Park which has a lakeside walk, wooden play equipment and small children's zoo. There are animals too at the pub itself – a pets' corner in the large garden which also has a play area. Inside the pub is an unusual display of carpentry tools. The conservatory doubles as a restaurant where the pub grub served is above average; a children's menu is available. A large family room can seat 30 people comfortably, and children's videos are often provided.

WHEATHAMP-STEAD
Wicked Lady

Tel. (0582) 832128
Nomansland (B651, towards St Albans)
Open 11–11

☺

🛏

✗ lunchtime and evening

🍺 **Boddingtons Bitter; Brakspear PA; Flowers Original; Marston Pedigree; Wethered Strong Country Bitter; Whitbread Castle Eden Ale**

When you are hungry, thirsty and wind-blown from an excess of kite-flying on Nomansland common opposite, retire to the Wicked Lady to recuperate. Parents can collapse on the grass or at the tables and benches provided in the large garden, while their offspring, whose energy of course knows no bounds, can scramble over the wooden equipment in the open adventure playground. The only problem is getting them home again (I know – I've often had to climb to the top of the slide to "persuade" my two year-old it's time to go). If it's too cold to sit outside – although youngsters rarely think it is – the pub has a pleasant conservatory where families may sit to drink and eat. A children's menu and highchairs are provided and videos are often shown to keep the little ones amused.

CLEETHORPES
Victoria

Grant Street (near station)
Open 11–11

○

✗ lunchtime

⚲ **Draught Bass, XXXX Mild;
Stones Best Bitter**

Once a large, seafront hotel, the Victoria has been refurbished to provide a single large bar area, which is popular with the young. It is a short stroll from the resort's amusement arcades, pier and gardens, and of course, the inevitable fish and chip shops. Fish is supplied direct from the famous Grimsby docks nearby, so is definitely worth a try. The family room is decorated and furnished to a high standard and due to be upgraded in 1989 with the addition of some play equipment. There are separate children's toilets, a full range of soft drinks and children's menu.

NEW WALTHAM
Harvest Moon

Tel. (0472) 822025
Station Road (off A16)
Open 11–3; 6–11

○

✗ lunchtime

⚲ **Ind Coope Burton Ale; Tetley
Mild, Bitter**

It is a shame that we have only managed to come up with two entries for Humberside, but the first edition had none at all, so things up there are slowly improving. The family room at the Harvest Moon is rather basic, but it does at least have its own toilets (with facilities for changing/feeding babies) which many so-called family pubs do not offer. The room opens on to a safe, enclosed garden which has a swing, slide and climbing frame. There is a set lunch for youngsters at £2.25. This is a large, modern pub which has recently been refurbished.

BRADING
Bugle Inn

Tel. (0983) 407359
56–57 High Street
Open 10.30–11

@

🍴

✗ all day

🍺

🍺 **Flowers Original ; Fremlins Bitter**

In the summer of '89 Whitbread spent £180,000 refurbishing the Bugle Inn, and I am pleased to say that the under-twelves have particularly benefitted. Outbuildings have been converted to make a children's club where a small kiosk, manned during peak periods, sells soft drinks, crisps and sweets. Drawing equipment, games and videos are also on tap. Outdoors there are swings and rides in the enclosed garden. A children's menu is on offer all day, highchairs are provided and the new toilet block has changing facilities for babies. If you can ever get the little dears out of the place, Brading itself has much to offer, including the Isle of Wight Wax Museum, "Animal World" next door and, right opposite the pub, the Lilliput Museum of Antique Dolls and Toys, housing one of Britain's largest private collections.

CARISBROOKE
Shute Inn

Tel. (0983) 523393
Clatterford Shute, off Newport-Shorwell road
Open 11–3 ; 7–11 (no children Sun eve)

@

✗ lunchtime and evening

🛏

🍺 **Burt VPA ; John Smith Bitter**

Just a mile from Newport, this delightful old inn enjoys a country situation with fine views of Carisbrooke Castle (where Charles I was once imprisoned). The family room is separate from the bar and has a pool table and juke box, but there are no facilities to cater for babies or very young children. Older children will undoubtedly find something from the bar menu to suit them, if a meal is required. The family room is closed on Sunday evenings. There is a beer garden and the inn also offers overnight accommodation.

CHALE
Wight Mouse Inn

Tel. (0983) 730431
On B3399, off A3055
Open 11–11

◎

🐌

✗ lunchtime and evening

🛏

🍺

🍺 **Burt VPA; Gales HSB; Marston Pedigree; Whitbread Strong Country Bitter**

The Wight Mouse Inn is attached to the Clarendon Hotel and children are most welcome in both parts of the establishment, which boasts a total of three family rooms. The licensees are very sensitive to the needs of all their customers and parents are considered as much as the children. Therefore only one of the children's rooms has noisy machines which are hard on the purse as well as the ear. Bar food, using mostly home-cooked local produce, is available all day (except Sunday afternoons). There is also a separate restaurant. Children's portions are provided as are highchairs. Holidaymakers staying at the hotel will also find cots and even pushchairs provided. Live music is performed every night of the week, and is enjoyed as much by the children as other customers. The garden has swings, slides and a climbing frame, but the particular favourite with the children is the menagerie. Dogs, rabbits and kittens are joined in season by pet lambs, which the youngsters find absolutely captivating.

NEWPORT
Wheatsheaf
Hotel

Tel. (0983) 523865
Open 10.30 (earlier for breakfast and coffee)-11

◎

✗ all day

🛏

🍺 **Flowers Original; Whitbread Strong Country Bitter**

This handsome sevententh-century coaching inn has Cromwellian connections – the republican leader once held a parliamentary meeting there. The family room which is on the ground floor and furnished as the rest of the pub, is also used as an overflow area for other customers at busy periods. Bar meals, which are available all day, can be taken here; a children's menu is offered. The inn is siutated at the centre of the town which is popular for its Tuesday market. Carisbrooke Castle is two miles up the road and it is no more than four miles to the nearest beach.

BEAN
Black Horse

Tel. (04747) 2486
High Street (B255, half mile off A2)
Open 11–2.30; 6–11

◎

🍴

✘ lunchtime and evening (not Sun)

🛡

🍺 **Ruddles Best Bitter, County; Webster's Yorkshire Bitter**

Bean is an attractive little village, close to the busy town of Dartford. The Black Horse is very popular with families, the main attraction being its mini-zoo whose monkeys keep children entertained for ages. There is also a very large aviary, a play area and a barbecue park in the spacious garden. The pub has a family room and restaurant where small portions and a children's menu are available. Baby changing/feeding facilities are provided. Nearby is a campsite.

BENOVER
Woolpack Inn

Tel. (089 273) 356
On B2162, one mile south of Yalding
Open 11–2.30; 6–11

◎

🍴

✘ lunchtime and evening (not Sun)

🍺 **Shepherd Neame Master Brew Bitter**

This splendid seventeenth-century country pub has a skeleton in the cupboard – literally! Most youngsters these days seem to have nerves of steel and are likely to be undaunted, but their parents can recover their composure in the small, comfortable family room. This is next to the main bar area which is part brick-floored and has an unusual double inglenook. Food here is good value and comes in generous portions; children's meals cost around £1 and a speciality is home-made ice-cream. Unfortunately, there is no particular play equipment for children, but the large garden gives them space to stretch their legs. An added attraction is the Whitbread Hop Farm which is just ten minutes' away.

Hop growing in the 16th Century, courtesy of Whitbread Hop Farm

BOUGHTON MONCHELSEA
Red House

Tel. (0622) 743986
Hermitage Lane (take right turn east of Cock Inn on B2163, then second left)
Open 12–3; 7–11 (11.30–11 summer Sat)

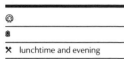

✕ lunchtime and evening

♨ range is rotated on six handpumps

Somewhat isolated in a rural setting, the Red House is well worth finding for the genuinely friendly welcome that is extended to all customers. The main part of the pub is eighteenth century ragstone with later extensions. It has two bars, one of which is for games (pool and darts). Children and even well behaved dogs, are welcome in the lounge/dining area which has an open fire, or in the conservatory. A selection of board games, cards, cribbage and dominoes are available, or in fine weather enjoy the garden, set in four and a half acres with a field for camping. Hot meals are served at lunch and in the evening, ploughman's and sandwiches are always available, prices range from 60 pence. The pub is popular with walkers on the local footpaths; other attractions nearby include Boughton Monchelsea Place, the Maidstone Carriage Museum and Kent Rural Life Museum.

EAST MALLING
Rising Sun

Tel. (0732) 843284
125 Mill Streeet (half a mile from A20)
Open 11–3; 6–11

✕ lunchtime and evening

♨ Shepherd Neame Master Brew Bitter, Stock Ale (winter)

This traditional village local is ideally placed for visitors touring the delightful Weald of Kent. It is close to the county town of Maidstone, the fairytale Leeds Castle and other places of interest. Pleasant country walks can be taken among the orchards at the back of the pub. The large family room doubles as a games room, with pool, snooker and football tables, or children may prefer to play out in the garden. Meals are reasonably priced and a children's menu is offered, as well as snacks.

ICKHAM
Duke William

Tel. (0227) 721308
*The Street (one and a half miles
off A257 Sandwich-Canterbury
road)*
Open 11–2.30; 6–11

ⓘ
🛏

✘ lunchtime and evening

🍺 **Adnams Bitter; Fuller London
Pride; Shepherd Neame
Master Brew Bitter; Young
Special; Biddenden Cider**

Visitors to Canterbury may like to sample some country air and come out to this free house in a picturesque village just a short drive from the city. There is an *à la carte* restaurant where you can eat for around £12 – children's portions are available, but families may prefer to choose something from the extensive list of bar snacks which cost around £2. The family room is at the rear of this sixteenth-century pub and leads out to a delightful garden where there are swings and a climbing frame.

MARSHSIDE
Gate Inn

Tel. (0227 86) 498
Open 11–2.30 (3 Sat); 6–11

ⓘ
🛏

✘ lunchtime and evening

🍺 **Shepherd Neame Master Brew
Bitter, Best Bitter, Stock Ale**

The Gate sounds more like a local community centre than a pub, but then that's just what pubs were before they invented the box that sits in your living room. Here customers enjoy all kinds of regular activities and team games such as quizzes and softball, while other entertainment such as Mummers plays are put on occasionally and "Fingers" can be heard tinkling the ivories on Sunday evenings. An amazing range of locally-made hand puppets, including the popular squashed hedgehogs, are sold in the bar, so there is never any reason to get bored. Games are also provided in the large family room where excellent food is available at all times – try the bean and vegetable hotpot for £2.85 or a black pudding sandwich for 90 pence. A stream runs through the garden and ducks, geese and chicken roam free. The pub is handy for Canterbury and the coast.

MONKS HORTON
Black Horse

Tel. (0303 81) 2182
Fiddling Lane
Open 11.30–2.30; 7–11

◎

🛏

✗ lunchtime and evening (not
Sun eve/Mon)

♚

🍺 **Shepherd Neame Master Brew
Bitter; Ruddles Best Bitter,
County; Webster's Yorkshire
Bitter; guest beer**

My mum and dad often visit this pub, because they say the food's really good! It is all home-made and there is always a daily special and the prices are reasonable too. They have not yet had a chance to take their grandsons there, but they assure me that the family/games room looks quite presentable. Most children though just love to be out in the large garden which has a pets corner and a play area with swings, etc. Summer barbecues are held here on Sunday lunchtime and evenings, weather permitting. The pub itself dates back to the late seventeenth century, but many later additions have produced a long bar with exposed brick and timbers.

SELLING
White Lion

Tel. (0227) 752211
*The Street (off A251, south of
Faversham)*
Open 11–3; 6.30–11

◎

🛏

✗ lunchtime and evening

♚

🍺 **Shepherd Neame Master Brew
Bitter**

This Shepherd Neame house is just a short drive from Faversham, where the brewery has recently restored a medieval hall as its visitor reception centre. It is a fine old brewery with many original features, and well worth a visit. The White Lion is not so young either – dating back some four hundred years, it is in the heart of Kent's hop country. It was refurbished a couple of years ago, but all its best features were retained. Families are welcome in a small carpeted room off the bar which has a video and fruit machines. Children's portions are served from the home-cooked menu, for which the pub is well regarded locally. There is a pleasant garden which is home to guinea pigs, rabbits and other domestic animals as well as a large aviary. The landord is a trumpet player and entertains the locals with his band every Monday evening.

SMARDEN
Bell

Tel. (0233 77) 283
*Bell Lane (approx. one mile from
village – follow pub signs)
Open 11.30–2.30; 6–11*

◎

⊗

✕

⋈

⊖ Brakspear Bitter; Flowers
Original; Fremlins Bitter;
Fuller London Pride;
Goachers Light Maidstone
Ale; Harveys IPA

At last, a Kentish free house that actually offers beer from a local independent brewery, Goachers. This pub is worth a visit just to try it! It is a very busy, sixteenth-century country inn with three bars, the public which is busiest, and two quieter bars at the rear. A large room off the public bar is set aside for families so they really feel part of the atmosphere. Meals from £1.25 are good value for money and the home-cooked specials are excellent; children's portions are available. Some games are provided and there is a play area in the garden.

WHITBREAD HOP FARM

When I was a young lass growing up in Kent in the fifties and sixties, hopfields were a very familiar sight. My mother, who is positively ancient of course, can remember even further back to the days when Londoners still used to come down in droves to pick the hops. Since then, sadly, the county has changed – whole farms have been replaced with housing estates, and the place is swamped, like most of the south-east, with people moving further and further out from London, only to commute back into it. Kentish hops are, however, still prized and the Whitbread Hop Farm at Beltring does an excellent job in educating the public about them, at the same time as providing an enjoyable day out for the family.

Although a working farm, it is extremely well organised for visitors, with a host of things to see and do, including several museums, a working craft centre, the oast houses, nature trail, and picnic areas. New for 1990 will be a restaurant, new stables with farriers shop and cartwright, a play area and pets corner. You can also see the Whitbread shire horses which are still used to deliver beer by dray in London; the highlight of their year is pulling the ceremonial coach at the Lord Mayor's show. There are 20 shires in all, and some of them can always be seen at the farm.

Special events are staged at the farm during the year, including traction engine rallies, the hop festival, and heavy horse shows. A list of the events can be obtained by writing to the Whitbread Hop Farm, Beltring, Paddock Wood, Kent;. tel. (0622) 872068. The farm is open to the public every day from 12th April until 21st October, 10am - 5.30pm; it is open on Bank Holiday Mondays. Admission in 1990 will be £2.50 per adult, £1.50 for children and senior citizens. School tours and group outings can also be arranged.

WALTHAM
Lord Nelson

Tel. (022 770) 628
In village, off B2068 from Canterbury
Open 11–2.30; 7–11 (closed all day Tue)

☸

✗ lunchtime and evening

🍺 **Adnams Bitter; Hall & Woodhouse Tanglefoot; Shepherd Neame Master Brew Bitter; Biddenden Cider; guest beer**

An attractive Georgian free house, this pub has been chosen really for its wonderful setting, rather than for its indoor facilities. It is situated in a small North Downs village in one and a half acres of lovely safe gardens with glorious views across the surrounding valleys and countryside. The traditional game of bat and trap is played here. It is just six miles from Canterbury and other local attractions include Chilham Castle, Howletts Zoo and the coast (just eight miles away). There is no family room as such, but children may eat with their parents in the dining room, either off their own menu or small portions of adult dishes; vegetarians are catered for. Otherwise, families are welcome in the snug. Mother and baby facilities are available in the ladies toilet.

ADLINGTON
White Bear

Tel. (0257) 482357
5a Market Street (A6)
Open 11–11

◎
🌮

✗ lunchtime and evening (not Mon)

🍺 **Matthew Brown Mild;
Theakston Best Bitter, XB, Old
Peculier**

This attractive old stone pub lies on the main road, close to the Leeds-Liverpool canal and White Bear Marina. Not surprisingly it is very popular with anglers and other canal users. It has two bars and two side rooms, one of which serves as the family area. An excellent range of home-cooked meals combines large portions with low prices; the children's menu starts at 80 pence. The family room opens on to a safe, enclosed garden where play equipment includes swings, climbing frame and a slide. This genuinely friendly hostelry is just ten minutes' away from the Rivington Pike, a noted beauty spot, and the Pennines.

CHARNOCK RICHARD
Bowling Green

Tel. Coppull (0257) 793732
On A49 Leyland-Coppull road
Open all day

___

◎
___
🛏
___
✗   at all times
___
🍺   **Marston Pedigree; Whitbread Castle Eden Ale**

Although very much an eating establishment, with most of the lounge given over to diners, the licensees do not fail to look after their other customers, particularly families. Meals may in fact be taken in the family room (except during the afternoon); highchairs and a children's menu are provided. This is a very large country pub and the family room is spacious with lots of toys and playthings to amuse young children. Outside, the facilities are also excellent. An exciting playground has slides, swings, rope ladders, climbing frames and a playhouse. What more could they wish for? An added bonus is that Camelot Fun Park is close by. Personally, I think I'd rather stay at the pub which is open all day, after all!

CLEVELEYS
Royal Hotel

Tel. (0253) 852143
North Promenade
Open 11.30–4 (5 Sat) 7–11

___

◎
___
🛏
___
✗   lunchtime
___
🍴
___
🍺   **Boddingtons Bitter; Higsons Mild, Moorhouses' Premier Bitter, Pendle Witches Brew**

A former seafront hotel with fine dark wood fittings, the accommodation here is now self-catering apartments. The pub is split into four main areas, one of which is the games area and another the family room. This latter is in fact, a spacious seafront sun lounge, so maritime activity can be observed while you sup or dine. Meals here are fairly plain but good quality; children are catered for too. Some games are provided indoors and outside the garden has a play area.

CROSTON
Black Horse

Tel. (0772) 600338
West Head Road
Open 11–11

___

◎
___
🛏
___
✗   all day
___
🍺   **Draught Bass; Thwaites Best Mild; guest beers**

Just ten miles from Southport, the Black Horse makes an ideal watering hole for a Sunday drive out into the country. It is an old free house in a picturesque village, and is also handy for the Martin Mere Wildfowl Trust and the West Lancashire Light Railway at Hesketh Bank – both popular with families. Children are welcome in the plainly furnished conservatory or in the restaurant where meals are served all day (including breakfast); a children's menu is available. The pub has its own bowling green out the back.

ELSWICK
Boot & Shoe Inn

Tel. (0995) 70206
Beech Road (one mile from A585,
near Preston)
Open 11.30–3; 6–11 (all day Sat)

ⓒ

🍴

✗ lunchtime and evening;

ᴹ

🍺 Thwaites Best Mild, Bitter

This large attractive, modern pub is the centre of village life, yet no more than eight miles from the bustle of Blackpool. A friendly welcome is assured, as is a good pint of beer. Amusements are provided for all the family – darts, dominoes and pool for the elder members, and a safe play area with swings, and a seesaw for the youngsters. The garden is also used for barbecues every Friday evening in summer; otherwise meals and snacks are served daily, with a separate menu for children.

GREAT HARWOOD
Victoria

Tel. (0254) 884810
St Johns Street
Open 11.30–3; 6–11

ⓒ

🍴

✗ luncthime

🍺 Matthew Brown Mild, Bitter;
Theakston Old Peculier
(winter)

On the outskirts of the town, this is a fine example of a Victorian pub which has been sympathetically restored to keep its original features, such as tiled walls, intact. No one particular area is set aside for children, but there are four bar-less rooms where families are welcome and thus really feel part of the pub. The snug, darts and pool room can all be used as well as the television room which overlooks the floodlit bowling green, so there is plenty to keep the whole family amused. The pub is surrounded by countryside which adds a pleasant aspect to the garden where there are picnic tables, a play area, pool table and table tennis. Meals (with children's portions if requested) are only served at lunchtime, snacks are available in the evening.

LONGRIDGE
Alston Arms

Tel. (077 478) 3331
Inglewhite Road (Chipping-
Inglewhite road, northern edge of
town)
Open 11–3; 6–11 (all day Sat)

ⓒ

🍴

✗ lunchtime and evening

🍺 Matthew Brown Mild, Bitter;
Theakston Best Bitter

Situated at the edge of the town, this old white-painted stone pub enjoys splendid views of Bleasdale and Longridge Fells. Also in sight is the Beacon Fell Country Park; and visitors to the area should not miss the picturesque village of Chipping nearby – the centre of the Lancashire cheese-making industry. You'll need a drink after all that sight-seeing and the Alston Arms is ideal if you have children in tow. An indoor room is set aside for families; but the real attraction here is the large fenced garden with timber swings, slide, climbing net, tyre bridge and log cabin. They'll need a drink too, after tackling that lot, so fortunately there is a kiosk selling tea, soft drinks and snacks. Oh, I forgot to mention the old Fordson tractor for children to play on and the wildlife that roams around the garden – goats, rabbits, doves and peacocks.

PILLING
Golden Ball

Tel. (0253) 790212
School Lane (near Pilling Mill and St Johns Church)
Open 11–3; 6–11 (all day summer Sat)

✕ lunchtime and evening

🍺 **Thwaites Best Mild, Bitter**

Bowling greens are obviously *de rigueur* in Lancashire – this pub boasts two of the Crown Green variety. It is, however, not compulsory to play; the pub also offers darts, snooker and pool while children have their own toys in the family room. There is a nice, safe beer garden and this too has play apparatus (of the junior variety). There is an extensive menu of reasonably-priced bar snacks, also set meals (for adults and children) are served in the large dining room. Pilling is a quiet country village, with a wide unspoilt beach, just eight miles from Blackpool. Other local attractions include Pilling Pottery and a large recreation ground right by the sands.

PRESTON
Continental

Tel. (0772) 51971
Riverside (just south of town centre on bank of Ribble)
Open 11–11 (11–3; 5.30–11 winter, all day Fri, Sat)

✕ lunchtime (not Sat)

🍺 **Boddingtons OB Mild, Bitter**

A popular pub on the banks of the Ribble, the Continental has been well modernised and caters properly for families. A spacious, warm conservatory serves as the family room and gives a complete view of the pleasant garden. This has a large lawn, picnic tables, flower beds and hanging baskets, and for children a sandpit, swings, and climbing frame with two slides. Children's portions or their own menu are served at lunchtime (only sandwiches are available on Saturday though) and highchairs are provided. The pub is set away from the town and traffic, but always busy, especially on Easter

Monday when "egg pacing" (rolling) takes place in the neighbouring Avenham Park. The park, together with the river and the Bac playing fields nearby (not to mention the pub), makes this an ideal spot for a family afternoon out. And in case you thought something was lacking, Preston Bowling Club is just close by.

ANNWELL PLACE
Mother Hubbards

Tel. (0530) 413604
Burton Road, Ashby-de-la-Zouch (A450)
Open 11–3.30; 5.30–11

☺

🛏

✘ lunchtime and evening

🍴

🍺 **Ind Coope Burton Ale; Tetley Bitter; guest beer**

Right on the border with Derbyshire and surrounded mostly by fields, this modernised pub was named after a former landlady, and not, as one might expect, after the nursery rhyme character. There is a large L-shaped bar/lounge which has an adjacent room used by families. This is available at any time except after 8.30 on a Monday evening, when it is used as a regular music venue; it may also be closed occasionally for functions. If you are making a special trip it may be worthing 'phoning to check. Food, including vegetarian dishes, can be ordered at any time until 9 pm; a children's menu is available. Babies may be changed in the ladies, but no provision is made to feed them. The enclosed garden has bench tables and a boot-shaped slide for the youngsters. Plenty of interesting places can be visited within a radius of ten miles, for example, the castle at Ashby-de-la-Zouch, Calke Abbey and Park, Twycross Zoo and Burton-on-Trent, famous for its brewing industry and home of the Bass and Heritage Brewery Museums.

BARROWDEN
Exeter Arms

Tel. (057 287) 247
28 Main Street (half mile south of A47)
Open 11–3; 6–11

🛏

✘ lunchtime and evening

🍺 **Bateman XB; Ruddles County; Ward Darley Thorne Bitter**

The Exeter, in common with thousands of other pubs, can adequately, and happily cope with children in the garden, but is hard put to cater for them properly indoors. That said, the Exeter is included because it is a delightful old world village hostelry in an idyllic setting overlooking the green and duckpond in what was formerly the county of Rutland. Families enjoying a fine day out at Rutland Water, Wakerley Woods or Rockingham Castle, would not wish to miss the opportunity of a visit to this free house (where the Batemans by the way, is excellent). Snacks and meals are available at both sessions, and a children's menu is served

CROFT
Heathcote Arms

Tel. (0455) 282439
Hill Street (off B4114)
Open 11.30–2.30; 5.30–11

@

🍴

🍺 Adnams Bitter; Everards
Burton Mild, Beacon Bitter,
Tiger, Old Original

This 300 year-old pub is set on a hill overlooking the village. Popular with the locals, a friendly welcome is also extended to visitors. The family room is used for games as well, with table skittles, pool and darts provided, so it would be wise to bring your own amusements for very small children. Food is restricted to snacks, but the range includes suitable dishes for children. The garden is safe for youngsters to roam in, but no play equipment is provided.

KILBY BRIDGE
Navigation

Tel. (0533) 882280
On the A50, one and half miles
from Wigston
Open 11.30–2.30; 5.30–11

@

🍴

✗ lunchtime and evening

🍺 Ansells Best Bitter; Ind Coope
Burton Ale; Tetley Bitter

A friendly, atmospheric, low-beamed canalside pub where there is always something going on, the Navigation is particularly popular on summer lunchtimes when drinkers and diners can enjoy the garden overlooking the waterway. There is a good choice of food, especially vegetarian dishes, all at reasonable prices. No particular concessions are made for children, but there is bound to be something to their liking on the menu, jacket potatoes or burgers, for example. A covered area at the side of the pub can be used by families in summer but as this has no heating, in winter one of the pub's many other rooms, for example the games room, can be used instead. Table skittles and a petanque pitch are among the amusements on offer here. The pub is not far from the city of Leicester.

OADBY
Firs

Tel. (0533) 888517
202 Oadby Road
Open 11–3; 5–11

🏠

✖ lunchtimes and evening

🍺 **Adnams Bitter; Everards
Burton Mild, Beacon Bitter,
Tiger, Old Original, Old Bill
Winter Warmer; guest beer**

The Firs was recently refurbished to include a large conservatory for family use, and much thought has gone into providing excellent facilities. This is one of the very few pubs in the country that really goes out of its way to cater for babes in arms. There are proper amenities for changing and feeding, even free nappies are available. Bottles can be heated and highchairs provided. Older children can choose something from either their own or the main menu; they also have their own "Pop Inn". The family room seats 50 and plenty more seating is provided in the huge enclosed garden. This has a large, well-equipped play area. An extra bonus is the children's entertainment that is laid on for Bank Holidays. Local attractions include the race course and Stoughton Farm Park. Leicestershire does not have many good family pubs, this one just shows what can be done.

BARHOLM
Five Horseshoes

Tel. (077836) 238
One mile off A16 at Tallington
Open 12–2 (not Mon); 7–11

🍽
🛏

🍺 Adnams Bitter; Bateman
XXXB; guest beer

This is a very "horsey" area, a fact that is reflected in the name and decor of this pub. A horse (and his friend, the goat) also gaze idly at the large patio and lawned garden. Barholm is a tiny village and this cosy, stone-built pub with its old lamps, beams and brassware, sits very comfortably in its surroundings. The family room is in an extension, but it is heated and carpeted to make it comfortable and congenial. Food is not generally served, but barbecues are held on Sunday evenings throughout the summer, when the country garden, which has a play area, really comes into its own. At least four guest beers are offered on a weekly basis, mostly from independent breweries. The Horseshoes is convenient for Tallington Water Sports Centre.

FREISTON
Castle Inn

Tel. (0205) 760393
Wainfleet Road
Open 10.30–3; 7–11

🛏

✗ lunchtime and evening

🍺 Bateman Mild, XB

Apprentice pirates can have a fine time in the garden here where the adventure playground includes an old fishing boat (in dry dock of course). Ideal for imaginative play, another exciting feature is the aerial runway (well I guess it makes a change from walking the plank). Unfortunately, this is really a fairweather pub; its single bar design does not allow for a family room, although children are welcome inside for meals. I do not think I would manage to get my own would-be Pugwash inside anyway, but children's portions of bar meals are provided for younger members of the crew. Freiston is roughly four miles from the centre of Boston.

OLD LEAKE
Bricklayers Arms

Tel. (0205) 870657
Main Road (A52)
Open 11–3; 7–12 (supper licence)

☺

✗ lunchtime and evening

🍴

🍺 Bateman Mild, XB

Children are welcome in this pretty country pub, but again, no family room is provided, so the 50–seater restaurant is the only legal area for them. As children's meals are priced at 95 pence, it would make a good value lunch stop on a day's outing to Skegness or other local tourist spots such as the Boston Stump and Sibset Windmill. The village is at the heart of Lincolnshire's market gardening area and abundant wildlife can be seen on the nearby marshes and the Friskney Decoy Wood to the north of Old Leake. The Bricklayers is a large pub, with a sizeable garden to match with swings and a sandpit for children to enjoy.

ROTHWELL
Nickerson Arms

Tel. (047289) 300
Hill Rise (off Horncastle road)
Open 11–3; 7–11

☺

✗ lunchtime (not Sat) and
evenings (not Sun/Mon)

🍺 Bateman XB; Marston
Pedigree; Rothwell Village
Bitter; Taylor Landlord; guest
beer

I do hope Lincolnshire has another good summer. Unfortunately, few of its pubs manage to offer indoor amenities for children. This is another that comes highly recommended by CAMRA members for its warm welcome to families, but with no separate room available it is suitable only in fine weather, or if you wish to eat. However, the enclosed garden has much to amuse youngsters, with swings, slides, roundabout, seesaw, climbing frame and other items that our surveyor professed to be much too old to identify!

A popular pub, the Nickerson Arms nestles amongst the Lincolnshire Wolds, three miles from Caistor and ten miles from the seaside resort of Cleethorpes. This is an area rich in wildlife, a short drive from the Humber Bridge. The Rothwell Village Bitter, by the way, is brewed by Hoskins and Oldfield in Leicester.

EAST LONDON

E9: HACKNEY
Falcon & Firkin

Tel. (01) 985 0693
360 Victoria Park Road
Open 11–2.30; 5.30–11 (11–11
Fri, Sat & summer)

⊚

🗑

✘

🍺 Falcon Ale, Hackney Bitter.
Dogbolter

A brew-pub, one of a chain built up in the eighties by David Bruce (mostly in London) which he later sold to Midsummer Leisure. Most of the pubs are family and fun-oriented, but without being the least bit tacky, and still managing to achieve a good pub atmosphere. Light and airy, with bare floorboards and church pews, the Falcon is typical of Bruce's style and was the first to receive the "Bo Junglies" treatment. This is the name given to the children's area which consists of an indoor adventure playground and seating area with tables. It is connected directly to the bar and has a separate entrance to the garden where there is more play equipment. The children's toilets have good amenities for dealing with babies. Meals and snacks are available at any time up until half an hour before closing; prices are very reasonable for the area.

CRANHAM
Thatched House

Tel. (04022) 28080
St Marys Lane
Open 11–3 (3.30 Fri); 5.30–11
(11–4; 6–11 Sat)

⊚

🗑

✘ lunchtime (not Sun)

🍺 Draught Bass; Charrington
IPA; Fuller ESB (winter); Tolly
Cobbold Original

This is a nice friendly, family local which is particularly popular for its food – mostly home cooked with regular special dishes. Vegetarian meals can be prepared on request and half portions are provided for children who like it when the food comes in little baskets so they can dig in with their fingers! Families are welcome in a room off the main bar. This is carpeted and has junior sized tables and chairs, but no special amusements. At time of writing, the pub was due to undergo some refurbishment which will entail increasing the size of the family room, but unfortunately, losing the garden.

UPMINSTER
Huntsman & Hounds

Tel. (04022) 20429
2 Ockendon Road, Corbets Tey
Open 11–3; 6–11

◎

⊗

✗ lunchtime

⊕ Ind Coope Burton Ale
(summer); Friary Meux Best;
Taylor Walker Best; Tetley
Bitter

Situated in the centre of Corbets Tey village, this is a congenial family pub that is very much the heart of the local community. The public bar is popular for darts and pool and teams take part in interpub competitions for these sports as well as quizzes. The family room is just off the main bar, so lacks nothing in pub atmosphere. What it does lack is any particular amusements for the youngsters, but this is compensated for in summer when the garden comes into use. Here a mini-zoo is home to various goats, chickens and other birds; there is also a fishpond and children's play area. Meals are served at lunchtime (children's menu provided), and snacks are available in the evening.

NORTH LONDON

NW1: KENTISH TOWN
Fuzzock & Firkin

Tel. (01) 267 4855
77 Castle Road (off Prince of
Wales Road)
Open 11–3.30; 5.30–11 (11–11
Thu–Sat)

◎

⊗

✗ (until 9.30)

⊜

⊕ Adnams Tally Ho; Bruces Ass
Ale, Fuzzock, Dogbolter;
Courage Directors; Hook
Norton Old Hookey

Situated in a quiet residential area, but handy for North London Polytechnic, this is one of the few former Bruce's pubs not to brew on the premises. It has a pleasant bar, simply furnished with lots of pictures of fuzzocks (donkeys). The children's room was closed at time of writing awaiting refurbishment, so do check if it has been re-opened as the "Bo Junglies" facilities are usually good. However, without that, the only place for children to go, is the garden, which is safe to run around in, but has no particular amusements. Hot food, as well as rolls and snacks are available any time the pub is open, up until 9.30. It is easy to get to by public transport (Kentish Town West BR), and not too far from Camden Town which is popular for the canal, antiques market and other attractions.

NW1: REGENTS PARK
Prince Albert

Tel. (01) 722 1886
11 Princess Road
Open 11–11

ⓐ

⊠

✗ lunchtime and evening

🍺 **Draught Bass; Charrington IPA**

The Prince Albert is ideally situated for families visiting London Zoo and is also handy for Regent's Park canal, Camden Lock and Primrose Hill. Not that you would get round all those in a single trip, but as the pub is open all day, you could pause for sustenance several times if you are determined to see as much as possible. Children are welcome in the conservatory which is small, but comfortable and where meals can also be taken. A good selection of food is offered and small portions are available on certain items at reduced prices. The pub also has a garden where barbecues are held on fine summer days.

NW3: HAMPSTEAD
Spaniards Inn

Tel. (01) 455 3276
Spaniards Road
Open 11–11

ⓐ

⊠

✗ lunchtime and evening

🍺 **Draught Bass, Highgate Mild; Charrington IPA; Fuller ESB; Young Bitter**

Another pub, chosen more for its position than its range of family amenities, but at least children are accepted here, which is still a rarity in London pubs. This historic hostelry is an attractive old building, right alongside Hampstead Heath and just a quarter of a mile from Kenwood House, so whether you fancy an energetic walk or a bit of culture, this pub will serve you well. The room commonly used for families doubles as a function room, so is sometimes closed, but in this case children are normally accommodated in other parts of the pub. No special amusements are provided, but there is a good sized garden which is safe for children. Meals are reasonably priced for the area and vegetarians are catered for, although no special concessions seem to be made for small appetites.

SOUTH LONDON

SE22: EAST DULWICH
Grove Tavern

522 Lordship Lane (junction with A205)
Open 11–11

⊛

✗

🍺 Courage Best Bitter, Directors

081 693 3661

The Grove has no special room set aside for families, but it is really a family restaurant as much as a pub. One of Courage's Harvester Inns, its restaurant seats 60 people and children are made very welcome with two different menus designed to appeal to different age groups. The garden here is also a big attraction and aims to achieve a rural feel with its aviary, rabbit hutches and haycart. There are swings and a climbing frame too. A separate ladies toilet in the garden has facilities for changing baby. The Horniman Museum, less than half a mile away, is very popular with youngsters for its collections of musical instruments and tribal masks and artefacts. It frequently features exhibitions of tribal life.

SE26: SYDENHAM
Dolphin

Tel. (01) 778 8728
121 Sydenham Road
Open 11–3; 5.30–11

🍴

⊛

✗ lunchtime (Mon-Fri)

🍺 Courage Best Bitter, Directors, John Smith Bitter

This is a typical Courage single-bar town pub in mock Tudor livery, but, hooray for Courage, it has a proper purpose-built children's room. Another bonus is that it sells the rarely found bottled Imperial Russian Stout. Traditional, home-cooked lunches are served, but not at the weekend. The family room opens onto a safe garden which has no access to the road. Here children can amuse themselves on the swings and slide and talk to the animals in the little menagerie. The pub is situated at the lower end of Sydenham's shopping area.

SW4: CLAPHAM
Tim Bobbin

Tel. (01) 622 1862
1 Lillieshall Road
Open 11–3; 5.30 (7 Sat) - 11

◎

🅱

✗ lunchtime Mon-Fri

🍺 **Ruddles Best Bitter, County;
Webster's Yorkshire Bitter**

Close to Clapham Common, this well established, prize-winning family pub particularly
welcomes children. It has attractive etched
windows and interesting artefacts all over the
walls and ceilings. The airy conservatory with its
surrounding courtyard is set aside for families,
with a particularly shady part especially reserved
for small babies. That is the sort of thoughtfulness
that wins prizes. This room is also available to
hire for meetings and parties. Lunches are served
during the week – children's portions available
"by negotiation", but snacks only are served on
Saturday. The enclosed garden is safe for little
ones to play in, but no special amusements are
provided either indoors or out. One niggle: the
beer is rather pricey.

SW12: BALHAM
Nightingale

Tel. (01) 673 0578
97 Nightingale Lane (B237)
*Open 11–3; 5.30–11 (all day Fri
& Sat)*

◎

🅱

✗ lunchtime (not Sun)

🍺 **Young Bitter, Special, Winter
Warmer**

The first in our capital selection to be owned by
the independent London brewery, Youngs. It is
always worth keeping an eye out in the
Wandsworth area, as Youngs still deliver some
of their beer locally by horse-drawn drays. These
magnificent animals are also kept for show and
to attend special events. This small but popular
pub is slightly off the beaten track, roughly half
a mile from both Wandsworth and Clapham
Commons. The rustic-style building lies almost
opposite the ruined walls of a supposedly
haunted abbey – so go in daylight! A small
conservatory at the end of the main bar area
serves as the family room. There is not enough
room to have toys in here, although a rocking
horse is available at Sunday lunchtime. The
room leads out on to a large walled courtyard
which is safe for children. The lunchtime menu
is simple fare, plaice and chips for instance and
portions can be provided for youngsters on
request.

SW13: BARNES
Red Lion

Tel. (01) 748 2984
2 Castelnau
Open 11.30–11

🗨

✗ all day

⌨ **Fuller Chiswick Bitter, London Pride, ESB**

The other London brewers, Fullers, own this pub where their full range of draught beers is on offer. It is a large, traditional, two-bar pub; the comfortable back bar leads into the restaurant where children are welcome even if not eating (but a menu for them, or small portions are available). A small bar is sometimes opened in the evening in the restaurant. However, this pub is really recommended for its outdoor amenities. The large garden has swings, a slide, seesaw and a small climbing frame. A pets' corner is home to some rabbits and guinea pigs. Barbecues are frquently held in summer. The pub is in fact great for a summer's day out as it is close to Barnes Common, Barn Elms sportsground and reservoirs – popular for fishing and bird watching and handy for riverside walks along the Thames.

SW16: STREATHAM
Greyhound

Tel. (01) 677 9962
151–153 Greyhound Lane
Open 11–3; 5.30–11 (all day Fri & Sat)

◉

🗨

✗ all day

☌

⌨ **Greyhound Pedigree Mild XXX, Special Bitter, Streatham Strong, Streatham Dynamite**

One of the pleasures of London, compared with many capital cities, is the abundance of parks and commons. Here is another pub set opposite another of London's green open spaces – Streatham Common. This one also has the added attraction of its own brewery, producing some pretty powerful ales, but also the only real mild brewed in the capital. It is a busy pub with a basic bar and sumptuous lounge, which caters for all comers at all times (particularly for food which is available all day, every day). The children's room, with its own toilets, is set in a solid conservatory at the back of the pub; some play equipment is provided. The enclosed garden is safe for children and often used for barbecues. Unusually for a London pub, there is overnight accommodation and cots are available.

SW19: WIMBLEDON
Broadway

Tel. (01) 542 1293
141 Broadway
Open 11–11 (11–3; 7–11 Sat)

◎

🎱

✗ lunchtime

🍺 **Courage Best Bitter, Directors;**
John Smith Bitter

This large former Hodgson's house is situated next to Wimbledon's only cinema and just up the road from the Polka Puppet Theatre. Across the Broadway the quiet, secluded South Park Gardens provides a tranquil spot if young children need an afternoon snooze in the pushchair. The pub has some interesting art deco features and a well-shaded conservatory where families are made welcome. A children's menu is available at lunchtime, but there are no other special facilities. The conservatory may be hired for parties.

Hand in Hand

Tel. (01) 946 5720
7 Crooked Billet (B281)
Open 11–11 (may vary)

◎

🎱

✗ all day (not Sun afternoon)

🍺 **Ruddles Best Bitter; Young**
Bitter, Special, Winter
Warmer

Another commonside pub – here the customers often spill over from the small front garden onto the common itself. It understandably can get very busy in summer, but it is not quiet the rest of the year either. It has one large bar with a separate, fairly basic family room. This is at the front of the pub leading on to the garden (which although it is open, is quite safe for youngsters). Traditional games, such as darts, shove-ha'penny, dominoes and crib are played – boards can be provided for children. Meals are professionally prepared and the menu caters for children as well as vegetarians.

Horse & Groom

Tel. (01) 542 3052
145 Haydons Road (A218)
Open 12–11

◎

🎱

✗ lunchtime (not Sun)

🍺 **Flowers Original; Marston**
Pedigree; Wethered Bitter

Just half a mile from the town centre, the Horse and Groom is handy for sports fans, as it is close to Wimbledon Stadium which features speedway, stockcar and greyhound racing, and the football ground (although it may be closed on some match days, so check). There is also a recreation ground opposite with swings and other equipment. It is a welcoming single-bar pub which is split-level to allow for a games area. There are games too in the small children's room at the back of the pub, including video machines and child-safe darts. The family room is also directly accessible from the car park. Ask staff about small portions of the lunch menu.

WEST LONDON

ISLEWORTH
Castle

Tel. (01) 560 3615
18 Upper Square
Open 11–11

@

🛏

✗ lunchtime (not Sun)

🍺

🍺 **Young Bitter, Special, Winter Warmer**

The only west London pubs we have managed to find are right on the edge, in what used to be called Middlesex, and in fact neither of these is brilliant, so if you dear reader, come across any better, please do write and tell us. The Castle is a friendly, roomy two-bar pub in the conservation area of old Isleworth. Children are made very welcome in the spacious conservatory or the garden. There are no special facilities for youngsters, but the pub is very close to Syon House and Park, and a hundred yards from the Thames. Children's portions can be provided at lunchtime; if you are peckish after 2.30, then you can order a toasted sandwich. Live jazz is served on Thursday nights.

Town Wharf

Tel. (01) 847 2287
Swan Street, Lower Square, Old Isleworth (ask for directions from Richmond tube)
Open 11.30–11 (children welcome until 9 pm)

@

🛏

✗ lunchtime and evening

🍺 **Samuel Smith OBB, Museum Ale**

A new (and successful) venture for Yorkshire brewers Sam Smith, the Town Wharf was built just two years ago on the site of a disused wharf, in a superb location overlooking the Thames, and just a stone's throw from Syon Park and Kew Gardens. Set in the middle of a new "development", the pub is away from the main road and the riverside terrace is quite safe for children. The upstairs lounge has a balcony with lovely views of the river. However, the family room, which is spacious and comfortable, is an area off the downstairs bar. The usual pub fare is served and children's portions can be provided, but it is more expensive to eat in the evening than at lunchtime.

BELLE VUE
Longsight

Tel. (061) 223 6470
*Kirkmanshulme Lane (A6010
between A6, Stockport road and
A57 Hyde road)*
*Open 11.30–3; 5.30–11 (11–11
Sat)*

◎

✕ lunchtime

🍺 Banks's Mild, Bitter

Sadly, Belle Vue as a family leisure centre, although still fondly remembered by many Mancunians, is long gone. However, the district still offers speedway, greyhound racing, ten-pin bowling, a multi-screen cinema and, right opposite the pub, a new athletics complex. The Longsight was built in the eighties with a quality of design and materials streets ahead of the national brewers' similar houses. The purpose-built family room, which shares an entrance with the off-sales counter, is smallish and simply furnished, but there are plans to extend it and provide a garden. Outdoors at present, there are just tables and chairs where children need to be supervised. Lunches cost around £2 and children's portions are avaible. Note that the children's room is sometimes used for meetings, so check if making a special visit.

BREDBURY
Ardern Arms

Tel. (061) 430 2589
*Castle Hill, (four miles from town
centre)*
*Open 11.30–3; 5.30–11 (all day
school summer hols; children
welcome until 8)*

◎

🛏

✕ lunchtime

🍺 Robinson Best Mild, Best Bitter

A cosy, comfortable pub with a rural feel to it, surrounded as it is by fields and farms, yet just four miles from central Stockport. Walkers can refresh themselves here before setting off along the Tameside valley. A room is set aside for families to use until 8 o'clock, but in the summer children prefer to be out in the garden. Here there is an enclosed play area with slide, swings, seesaw and climbing frame, as well as ample seating for adults. Both the snack menu and full meals can be adapted to suit small appetites.

CHEADLE
Queens Arms

Tel. (061) 428 3081
177 Stockport Road (A560)
Open 11.30–11

◎

🛏

✕ lunchtime

🍺 Robinson Best Mild, Bitter,
Old Tom

Beer buffs will note that the Queens Arms is a rare outlet for Robinson's ordinary bitter. That being of no interest to children, let's get on with the really important facts about the pub. A multi-roomed building, the family room is at the rear, where indoor games are provided. The large garden has swings and slides, tables and seating. A children's menu is available at lunchtime.

HOLLINWOOD, OLDHAM
Woodman Inn

Tel. (061) 682 4005
684 Manchester Road (A62)
Open 11–6; 7.30–11

◎

🕏

✗ lunchtime Tue - Fri

🍺 **Lees GB Mild, Bitter**

This terraced public house is situated on the main Oldham road, directly opposite the Roxy Cinema. It has a pleasant family room with a television and dartboard, which opens on to a nicely landscaped garden. There is also a separate access to the garden for prams and pushchairs. Barbecues are offered in fine weather; otherwise lunchtime meals (snacks only Monday and Saturday) cost from 55 pence.

MIDDLETON
Tandle Hill Tavern

Tel. (0706) 345297
14 Thornham Lane, Slattocks
Open 12–3; 7 11 (check for winter opening)

◎

✗ lunchtime and early evening

🍺 **Lees Bitter**

The Tandle Hill Tavern is not included for its excellence of family facilities, but for its position. It stands in an isolated spot on a quiet country lane surrounded by open farmland. It is reached by a field path, or bumpy road (children will love the adventure). Visitors to the Tandle Hill Country Park will find it a godsend, and despite its isolation it can get very busy on summer weekends, but maybe that has something to do with the warm welcome. Very reasonably priced snacks and meals are served; children are welcome at lunchtime and in the early evening.

RINGWAY
Airport Hotel

Tel. (061) 437 2551
Ringway Road, Wythenshawe
Open 11–11 (11–3.30; 5.30–11 Sept. - Easter)

◎

🕏

✗ lunchtime

⋈

🍺 **Robinson Best Mild, Best Bitter**

This multi-roomed pub has two advantages for families. The first is that it makes a change from the airport lounge if you are waiting for a delayed flight; the second is that children will love to visit it, just to observe the planes from close quarters. The garden is carved out of the airport itself – if you lean over the fence you could shake hands with the pilots! Not recommended for those with sensitive hearing. Children's portions are served at lunchtime; other than that facilities are a bit limited. The family room is somewhat basic (children are welcome until 9 o'clock), but if you really are delayed the accommodation includes cots. A somewhat quieter pub, also offering a children's room, is the **Romper** on Wilmslow Road.

ROYTON
Halfway House

Tel. (061) 624 0166
613 Rochdale Road
Open 12–3 (4 Fri, Sat);
6 (7 Sat) - 11

@

⊗

✗ lunchtime

⊌ **Lees GB Mild, Bitter**

A mile's walk from here through the Tandle Hill Country Park would lead you to the **Tandle Hill Tavern,** but if the troops are tired and hungry, this makes a good watering hole. It lies on the main road, two miles from Rochdale. The family room has its own entrance, but also connects with the main bar area. It can seat 30, and leads out on to the patio. Hot meals and snacks are served at lunchtime; half portions are available at half price which makes for very good value.

WIGAN
Seven Stars
Hotel

Tel. (0942) 43126
262 Wallgate (follow road to pier
on one-way system)
Open 12–4; 7–11

@

⊗

♜

⊌ **Thwaites Best Mild, Bitter**

The Wigan Pier complex is very popular with families, and this pub, just 200 yards away is a haunt of CAMRA members. Also handy for the town-centre shops and new market, this late Victorian Magee Marshall's house has a large lounge which opens onto the garden where there is a swing. Two pool tables, darts and dominoes are also available. Families may use the club room upstairs which offers baby changing/feeding facilities. Bar snacks are served from 12–2.

PUB GRUB FOR KIDS

Where will you find meteorites, depth charges and cosmic rain?

On pub menus of course. All are pubspeak for baked beans and are dreamed up by publicans who think they will strike the right note with their under-age customers.

These high-fibre convenience pellets from galactica will beam down with space invaders or rockets (sausages); UFOs or flying saucers (burgers); submarines or Jaws (fishfingers); if you are lucky, maybe gold nuggets (chicken nibbles).

They have their own place on the menu too, generally towards the end (after puds but before the liqueur coffee). Usually it is labelled Children's Menu because the imagination of mine host, or hostess, has happily fizzled out by now – but if he's still feeling creative you may find your offspring patronised in Kidstuff, Kiddies Korner, the Young Ones or – yes I really have come across this – Little Customers. Yuk!

Still, never mind what they call it. What do pubs provide for children to eat and is it what they – or we – want? The average pub's approach to children's food is strictly unimaginative, however frolicsome the descriptions might be. Put simply, you fall between two (bar) stools: the pubs which graciously allow children to eat on their premises but make no concession to them whatsoever, and those which seek to show they welcome children by printing a brief menu for them.

Those in the first camp say kids can eat there but the same fare as their parents, however rich, heavy and unappealing to youngsters that might be (and at worst without any price reduction either). Those in the second provide a menu more or less summed up by the above descriptions, though not always in such colourful terms — ie beans 'n' chips, saus 'n' chips, burger 'n' chips, chicken fingers 'n' chips, chip butties 'n' chips, or chips 'n' chips.

Before I go any further I am afraid I must nail my colours to the mast and alienate many. When I take my son to a pub for a meal what is my main concern? Is it his health, his teeth and his diet? No. It is peace at any price. And that, I'm afraid means junk food. As editor of "Good Pub Food" I may — indeed I do — want braised offal, steak and kidney pudding, rabbit casserole, fresh fish, hearty pies and beautiful vegetables. Sadly, this is just the sort of menu that seems to bring out the worst in some children. The words "won't eat that" force themselves through clenched lips, which among the very young can so quickly change to quivering lips. The last thing you want in a pub, where children still tend to be let in under sufferance (by fellow customers if not by publicans), is a noisy scene. So I have to confess a soft spot for Chips Corner, particularly as it generally comes pretty cheap, allowing us adults to indulge our more expensive appetites without a family outing costing an arm and a leg. Assuming that this is an occasional treat — like a children's party at McDonald's — then on the "little of what you fancy" principal, junk food cannot do much harm.

That said, any pub which reckons it can get away with a couple of chippy choices to keep the kids happy is copping out. For one thing, some children have the sense to enjoy more interesting food; for another, eating out socially should be a way to introduce "faddies" and the burger brigade to something different.

Pubs actually have advantages over restaurants in this respect. They are informal places, so children can act naturally — use their fingers if they want — and there is the flexibility of the snack menu. Suppose your child does not fancy any of the set main dishes; among the snacks you are likely to find bowls of soup (hopefully home-made) with big chunks of bread, jacket potatoes, ploughman's with Cheddar cheese or just Yorkshire pudding with gravy. Followed by one of the scrummy desserts many pubs offer, it should satisfy most children's appetites. One quibble: I do wish they would provide fresh fruit as an alternative to pudding, as many children like to finish with an apple.

If a pub does not specifically set out to cater for children and you are faced with what might be called an "adults only" menu, do not despair, many publicans can be very accommodating. The choice of dishes may seem unpromising, but the constituents generally have possibilities. For instance my son will eat pasta, but not the sauce. So far, my request for "plain spaghetti please, with butter and grated cheese" has never been refused. When I was researching "Good Pub Food" I recall a pub where my son stoically turned down everything on the excellent menu and, even though it was packed, the young barman persevered until he elicited enthusiasm for potatoes in their skins. A large bowl of new spuds was cheerfully produced with an accompanying plate of grated cheese so he could do his own sprinkling. Moral for pubs: if you've got it on the premises then supply it, instead of the stock reply, "sorry we don't do that".

All pubs allowing children in to eat should offer half portions of adult meals at half price. You think that goes without saying? Happily nearly all the pubs listed in this guide do, but you would be surprised that the number which do not. I was deeply intrigued by one menu stating that all starred items were available in small portions for kids. I still fail to understand why stuffed lambs' hearts were among those suggested ... I also admire the landlady who told me she would try to cook children whatever they wanted adding: "Though they seem to like mash mountain and bean sea, followed by strawberry milkshake." Which is where we came in.

Sadly, I only came across one pub which offered my ideal toddler's choice: "Finger food – a picnic box filled with a selection of tasty morsels." Why don't more pub cooks have the savvy to provide what is, after all, a fairly easy option; a dish with loads of "bite" foods from raw carrots to cheese straws, cocktail sausages to chunks of fruit? It is entertaining as well as satsfying. And why don't more plubs offer children alternative drinks? Shame on the licensee who keeps six real ales but only provides standard fizz for the youngsters; and cheers to the few pubs now dreaming up sophisticated kids' cocktails. I've come across Sahara Sunrise of orange, lime and lemonade and Kids Kir of blackcurrant and lemonade.

I was heartened to see the burgeoning pub barbecue really come into its own during our last glorious summer. This is another perfect way to feed children – all that noise, energy and mess banished to the great outdoors where they seem to eat more anyway.

A final moan. All too often I see on pub menus the words "Children catered for". Almost invariably it means they are not properly catered for and worse, makes them sound like some alien species. So that's why they feed them on Outerspacers.....

Susan Nowak
Susan Nowak is editor of "Good Pub Food",
published by Alma Books

CHILDER THORNTON
White Lion

Tel. (051) 339 3402
New Road (200 yards off A41)
Open 11.30–3; 5–11 (11.30–11
Fri, Sat) children welcome until 7

@ lunchtime

🍴

✖ 12–2 (not Sun)

🍺 **Thwaites Best Mild, Bitter**

A classic little country pub which is very popular with families at the weekend. The pub serves, in the best tradition, as a local community centre, but visitors are also warmly welcomed. The family room offers no special facilities, but the fact that children are really accepted, not just tolerated, by the locals as well as the licensees, makes up for that. This is an area where most publicans shut their doors at the mere sight of pint-sized customers. The garden has a recently renewed slide and swings. Small, half-price portions of the lunchtime menu are available. There are no special baby facilities, but mothers will find the toilets more pleasant than many in an emergency.

LYDIATE
Running Horses

Tel. (051) 526 3989
25 Bells Lane (off A5147)
Open 11–11

@

🍴

✖ 12–2 (not Sun)

🍺

🍺 **Ind Coope Burton Ale;**
   Walker Mild, Best Bitter

Situated on the Leeds-Liverpool canal, this pub is popular with coarse anglers and organises fishing competitions at both senior and junior level. Non-angling members of the family will also find plenty to keep them occupied here. There are lots of tables overlooking the canal which is home to geese and ducks and busy with pleasurecraft. More seating is provided in the play area of the garden where children can amuse themselves safely on the slide and swings. Pens house goats and hens; and the garden also has a boules pitch. Inside, the pub has been much enlarged and extended over the years, whilst keeping its character intact. A spacious family room is available, but children are advised to bring their own toys. The reasonably priced lunchtime menu includes children's dishes.

NEW BRIGHTON, WALLASEY
Albion Hotel

Tel. (051) 639 1832
104 Albion Street (off A554)
Open 11–11 (children admitted until 8)

◎

🍽

✗ lunchtime and evening

🛏

🎭

🍺 **Courage Directors; John Smith Bitter**

The Albion is a well maintained and superbly run residential hotel with a good "local" feel to it. It is situated in a quiet residential district, within ten minutes' walk of the open air swimming pool, bowling green, tennis courts and other entertainment. Children are welcome in the function room where the bar is closed at family hours. The best time is Sunday lunch which is "Albion Showtime" with a clown and other children's entertainment – other pubs please copy. Highchairs are provided and children may pick small portions of adult dishes or from their own menu.

WEST KIRBY
Ring o' Bells

Tel. (051) 625 8103
Village Road (100 yards from A540, left after war memorial)
Open 11–11

🍽

✗ lunchtime and evening

🍺 **Marston Pedigree; Whitbread Castle Eden Ale**

This is a quaint old pub, built in the early nineteenth century, in a picturesque setting close to the shore of the River Dee and Hilbre Island. Other local attractions are West Kirby Marina, popular for wind-surfing, which is only a mile away, and a nature reserve within walking distance of the pub. The best facilities for children at the pub are in the large enclosed garden where the play equipment includes a tunnel slide and flying fox! There is a separate play area for the under fives. There is no family room but children are welcome in the bar for meals where highchairs and a children's menu are provided.

BILLINGFORD
Forge

Tel. (036 281) 8980
Bintree Road, 200 yards off
B1145
Open 12–2.30; 7–11

⊕

🕮

✗ lunchtime and evening (not
Mon)

🍺 **Adnams Bitter; Greene King
IPA, Abbot Ale; weekend guest
beer**

As its name suggests, this free house is a former blacksmith's forge. A long, low brick building, the Forge is a quiet, friendly village local with open fires, where families are made very welcome. The room set aside for families (and games) is in the main part of the building, but only accessible from the courtyard at the back. It is comfortably furnished with tables and chairs, and has a pool table, dartboard and a fruit machine. The menu offers a range of children's dishes; baby feeding and changing facilities are also available. The pleasant garden is equipped with slide, seesaw and swings, watched over by goats.

Ribs of Beef, Norwich

BRANCASTER STAITHE
Jolly Sailors

Tel. (0485) 210314
On A149
Open all day

ⓖ

🕭

✖ lunchtime and evening

🍺 **Greene King IPA, Abbot Ale**

Staithe is the local term for a mooring place and this pub, almost on the harbour, is a mile or so away from the village of Brancaster itself. The family room is attractively furnished in keeping with the rest of the pub. Older children can enjoy the traditional games available, cards, dominoes and so on; for those not old enough to cope with these, parents would be wise to bring a few small toys. Three highchairs are provided and children's dishes are offered on the bar menu, while in the restaurant half portions of adult dishes are generally served. There is ample space for changing babies in the ladies' WC. Outside the garden has a playhouse and slides.

BRUNDALL
Yare

Tel. (0603) 713786
Station Road (A47)
Open 10.30–2.30; 5.30–11 (all day summer Sat)

ⓖ

🕭

✖ lunchtime and evening

🍺 **Courage Directors; John Smith Bitter; Woodforde Wherry Best Bitter, Phoenix XXX; weekend guest beer**

Situated at the heart of Broadland, this rambling riverside free house is popular with locals and visitors alike. Brundall is the main embarkation point for hire cruisers and is also handy for Norwich (five miles), the coast and other local attractions. The large lounge has a "wicker fenced" ceiling and is decorated with pictures and other artefacts relating to the Broads. The separate family room is fairly spacious too and equipped with a football machine and other amusements. Children may also accompany parents into the sun lounge and restaurant where suitable meals can be ordered.

HAPPISBURGH
Hill House

Tel. (0692) 650004
The Hill, by the church, off B1159
Open 11–3; 6.30 (7 winter)-11

ⓖ

🕭

✖ lunchtime and evening (not winter Mon)

🍺 **Adnams Bitter; Greene King Abbot Ale; Woodforde's Wherry Best Bitter; guest beer**

Halfway round the Norfolk coast, the Hill House at Happisborough (pronounced Haisborough) is situated close to the beach. Built in the sixteenth-century, it has a timbered lounge with a pool area and inglenook with woodburning stove to keep off the chill winds. Bar snacks and daily home-cooked specials are served, or you can dine in the silver service restaurant. Half portions are available for children. The family room is quite separate in converted outbuildings where access is via the car park. To make up for its somewhat isolated position, this room offers loads of things to keep youngsters amused including a football table and boxes with a good selection of toys. The large garden has bench tables.

HEVINGHAM
Marsham Arms

Tel. (0605) 48268
Holt Road (B1149, four miles from Norwich airport)
Open 11–3; 6–11

🏠

✖ lunchtime and evening

🛏

🍺 **Adnams Bitter; Draught Bass; Greene King Abbot Ale; Woodforde's Wherry Best Bitter; guest beer**

Set in a lovely part of rural Norfolk, handy for Norwich, the broads and the coast, this pub really sets out to cater for the whole family. If you want to use it as a touring base, it now has eight bedrooms and cots can be provided. These were added when the pub was extended and modernised recently. Another new feature is the family room, decorated in the same style as the bars, so retaining the atmosphere of the pub. This room is very popular and the licensees have a hard job keeping childless customers from using it. Facilities for nursing mothers are provided and most dishes on the menu can be reduced to child-size portions, so there is a good choice of home-cooked food – not just chips with everything. There is a safe garden and play area outside.

NORWICH
Ribs of Beef

Tel. (0603) 619517
24 Wensum Street (near cathedral)
Open 10.30–11

✖ lunchtime

🍺 **Adnams Bitter; Bateman Mild; Marston Pedigree; Reepham Rapier Pale Ale; Woodforde's Wherry Best Bitter, Ribcracker; guest beer**

This famous pub, which specialises in local beers (up to 11 are on at a time, including guests), is situated a stone's throw from the cathedral. On the bank of the Wensum it offers fine views of the river and has mooring facilities. The recently completed riverside walk enables visitors to follow the river, to Elm Hill and St Andrews Hall, or cross the bridge into the merchants' quarter of Colegate. There are no particular amusements for children at the pub, but it is rare enough to find a city-centre pub that caters for youngsters at all. Here a downstairs room is open for families to eat and drink; children's portions and highchairs are available on request.

SNETTISHAM
Rose & Crown

Tel. (0485) 41382
Old Church Road (off A149 Kings
Lynn-Hunstanton road)
Open 11–3; 5.30–11

ⓒ

⊗

✗ lunchtime and evening

🍺 **Adnams Bitter, Broadside;
Draught Bass; Greene King
IPA, Abbot Ale; Woodforde's
Wherry Best Bitter**

Yet another free house, as all the family pubs in Norfolk seem to be! Hooray for that. This one dates from the fourteenth century and it shows, with its flagged floors and open fires. It is one of the best family pubs in the county, and possibly one of the best in this book. The family room can seat up to a hundred people and includes an indoor barbecue from which children can help themselves. Highchairs and baby changing/feeding amenities are also provided. If a proper sit-down meal is what you want, then visit the restaurant (children's menu available); bar snacks offer a more speedy alternative. The walled garden has an excellent play area with sandpit, monkey bars, swings and other playthings.

Darby's at Swanton Morley

SWANTON ABBOT
Jolly Farmers

Tel. (0692) 69542
*Off B1150, Norwich-North
Walsham road
Open 11.30–3; 7–11*

☺
⑧
✘ lunchtime and evening
🍺
🍺 **Greene King Abbot Ale; Hall &
Woodhouse Tanglefoot;
Theakston Old Peculier;
Wethered Bitter**

An old building with modern additions, this free house has a warm, friendly atmosphere – exactly how a country pub should be. It is situated in a pleasant village with a campsite nearby. The public bar offers traditional games and there is a separate family room and a restaurant. The food is good and can be provided in child-size portions. The enclosed garden has a safe play area with an enchanted tree, swings and a slide.

SWANTON MORLEY
Darby's

Tel. (036 283) 647
*Elsing Road (B1147)
Open 11–3; 6–11*

☺
⑧
✘ lunchtime and evening
🛏
🍺 **Adnams Bitter, Broadside;
Hall & Woodhouse
Tanglefoot; Woodforde's
Wherry Best Bitter; guest beer**

When Watney's threatened to close down one of the two pubs in the village, this new one was created. But in fact, it looks anything but new – it has been beautifully converted and extended from two adjoining cottages. The bar has an old beamed ceiling and brick walls, on which much local memorabilia is hung. Old pine furniture has been used instead of standard modern pub fittings. All the beers come from independent breweries. What's more, when planning the pub, much thought was given to the growing demand for proper facilities for families. The separate family room is equipped with Lego and other toys and games; and the function room upstairs is available for children's parties. The pub is set away from the road and has a safe garden with more playthings. The restaurant and bar menus also cater for children. Overnight accommodation at a neighbouring farmhouse includes cots and it is well situated as a base to explore the county. What more could one wish for. I think I'll take up residence.

THORNHAM
Lifeboat Inn

Tel. (048 526) 236
Ship Lane (off A149)
Open 11–3; 6–11

@

🖾

✗ lunchtime and evening

🛏

🍺 **Adnams Bitter; Greene King
IPA, Abbot Ale; Tetley Bitter;
guest beers**

This sixteenth-century inn offered a haven for smugglers and travellers in days gone by. Now the smugglers have departed, but travellers still go out of their way to visit this welcoming inn which is lit by oil lamps. Bar food is served at both sessions and includes a children's menu. Home-made ice-creams are a particular treat, but in fact most of the food is home cooked and all the fish comes fresh daily from Billingsate and Grimsby. The restaurant is open only in the evening. Outside, the safe garden has a play area.

BRACKLEY HATCH
Green Man

Tel. (02805) 209
On A43 between Syresham and Silverstone
Open 11–11

◎

⊗

✗ lunchtime and evening

◄

♨

⊕ **Hook Norton Best Bitter; Marston Pedigree; Morrell Bitter**

Ideal for those with sporting interests, this small country hotel is close to both the motor racing circuit at Silverstone, and Towcester Race Course. If your interests are slightly more aesthetic, then take a trip to Sulgrave Manor (the Washington family home) or Stowe School – noted for its gardens laid out by Capability Brown. Children are made very welcome at the Green Man, which won the Publican/Schweppes 1989 Family Pub of the Year Award. Cots are available for overnight stays. Otherwise families are invited to use the lounge (which has no particular amusements) or the conservatory where the menu caters for small appetites and highchairs are provided. The garden has a large play area with novelty slides, swings and even a Dr Who "time capsule". There is a cabin with soft drinks bar and table and chairs and a marquee where regular entertainment is provided free of charge on Sundays: perhaps Punch and Judy, or a magician.

DEANSHANGER
Fox & Hounds

Tel. (0908) 563485
High Street (off A422)
Open 12–2.30 (3.30 Sat); 6 (7 Sat)-11

◎

⊗

✗ lunchtime and evening (not Sun eve)

◄

⊕ **Draught Bass; Halls ABC Bitter; Wadworth 6X**

This well-lit, country local consists of a fairly basic public bar and a cosy lounge with open fire, which doubles as a restaurant. Very reasonably priced meals are available until half an hour before closing time. In addition to the main building, the former stables have been converted as a barbecue area at the back of the pub. There is a play room for children in the rear stable which leads out to the patio and garden. Toys and playthings are provided inside and out. Highchairs are available as is a children's menu for families wishing to eat; changing and feeding facilities for babies can be provided on request.

ECTON
Worlds End

Tel. (0604) 414521
*Main Road (A4500 from
Northampton to Wellingborough)
Open 11–11*

◎

🌲

✗

🍺 **Ruddles Best Bitter, County;
Webster's Yorkshire Bitter**

This main road pub was completely refurbished in 1989 to a high standard, and decorated with a medieval theme, incorporating a multi-level bar and separate dining area. Meals are served at any time, including a children's menu. A real effort has been made here to appeal to families. Twin play rooms situated on the patio offer Lego, television, video and other amusements – it is hard to keep the adults away! Outside the play equipment includes swings and slides.

HELMDON
Chequers

Tel. (0295) 768175
*Station Road (village centre, two
miles from A43)
Open 11–3; 6–11*

◎

🌲

✗ lunchtime and evening

🍼

🍺 **Mansfield Riding Bitter; Wells
Eagle Bitter, Bombardier**

A homely village pub in the centre of a small village, where families are given a warm welcome. The cosy bar has a large stone inglenook where a real fire blazes in chilly weather. The small room next door serves as the family room, and this too has an open fire, as well as a pool table. Half-price portions for children are served here. Babies can be changed in the ladies' loo. There is some play equipment in the large garden. This is surrounded by a dry stone wall over which is a fine view of the impressive nine-arch Helmdon viaduct, ex-Great Central Railway.

WHITFIELD
Sun

Tel. (02805) 232
*Farrer Close (off A43)
Open 12–2.30; 6.30–11 (children
until 9)*

◎

🌲

✗ lunchtime and evening (not
Sun)

🍼

🍺 **Bateman XXXB; Hook Norton
Best Bitter**

This pleasant local, built of Cotswold stone, is tucked away off the main street in a small hamlet. It makes a good, quiet break from the main A43, either just for some quick refreshment, or overnight (cots are available). The former restaurant is now used as a family room, but the Sun still offers food. In fact it is all home-cooked by the landlady and her son, and includes a children's menu (the usual, with chips). Highchairs and proper facilities for nursing mothers are provided. No amusements are supplied for youngsters, but there is a safe garden, so come armed with your own playthings.

BAMBURGH
Victoria Hotel

Tel. (066 84) 431
Front Street
Open 11–11

✗ lunchtime and evening

⊶

🍺 **Halls Harvest Bitter; Marston Pedigree; Tetley Bitter; guest beer**

Bamburgh, the ancient capital of Northumberland, is now no more than a village, albeit a very attractive one, which stands in the shadow of its spectacular castle. The Victoria is not quite such an imposing building, but is still a fine looking hotel. Families are welcome in the snug which has an inglenook and is served by a hatch to the bar, and the games room where pool, table tennis, pin ball and video games machines can be played. This latter room leads out on to an enclosed patio. The food here is highly recommended; a varied selection of home-made dishes is served at very reasonable prices; children are catered for on the menu, as are vegetarians. Overnight accommodation includes cots and Bamburgh is a good base for exploring the Northumberland coast with its superb beaches and fascinating islands such as the Farne islands (a must for birdwatchers) and Holy Island, also known as Lindisfarne.

BLANCHLAND
Lord Crewe
Arms

Tel. (043 475) 251
Open 11–3; 6–11

⊚

🛏

✗ lunchtime and evening

⊶

🍺 **Vaux Samson**

Although I last visited it some 15 years ago, Blanchland has always stuck in my mind as being one of the most timeless places I have ever seen, and I doubt that it has changed drastically since my visit, as it hadn't over the preceeding centuries. I remember being very disappointed at visiting the place out of licensing hours, as the warm sandstone village local beckoned so welcomingly. Built in fact as the Abbot's lodgings in the Middle Ages, the pub once formed part of Blanchland Abbey and the beer gardens were the cloisters. Later, in 1715, it was strongly connected with the Jacobite Rebellion. These days the pub concentrates on the needs of the tourists who flock to this idyllic spot in the Derwent Valley. Families are welcome in the Derwentwater Room, off the main bar, and furnished with tables and benches. It has log fires and direct access to the garden. Bar meals, with suitable portions for children are served in this room, and highchairs are provided. Convenient for the Beamish Open Air Museum and Hadrian's Wall, both exciting venues for children, the pub is also within easy driving distance of Durham City with its superb cathedral and other historic attractions. The overnight accommodation at the pub includes cots.

HEDLEY ON THE HILL
Feathers Inn

Tel. (0661) 843268
North of Stocksfield
Open 6–11 (closed lunchtimes
except Sat 12–3.30 and Sun)

◎

✗   Sat/Sun lunchtime

🍺   **Marston Pedigree; Ruddles Best Bitter; guest beer**

This is a small country pub, about a mile up the road from Stocksfield Golf Club. It is quite unspoilt, and no electronic machines or music upset its peaceful atmosphere. The only concession is one small video game in the family room. This is one of three rooms in the pub, the others being, traditionally, the bar and lounge. The Feathers boasts an active Leek Club; other attractions more likely to draw families to the area are the nearby Beamish Museum and Hadrian's Wall. The pub is closed at lunchtime during the week, but weekend lunches include children's portions, or the usual fishfingers and baked beans selection. A good range of guest ales is served on a two-weekly cycle.

COSTOCK
Red Lion

Tel. (0509) 852535
Old Lane Road (Loughborough road)
Open 11–2.30 (3.30 Sat); 6–11

◎

⛟

✗ lunchtime daily; evenings Thu-Sat

⛉ **Shipstone Mild, Bitter**

This is a traditional country pub, set back from the main road with real fires and real beams in its two bars. The family room is fairly small and was in the process of being redecorated as we went to press, so should be looking fairly spick and span by the time you read this. Tables and chairs, some toys and a video machine are provided for amusement. A children's menu is served at lunchtime. The garden has some swings and a climbing frame.

CROPWELL BISHOP
Lime Kiln Inn

Tel. (0949) 81540
Kinoulton Road (one mile off A46)
Open 12–3; 6–11

◎

⛟

⛉ **Home Mild, Bitter**

A small, friendly country pub, situated just outside the village, the Lime Kiln was established in 1840 as a coaching inn. The whole pub is not exactly spacious and the family room is described as "small, but very cosy". Space allows for a juke box, but no other amusements. No meals are served, but bar snacks, ranging in price from 50 pence to £2.50 are available from midday until 2 pm. There is some play equipment out in the garden which is currently home to two ducks, two rabbits and two dogs. I don't *think* the landlord's name is Noah. The pub is ideally located for visitors to the Vale of Belvoir and the National Water Sports Centre at Holme Pierrepoint.

EPPERSTONE
Cross Keys

Tel. (0602) 663033
Main Street
Open 11–2.30; 6–11

◎

⛟

✗ lunchtime and evening (not Sun eve or Mon)

⛉ **Hardys & Hansons Best Mild, Best Bitter**

The Cross Keys serves as a reminder of what a village pub should be: a many roomed local with a welcoming atmosphere. That means families, too, are welcome in a lounge which is decorated as the rest of the pub, so you do not feel segregated. Unfortunately, no amusements are provided either indoors or out, so bring something with you. Standard pub fare is provided – children's portions on request. Set well away from any main road, the garden is quite safe for youngsters. Epperstone is convenient for visitors to Sherwood Forest and Nottingham Castle as well as the National Water Sports Centre.

LOWDHAM
Old Ship

Tel. (0602) 663049
Main Street
Open 11.30–2.30; 5.30–11

@

🖂

✖ lunchtime and evening

🍺 John Smith Bitter

CAMRA's "Good Beer Guide" describes this as a "deservedly popular pub". This high praise is due to the fact that the Old Ship feels like a real pub and makes a real effort to cater properly for all its customers (including those whose heads do not yet reach the bar). An attractively and well furnished lounge complements the bar which has a pool table. The family room, off the lounge, is comfortably furnished and being at the rear, gives easy access to the garden and play area. There is a door leading directly onto the car park. Good value, home-cooked meals are served at both sessions and a children's menu is available.

LOWER BLIDWORTH
Fox & Hounds

Tel. (0623) 792383
Off A614
Open 11–3; 6–11

@

🖂

✖ lunchtime (Mon-Thu)

🍺 Hardys & Hansons Best Mild, Best Bitter

The first edition of this guide listed the Fox and Hounds at Blidworth Bottoms, but this apparently is the familiar name for the village. It has much more appeal I think than Lower Blidworth which sounds rather stuffy, and the atmosphere at this pub is anything but that. It is a true country local, a fine example of a traditional multi-roomed village pub that has not been ruined by "tasteful redecoration". Although the family/games room is on the small side, children are always made most welcome. A children's menu or small portions are available; when meals are not being served, bar snacks or rolls can usually be provided. There is a very large garden with play equipment, and the pub is close to a riding centre and Sherwood Forest.

NOTTINGHAM New Market Hotel

Tel. (0602) 411532
40 Broad Street
Open 11–4; 5.30–11

◎

✖ lunchtime

◁ **Home Mild, Bitter; Youngers Scotch, IPA, No. 3**

This large city-centre pub might be mistaken for a bank from the outside, but the landlord is the unlikeliest bank manager you are likely to meet as he is considered by regulars to be mildly eccentric. The basic public bar is a must for railway buffs as it has many interesting railway items on display. The two lounge bars are pleasant and comfortable. There is a sliding door between them and the further one is used by families. It has a serving hatch to the bar. If baby needs changing then mum will enjoy a trip to the splendid Victorian-style loo. A children's menu is provided at lunchtime.

Travellers Rest

Tel. (0602) 264412
Mapperley Plains (off A614)
Open 11–11

◎

▯

✖ lunchtime and evening

◁ **Home Bitter; Younger IPA, No. 3; guest beer**

The landlord of the Travellers takes great pride in the high quality of the service and facilities he provides – and justly so. Since he took over, the pub has been completely transformed and is exceptionally clean and well-kept. It is a large old coaching inn in a rural setting, but on the main road. Hot meals are served until two o'clock, but a cold buffet, which is a speciality here, is available until 8 pm. A children's menu or small portions are readily served. The Pop Inn family room is extremely good. Nicely furnished and carpeted, it can seat 70 comfortably. Amusements include a video game, juke box and pool table; and there is a tuckshop and non-alcholic bar. It is reserved exclusively for families to use and has its own toilet with baby changing facilities. Highchairs are provided. The garden, which is partly grassed, has some swings and other equipment.

UPTON
Cross Keys

Tel. (0636) 813269
Main Street (A612 to Southwell)
Open 11.30–2.30; 6–11

◎

🕮

✖ lunchtime and evening

🍺 **Bateman XXXB; Boddingtons Bitter; Marston Pedigree; Whitbread Castle Eden Ale; guest beer**

A characterful pub, situated in a conservation area, opposite the HQ of the British Horological Institute at Upton Hall. Recently restored and extended in keeping with its seventeenth-century origins, the pub has an upstairs restaurant in what was originally a dovecot. The restaurant is only open Thursday and Friday evenings; at other times the room can be used by families. A large foyer, set with tables and chairs, is also always available for family groups. A good range of bar meals is served at both session; children's portions and highchairs can be provided. The safe garden has some play equipment. Many places of interest to children are all within half an hour's drive, including Belton House Adventure Playground, White Post Modern Farm Centre, Sundown Pets Corner, Rufford Country Park and Sherwood Forest.

CHIPPiNG NORTON
Albion Tavern

Tel. (0608) 2860
On A361, Burford road
Open 11–2.30 (maybe longer);
6–11

◎

🊳

✗ lunchtime (not Mon)

🍺 **Hook Norton Mild, Best Bitter**

Set on the edge of the town, this pub is close enough to the open country for it to be suitable for a drink and maybe a bite to eat after a ramble. It is also convenient for the town's shops and indoor swimming pool. Recently rejuvenated, this friendly local has limited facilities for children, but they are none the less welcome. A clean, tidy front room provides seating for families and will be opened on request. Good value meals are served at lunchtime, but only snacks in the evening. Children's portions and vegetarian dishes are available on request. The garden, home to a traditional Aunt Sally, is enclosed and safe for youngsters.

FYFIELD
White Hart

Tel. (0865) 390585
Off A420, near Abingdon
Open 11–2.30; 6.30–11

◎

🊳

✗ lunchtime and evening

🍺 **Boddingtons Bitter; Gibbs Mew Bishop's Tipple; Morland Bitter; Ruddles County; Theakston Old Peculier; Wadworth 6X, Farmers Glory, Old Timer (winter); Weston Medium Cider**

A free house, as may be inferred from the wide range of real ales available, the White Hart is featured in CAMRA's "Good Pub Food" guide, and rightly so. Food is the priority here, even the bread is baked daily on the premises. For families there is a choice of three different rooms without a bar, all of which also serve as dining areas. As the emphasis is on meals here, no amusements are provided for children, but there are high-chairs and facilities for dealing with babies. Children will normally find something to their taste from the extensive bar menu, but no particular dishes are created for them. So if your offspring are the kind who really enjoy a good meal out, this is an ideal choice. Not all the customers at this fifteenth-century hostelry go to dine however; it is also a popular pub with the bar and main drinking area situated in the original timbered arch-braced hall. The building started life as a chantry house and has a 30 feet high gallery where drinks may be taken, to give an extra "heady" sensation maybe. On fine days the extensive gardens at the rear of the pub come into their own. These are enclosed, so safe for youngsters.

LEWKNOR
Olde Leathern
Bottel

Tel. (0844) 51482
I High Street (off B4009)
Open 11–2.30; 6–11

◎

✉

✗ lunchtime and evening

⍋ Brakspear Bitter, Special, Old

The name of this pub seems to vary from what is given here down through various permutations to simply Leather Bottle (even the inn signs vary), but I am sure you will know it when you get there. Situated close to the M40 (junction six) and half a mile from the Ridgeway Path, this oak-beamed rural pub attracts a complete cross-section of customers – from hikers to business people. Families are welcome too, in a clean, well-appointed, but rather small annexe to the public bar. Here are tables and seating for 15, but as it leads onto the garden, there is extra scope in fine weather. An extensive menu offers small portions for children; steaks are a particular favourite with the local customers. This welcoming and friendly pub has a good reputation for its well-kept ales and is listed regularly in CAMRA's "Good Beer Guide". It also boasts Cromwellian connections.

LONG
HANBOROUGH
Swan

Tel. (0993) 881347
Millwood End (via Combe Road, off A4095)
Open 11–2.30; 6–11

✉

✗

⍋ Morrells Light Ale, Best Bitter

Facilities for children are limited here, but it is, nevertheless, popular with families, particularly on summer weekends when barbecues are held. It is also nice to be able to include pubs owned by local breweries, this one being tied to Morrells, based in Oxford itself. A good, one-bar village local, the Swan caters well for families in fine weather, so do not go on a rainy day. It has a superb, large fenced-in garden which is a children's paradise. Not only is there an assault course designed for youngsters, an Aunt Sally, outdoor skittles and a wendy house, but also domestic pets to enjoy, such as goats and ducks and some birds in an aviary. If it does get chilly, then families can retreat into the outhouse which has a pool table. Bar snacks are available at all times and with prices starting from 50 pence, children can be fed quite reasonably. Many tourist sights are nearby too, including Blenheim Palace and the Roman villa remains near Coombe. Country walks can be had in Wychwood Forest or on Stonesfield Common, which is ideal for picnics.

LONG WITTENHAM
Machine Man Inn

Tel. (086730) 7835
Just off High Street (A415)
Open 11.30–3; 6–11

—

◎

🛏

✖ lunchtime and evening

🍺 **Buckley Best Bitter; Hook Norton Best Bitter; Marston Pedigree; guest beer**

Goodness knows how this pub got its name; the inn sign shows a robot standing menacingly against a stormy sky. The sort of thing that would have great appeal for my young sons, who might then be disappointed that the pub is not full of beings from another world. It does not give the impression of "ye olde worlde local" beloved by many pub-goers, but this is in fact a friendly, comfortably furnished village free house. It is basically a large, single-bar pub, but there is a spacious room at the side of the bar which doubles as a dining-cum-children's area. Families are not, however, obliged to have a meal. For those who are hungry, the menu includes children's portions or their own dishes. There are some swings in the open garden at the back of the pub. Long Wittenham is an attractive Thameside village; the Pendon Museum, open at weekends has an impressive collection of intricately landscaped railway models which appeals even to children weaned on "machine man" toys. A former hill fort, Wittenham Clumps, is also a popular spot for walks, kite-flying and just admiring the view.

Plowden Arms, Shiplake

NORTH LEIGH
Woodman

Tel. (0993) 881790
New Yatt Road (off A4095)
Open 11.30–3; 7–11

◎

🍴 lunchtime and evening (Mon snacks only)

🍺 **Hook Norton Best Bitter; Glenny Witney Bitter, Wychwood Best; Wadworth 6X; guest beers**

This free house offers beers from another small independent brewer, Glenny, based at Witney. It is a smallish local, built at the turn of the century, in a country village which enjoys scenic surroundings and picturesque views. Easy country walks can be had locally, and it is worth ambling the mile it takes to get to the important roman settlement that has been excavated at the east end of the village. A one-bar local, the Woodman offers a small comfortable lounge for use by families, just off the main bar. Here children can enjoy the toys provided and the special menu of all their favourite things (including lots of chips!). There is a large, terraced garden which is enclosed, so safe for youngsters, who may enjoy having a go at the Aunt Sally. I think it is time, in these days of equality, that someone set up an Uncle Fred in the garden for a change – why should the women take all the punishment!

SHIPLAKE
Plowden Arms

Tel. (0734) 402794
Reading Road (A4155)
Open 11.30–2.30; 6–11

◎

🍴 lunchtime and evening (not Sun/Mon)

🍺 **Brakspear Mild, Bitter, Special Bitter, Old Ale**

Dating back to 1580, this roadside pub has recently been renovated and extended to provide up-to-date facilites, including a family room. Fortunately, the work has been done sympathetically to maintain original features and it has been tastefully decorated and well furnished. The large bar has a pleasant atmosphere and customers are not disturbed by children as the family room is in the former stable and coach house. This, too, is newly decorated and comfortably furnished and opens on to a large attractive garden (formerly the village bowling green). Unfortunately no amusements are provided for youngsters either indoors or out, so parents are advised to bring something to keep them busy. Food will, of course, occupy them for a while; the children's menu here costs around £2. A footpath from the pub leads down to the River Thames, 500 yards away, where moorings are available. Also nearby is the famous twelfth-century church where Alfred Lord Tennyson was married. The pub is three miles from Henley-on-Thames, home of Brakspear's brewery and a very worthwhile town to visit.

STOKE ROW
Cherry Tree

Tel. (0491) 680430
Off B481
Open 10-2; 6-11

🍺 **Brakspear Mild, Bitter, Special Bitter**

An unusual feature of this pleasant village is the Maharajah's Well, donated by the grateful Maharajah of Benares to the people of the village in the nineteenth century for work done by a local irrigation engineer in India. I do not know if the Maharajah stopped off for a drink at the Cherry Tree, if he had he would have experienced the true English village pub. A picturesque, three-roomed local, with real fires, beams and flagstone floors, little has changed since the Maharajah's time, except that nowadays children are allowed in. The family room is a small, comfortable and well-furnished room next to the main bar. There is also a games room, but this is for adults only. Children can however, enjoy the large open garden at the front of the pub which has a safe play area with slides and swings. No meals are served here, but the snacks available at lunchtime should appease most appetites; prices from 50 pence. A popular local attraction for families is the small zoo near Ipsden, about two miles away. This has a large collection of birds and wildfowl as well as animals.

TRAVEL PURSUITS

Pipe cleaners – there's an old fashioned image for you. But they are still around. In fact the Early Learning Centre sells them in colourful packs. Not to be recommended for the very young, who are likely to poke them where they shouldn't, or just get too frustrated trying to manipulate them. However, children from around six years up, can pass quite a few miles making models – anything from stick people and animals to intergalactic space transporters.

THAME
Swan

Tel. (0844) 261211
9 Upper High Street
Open 11–11

✗ (not Sun)

⋈

🍺 **Brakspear Bitter; Flowers Original; Hook Norton Best Bitter; guest beer**

Originally a fifteenth-century hostelry, the Swan was re-opened in 1987 after being completely redesigned. Now bare boards, rugs and unusual furnishings and fittings have given the pub a new lease of life. The separate restaurant which has retained its medieval ceiling, provides fresh, adventurous food, while an ever-changing selection of real ales is offered from far and wide; some 120 different beers are served over the year. Understandably popular with adult customers, the Swan also caters for children. There is a separate family room and if the restaurant menu is a little on the pricey side, then youngsters will no doubt be happy with something from the bar menu where prices start at 90 pence. Facilities for changing and feeding babies are provided. Amusements at the pub include shove-ha'penny and miniature croquet. If you visit on Tuesday, you can enjoy the town's bustling market.

WYTHAM
White Hart

Tel. (0865) 244372
Off A34 bypass
Open 11–2.30 (3 Sat); 6–11

🍴

✗ lunchtime and evening

🍺 **Ind Coope Burton Ale; Tetley Bitter**

The road from north Oxford, through Wolvercote takes you into this charming village, just three miles from the famous university city. So if you want to get away from the crowds – and certainly Oxford offers little in the way of family pubs – try this one. Three hundred years old with a flagstone floored bar, the White Hart has two rooms which are suitable for parents with children. One serves as a dining room/cold buffet servery, but if you do not wish to eat, then you can use the outdoor patio area, which has been totally enclosed for all-year use. It has a coal burner, so you will not feel the winter chills. The pleasant garden is fenced, so safe for children to enjoy; it boasts a fine example of a sixteenth-century dovecot.

HENGOED
Last Inn

Tel. (0691) 659747
*On back road, Oswestry to
Weston Rhyn
Open 7–11 (closed lunchtimes
except Sun)*

✕ evenings (not Tue)

🍺 **Marston Border Bitter,
Pedigree; Wood Special;
Weston Country Cider; guest
beer**

CAMRA members are fondly welcomed at this pub – by Ben, the only dog to become a life member of the Campaign! Close to the Welsh border (as its name might suggest), this large country pub is closed during the day, except on Sundays. Nevertheless, it does have a separate family room and children are welcome in the evening in any part of the pub away from the bar. Small portions are served for children in the restaurant area. This makes a good place to eat after visiting the nearby sites of Offa's Dyke, Chirk Castle or the Old Oswestry earthworks. Oswestry is also nearby.

HOPTON WAFERS
Crown Inn

Tel. (0299) 270372
*On A4117 between Cleobury
Mortimer and Ludlow
Open 11–3; 6–11 (children under
five until 9 pm)*

🕸

✗ lunchtime and evening

🛏

🍺 **Ansells Mild; Flowers
Original; Marston Pedigree;
Wood Parish Bitter**

This quaint, ivy-clad free house is just as everyone imagines an English country pub should be. Situated on the main road between Cleobury Mortimer and Ludlow, it has a low-beamed restaurant warmed by an open fire, offering freshly cooked meals (including a menu or portions for children). Children are welcome in the pub to eat, but there is no specific family room. However, in fine weather the four acres of grounds are ideal for youngsters to explore. The outside terraces provide seating for a hundred and 200 more can be accommodated in the garden itself. A duckpond and trout stream complete this idyllic scene. Wyre Forest, Ludlow Castle and the West Midland Safari Park are all within a radius of eight miles.

TREFLACH
Gibraltar Inn

Tel. (0691) 650111
*Gibraltar Lane
Open 7–11 (closed lunchtime
except Sat, 11–3 & Sun 12–3)*

⊚

🕸

✗

🛏

🍺 **Ind Coope Burton Ale; Tetley
Bitter**

The small hamlet of Treflach is one mile past Trefonen on the road from Oswestry and just a stone's throw from Offa's Dyke. The Gibraltar Inn is one of the few surviving examples of a timbered Welsh long house. Dating back to the seventeenth century, it has retained all its original features. Overnight accommodation is available at the pub, and two cots are provided. You may think twice about booking though, if you are of a nervous disposition as it is said to be haunted by not one, but two ghosts. Children are made very welcome in the family room here where playthings include especially handknitted toys, made locally. Outdoors there is a skittle alley, putting green and boules track, all watched over by a selection of small, furry pets. A special list of meals to appeal to young appetites is available, and other requests will be catered for, providing the kitchen has the necessary in-gredients.

BISHOPS LYDEARD
Bell Inn

Tel. (0823) 432968
*West Street (off Taunton-
Minehead road)*
Open 11–3; 5.30–11

ⓒ

🛏

✕ lunchtime and evening

🍺 **Boddingtons Bitter; Butcombe
Bitter; Exmoor Ale; Hall &
Woodhouse Badger Best
Bitter; Marston Pedigree;
Wadworth 6X**

Situated in the Quantock Hills, this fourteenth-century free house, complete with beams and inglenooks, caters for a wide range of customers. There is plenty to occupy youngsters on a dull day: the family room has videos, pool tables, juke box, pin ball machines and a full-size skittle alley. It sounds like a games room, and it is, but children are made very welcome here and are also catered for in the conservatory/dining area (children's meal costs around £1.40). There is a floodlit patio and garden too. A visit to the West Somerset Steam Railway, half a mile away, is an absolute must.

BRIDGWATER
Quantock
Gateway

Tel. (0278) 423593
*95 Wembdon Road (A39, just out
of town)*
Open 10.30–3; 6–11

ⓒ

🛏

✕ lunchtime and evening

🍺 **Draught Bass; Flowers IPA,
Original; Marston Pedigree**

This large pub on the Minehead road makes an ideal halt for families on their way to the Somerset coast. The beer is good (guest beers are regularly featured) and so is the food – children as well as vegetarians are catered for on the menu. There is a super, very large family room and a play area in the garden with swings, slides and other playthings.

CANNINGTON
Malt Shovel Inn

Tel. (0278) 653432
*Blackmoor Lane (four miles from
Bridgewater on A39)*
Open 11.30–3; 6.30–11

ⓒ

🛏

✕ lunchtime and evening

🛏

🍺 **Butcombe Bitter; Wadworth
6X; Lanes cider; Rich's cider;
guest beer**

Set in a quiet country road off the main thoroughfare from Bridgewater to Minehead, this multi-roomed pub is well worth a visit. There are two bars and families can use either the spacious family room or the skittle alley or eat in the restaurant. Bar meals are also served and highchairs provided. Children's meals cost around £1.50. Should you wish to stay, cots are available and the bedrooms offer pleasant views of the Quantock Hills. Alternatively, there is space for a few caravans alongside the beer garden. In common with many villages around here, Cannington is rich in historical associations – this area of Somerset was involved in the famous Pitchfork Rebellion of 1685, where opposing forces finally met in the Battle of Sedgemoor at Bridgewater.

MONKSILVER
Notley Arms

Tel. (0984) 56217
On Wiveliscombe-Watchet road
Open 11–2.30; 6–11

ⓐ

⬧

✗ lunchtime and evening

⬧ **Ruddles County; Usher Best Bitter**

At the centre of a small village, this old inn is very popular both with locals and visitors for its interesting and inexpensive meals. Children are made very welcome (and catered for with smaller portions); the comfortable family room has recently been improved and redecorated. Toys and books for all age groups are thoughtfully provided. The attractive garden is enclosed, but as it has a stream, some supervision of youngsters is required. Monksilver enjoys a beautiful rural setting and is close to Exmoor and the coast.

NORTON ST. PHILIP
George Inn

Tel. (037 387) 224
At junction of A366/B3110, six miles south of Bath
Open 11.30–2.30; 6–11

ⓐ

⬧

✗ lunchtime and evening

⬧ **Draught Bass; Wadworth 6X, Devizes**

Dating back to 1223, this historic pub is one of the oldest inns in England. The Duke of Monmouth made the George his headquarters in June 1685 after he had abandoned his attack on Bristol. Samuel Pepys was also a customer. It now enjoys a quiet atmosphere, enhanced by real fires. There is a public bar and a separate room where families are welcome, but no amusements are provided. Several items on the bar snack menu are suitable for children, or small portions may be ordered for them in the restaurant where there are two highchairs. The enclosed garden and courtyard are safe for youngsters. Norton St Philip is just six miles from Bath (and the Post Office reckons it is in fact in Avon); the nearest railway station is also at Bath.

PORLOCK
Ship Inn

Tel. (0643) 862507
High Street (A39)
Open 10.30–3; 5.30–11

◎

🍴

✗ lunchtime and evening

⌣

⬥ **Draught Bass; Courage Best Bitter; Cotleigh Old Buzzard**

This rambling old pub is on the road to Lynmouth, just one mile from the sea. Family accommodation is provided (with a cot), so it makes a good base for a holiday in the Exmoor National Park which offers many outdoor pursuits. Seafishing trips can be arranged with the licensees and riding for novices upwards. Casual visitors will find this a cosy pub, full of character and a warm, friendly atmosphere. Families are welcome in the Smoke Room (not true to its name I trust) which is off the bar. Some playthings are provided here as well as high-chairs and a children's menu. Extra plates will be given to share adults' meals if preferred. The beer garden is enclosed and safe for children and has some swings. Ask at the bar for baby changing/feeding facilities.

WEST PENNARD
Red Lion

Tel. (0458) 32941
On A361, three miles from Glastonbury
Open 12–2.30; 6–11

◎

🍴

✗ lunchtime and evening

⬥ **Butcombe Bitter; Hall & Woodhouse Tanglefoot; Red Lion Best**

The house beer served here is not brewed on the premises, but by the little independent brewery, Ash Vine, based near Frome. A free house, built in 1678, the Red Lion has recently been restored to give modern amenities in a traditional setting. These include a family dining room, but families are also welcome just to come in for a drink. A children's menu and highchair are provided, as are baby facilities. Both the pub's gardens are safe for children, but have no particular amusements for them. The Red Lion benefits from a lovely setting, surrounded by farms and cider apple orchards, and is just three miles from Glastonbury, famous for its Tor and abbey. Cheddar Gorge and Wookey Hole are also close at hand.

BURTON-ON-TRENT
Wyggeston

Tel. (0283) 68250
Calais Road (near hospital)
Open 11–3; 6.30–11

☼

☞

✗ lunchtime Mon-Fri

∱ **Draught Bass**

This large urban Victorian pub was renovated recently and purpose-built family facilities were installed at the same time. The works made the pub accessible to the disabled. The large family room has some games and opens via patio doors on to the enclosed garden which has a wendy house, slide and a swing. Children's toilets are provided and there is ample space to deal with babies in the ladies' toilet. Small portions can be ordered from the lunch menu, but no food is served at weekends. The pub is handy for a visit to the Heritage Brewery Museum (see below).

CAULDON
Yew Tree

Tel. (0538) 308348
Off A52/A523, near Waterhouses
Open 10–3; 6–11

☼

∱ **Draught Bass; Burton Bridge Bitter; M & B Mild**

Dating back to the seventeenth century, this multi-roomed pub is stuffed full of antiques and curios including working polyphonia, a pianola, grandfather clocks and a pair of Queen Victoria's stockings! The family room is slightly less exciting, but does have table skittles to amuse the youngsters. Food is restricted to snacks. The pub is handy for the Manifold Valley and is just five miles from Alton Towers. Oh, and don't let the cement works nearby put you off – this is one of the finest pubs in the country.

MORETON
Rising Sun

Tel. (0952) 70251
Three miles east of A41
Open 11–3; 6–11

☼

☞

∱ **Marston Best Bitter, Pedigree**

This is a very friendly country pub, well worth a visit, even though facilities are a little bit limited. Family pubs in Staffordshire altogether seem to be rather rare – this one does at least welcome youngsters. It boasts fine views over the surrounding countryside and although the garden is open it is safe for children. The family room has no particular amusements, but it is very comfortable and children could bring a few small toys of their own in.

TATENHILL
Horseshoe Inn

Tel. (0283) 64913
*Tatenhill Road, one mile from
A38/A5121*
Open 11.30–3; 5.30–11

◎

---

⑧

✗ lunchtime and evening (not
Sun or Mon eve)

---

⑭ **Marston Pedigree, Owd
Rodger (occasionally)**

An old village inn which is popular with visitors from nearby Burton-on-Trent, particularly for its excellent food. A children's menu is served and prices start at £1.50; no food is served at all on Sunday though. The totally unspoilt beamed lounge also contains the family room, so although it is segregated it still has a good pub atmosphere. There is a large enclosed garden where the children's play area has a bark base for safety.

WHISTON
Swan

Tel. (0785) 712460
Two miles west of A449
Open 11–3 (not Tue); 6–11

◎

---

⑧

---

⑭ **Ansells Bitter; Ind Coope
Burton Ale**

This attractive country pub is in a quiet location, surrounded by farmland. It is well-thought of locally – the bar is especially popular, although the lounge is more comfortable. The small family room has a limited number of tables and chairs, some electronic games and a toybox with a few toys. The garden is not enclosed but it is safe for children to play in and equipment such as swings, is provided. No meals are served, but snacks are available.

Illustrations reproduced by kind permission of the Heritage Brewery Museum (see over)

YOXALL
Golden Cup

Tel. (0543) 472295
Main Street (A515)
Open (11–3; 5.30–11 (all day Sat)

ⓐ

⌷

✘ lunchtime daily, evening Tue-
Sat

⌷ **Draught Bass**

A large, well-appointed road house which makes a good halt for visitors to Ashbourne, Derbyshire and the Peak district. It is set in a country village, just 20 minutes' drive from Lichfield and Burton-on-Trent. Families are welcome in the small conservatory. The pub has all the usual traditional games (none specifically for children), as well as a purpose-built petanque pitch. There is a large enclosed garden where amusements include a play house, slide, swing and climbing frame. The garden is well-kept and attractive, so makes a pleasant place for parents to sit and watch their offspring play. A children's menu is served and the pub offers a full range of meals.

HERITAGE BREWERY MUSEUM

Burton-on-Trent lies at the heart of the British brewing industry – not only are the giants, Allied and Bass based here (practically next door to each other) – but other independent breweries manage to exist in their shadow. Two which survive very well are Burton Bridge, and Marston, which is the only brewery to use the unique Burton Union system of fermentation for their stronger ales.

Another very small brewery is Heritage which now brews beers under licence for Everards. This is in fact the brewing company of the Heritage Brewery Museum which is open to the public and is a fascinating place to go if you are interested in the process and history of brewing. A vist to the museum starts off with a short introductory video, then a guided trip round the brewery itself; followed by a chance to observe the restoration work in progress. You can also see one of the country's largest collections of bottled beers and partake of liquid refreshment in the function room. There is a well-stocked shop full of interesting gifts and souvenirs.

Entrance costs £2.50 for adults and £1 for children, although a family ticket is available for £5.50. It is open from 10 am-2 pm from October until Easter, then 10 am-4 pm the rest of the year (closed Christmas and Boxing Days and New Year's Day).

BRANDESTON
Queens Head

Tel. (072882) 307
*Two miles off B1120 at Earl
Soham*
Open 11.30–2.30 ; 5.30–11

✕ lunchtime and evening

🍺 **Adnams Mild, Best Bitter, Old
(winter), Broadside (summer)**

Ray and Myra Bumstead have run the "Queen"
for 13 years now and during that time they have
built up a reputation for good home-cooked
food, and an especially warm welcome for
families. The pub stands well back from the road
amidst well-kept gardens of trees and flower
beds. A secluded campsite is available at the
rear of the premises, and special prices are
offered for children using the bed and breakfast
accommodation in the pub itself. The family
room, which seats around 30 people has no
noisy space invaders or other machines; it looks
out on to the enclosed garden which has a
children's play area with a fun tree and climbing
frame. Small portions of the main menu are
offered for growing appetites.

IPSWICH
Lord Nelson

Tel. (0473) 254072
81 Fore Street
Open 11–11

◉

⋈

🍺 Adnams Mild, Bitter,
Broadside (winter)

This seventeenth-century pub is very eye-catching, with its half-timbering and dormer windows. It has two distinctly different bars: a quiet lounge decorated with Nelson memorabilia, and a rather more noisy public bar where voices have to be quite loud to be heard above the background music. The large family room comes somewhere between the two, noisewise that is. The usual range of pub games, cards, dominoes, draughts, etc. is available for children (or anyone else for that matter) to amuse themselves with. Children are welcome at any time and if hungry something from the bar snack menu should fill a hole. Babies may be changed in the ladies.

LONG MELFORD
Crown Inn

Tel. (0787) 77666
Hall Street (A134)
Open all day

◉

🍴

✗

⋈

🍺 Adnams Bitter; Greene King
IPA; Mauldon Bitter

Long Melford boasts the longest village street in England and has some fine Tudor architecture. The Crown (circa 1610) caters for the tourists who use it as a base to discover the many famous attractions in the area: Melford and Kentwell Halls, the old market town of Lavenham to name but a few. Children particularly enjoy a visit to the Clare Country Park nearby. Families are welcome in either of the two comfortable lounges. Meals are served from noon, including afternoon tea and children's meals at 6.30 pm. Highchairs are provided, along with facilities for changing and feeding babies. Families staying at the hotel can take advantage of the baby listening service. There is a safe, enclosed garden where the play area has a big plastic climbing frame.

ORFORD
Jolly Sailor

Tel. (0394) 450234
Quay Street, off B1078
Open 11–2.30; 6–11

@

&

✗ lunchtime and evening

~

⊕ **Adnams Bitter, Old (winter)**

Built in the sixteenth century to offer sustenance to the sailors at Orford's then thriving port, the pub has outlived its original purpose and now serves locals and tourists alike. Constructed out of old ships' timbers, the Jolly Sailor has a flagstoned bar and a comfortable lounge, as well as a snug. A further room, furnished in keeping with the rest of the pub, but without a bar, is open to families. Meals, with small portions for children, may be taken here, but as there are no other particular amenities, it is perhaps more suitable for older children than toddlers. While one might expect a display of seafaring artefacts, the pub somewhat idiosyncratically boasts an unusual collection of stuffed miniature dogs.

PIN MILL
Butt & Oyster

Tel. (047 384) 764
Off B1456, Ipswich-Shotley road
Open 11–2.30; 7–11 (open all day in summer)

@

& terrace

✗ lunchtime and evening

⊕ **Tolly Cobbold Mild, Bitter, Original, XXXX, Old Strong (winter)**

This famous pub is set right on the River Orwell, enjoying splendid views of sailing barges and smaller craft. Very much a local waterman's pub, dating back to the seventeenth century, it now also attracts weekend yachters and other visitors from further afield, despite its rather isolated position. They come because it is simply a superb pub, where the ale is taken from casks racked behind the bar. A terrace outside provides bench tables for summer drinking. The former smoke room, which leads off the main bar, is now used as a family room. A wide range of board games and traditional pub pastimes such as shut-the-box can be played here. Children are also welcome in the dining room where a special menu is served. Food is excellent and the menus are changed daily.

SOMERLEYTON
Duke's Head

Tel. (0502) 730281
Sluggs Lane, off B1074
Open 11–2.30; 6–11

◎

🎱

✗ lunchtime and evening

🍺 **Flowers Original; Wethered Bitter**

A 300 year-old Suffolk long house, this pub lies set back off the road on the church green, a hundred yards from the River Waveney. Somerleyton itself is a most unusual village built for workers on Sir Morton Peto's estate and all the houses have the same Victorian style. The Duke's Head is a large, popular pub which offers for sale paintings by local artists. It has a spacious children's room equipped with a pool table and some electronic games; the usual type of menu is provided for them, fishfingers, sausages, etc. with chips. The garden has seats and swings and backs on to fields leading down to the river. Sir Morton Peto was also responsible for rebuilding Somerleyton Hall, now open to the public, with state rooms to view and grounds to explore. For children, there is a maze, nature trail and a miniature railway.

SOUTHWOLD
Red Lion

Tel. (0502) 722385
2 South Green
Open 11–11 (11–3; 7–11 winter)

◎

✗ lunchtime and evening

🍺 **Adnams Bitter, Broadside**

This homely sixteenth-century pub overlooks the large green of a very quaint town, which becomes busy with tourists in the summer months. It is close to the sea and its lively harbour – places of interest to visit include a lighthouse, nature reserve and two museums. The Red Lion has a single bar and a large comfortable family room, warmed in winter by an open fire and furnished with high-backed settles; no particular amusements are provided here, so parents would be well advised to bring some along. A cold buffet is served in summer, and bar meals in winter, but then at lunchtimes only. Children's portions are available (chip-lovers should note that this is chip-less establishment)

WETHERINGSETT
Cat & Mouse

Tel. (0728) 860765
*Pages Green (off A140 and
B1077). OS 145652
Open 11–3; 5–11*

🏠

🅿

✖ lunchtime (evenings by
  arrangement)

🍺 **Adnams Bitter, Broadside,
Draught Bass; Brakspear
Bitter, Hall & Woodhouse
Tanglefoot; Mauldon Cat &
Mouse Bitter; Whitbread
Castle Eden Ale, Flowers
Original; Woodforde's
Wherry Best Bitter; James
White, Wilkins and Thatcher
ciders**

The catholic range of beer here is particularly laudable in that many of the small local breweries are represented, and the range listed above is liable to vary, to give an even wider choice for regulars. My colleague at CAMRA, Roger Protz, praised landlord Roy Booth is his "Best Pubs of East Anglia", saying that he deserves honorary life membership of the Campaign for his devotion to the cause. Casual visitors have to be fairly dedicated too, as the Cat and Mouse is devilishly difficult to find (take the Thorndon and Eye road from Debenham). The pub is old world, in the best sense: nothing fake, just little rooms, old beams, flagstones and whitewashed walls. To their credit, the Booths are not just ale buffs, they also provide some pretty good nosh and a cosy family room with armchairs, a piano and comics and books for the children. Outside children can get a real taste of the countryside as many domesticated animals – goats, rabbits, donkeys, ducks and geese live in the grounds.

Olde Bell and Steelyard, Woodbridge

WOODBRIDGE
Olde Bell & Steelyard

Tel. (03943) 2933
103 New Street
Open 11–2.30; 6–11

@

🏠

✘ lunchtime and evening

🍺 **Greene King IPA, Abbot Ale**

A classic pub, in fact, one of three Grade I listed buildings in the historic, riverside market town of Woodbridge, the Olde Bell and Steelyard takes its name from the seventeenth-century weighbridge that used to be worked by the publican, and whose machinery still stands (minus its weight) in front of the premises. Another unusual feature of this ancient pub, is that it specializes in pizzas – in fact if you want to eat, there is nothing else on offer. They are extremely popular with children and come in a variety of toppings and sizes; a large family pizza costs £6.95. The 20–seater family room is a no-smoking zone and some of the pub's wide selection of traditional games can be found here, namely Ring the Bull and Devil among the Tailors. Children may also be taken into the conservatory, but this only has seating for six, and of course the garden which has tables and benches. Old as it is, the pub caters well for the disabled; the wheelchair entrance is at the rear of the pub; there is a ramp to the lounge bar and a suitable WC.

Seckford Arms

Tel. (03943) 4446
Seckford Street
Open 11–11 (children until 6.30)

@

🏠

✘ lunchtime and evening

🚻

🍺 **Adnams Bitter, Broadside; Draught Bass; Felinfoel Double Dragon; Young Bitter, Special Bitter**

Originally a small cottage, the Seckford Arms has recently been extended to provide a large conservatory for families to use. Thankfully a smoke-free zone, the room is furnished in the same style as the rest of the pub, which, for a pub in Suffolk, is unusual to say the least. The owners, the Holyoaks, travelled widely before settling in Woodbridge and the pub is full of mementoes of their travels, in particular Mayan wood carvings from South America. In fact there is a carving of a Mayan indian on the front door. Facilities for children include highchairs and meals; if you wish to dine in the restaurant it is advisable to book. The pub is situated opposite the parkland of Fen Meadow.

BUCKLAND
Jolly Farmer

Tel. (0737) 242764
On A25 outside village
Open 11–11

◎

☎

✖

🍺 Friary Meux Best; Ind Coope
Burton Ale

The Jolly Farmer is situated on the main road away from the village which comes complete with a green and pond, as well as a curious towered tithe barn. The pub aims to have jolly children too by providing all sorts of amenities for them. The huge family room has video games and other playthings – even balloons if the children would like them. In the garden there are swings and an old, full-sized fire engine – to appeal to all devotees of Fireman Sam. The pub offers a comprehensive menu which allows for children's portions, or standard "kiddy fare" of beefburgers, fishfingers and so forth.

CHARLWOOD
Greyhound

Tel. (0293) 862203
The Street (off A23 near Horley)
Open 11–3; 5–11

◎

☎

✖ lunchtime and evening

🍺 Draught Bass; Charrington
IPA; Fuller ESB (winter);
Stones Best Bitter

Situated close to Gatwick Airport, the Greyhound is nonetheless a village pub. It is within walking distance, too, of Gatwick Zoo, so is useful for a day out in the area. The pub has a good local reputation for food, and can get very busy. Non-smokers will be pleased to note that the dining area is designated a smoke-free zone. Children's portions are available on most dishes at half-price. The purpose-built family room is not very large, but attractively furnished and leads out onto the patio; bring your own toys. There is a separate toilet for children.

COLDHARBOUR
Plough

Tel. (0306) 711793
Coldharbour Lane, near Dorking.
OS152441
Open 11.30–3; 6.30–11

◎

☎

✖ lunchtime and evening (not
Mon eve)

🍺 Adnams Broadside; Buckley
Best Bitter; Hall & Woodhouse
Badger Best Bitter; Ringwood
Old Thumper; Theakston Old
Peculier; Churchward
Medium Dry Cider; guest
beer

As may be guessed from the wide range of real ales available, this is a free house. It is a family-run, 350 year-old establishment near Leith Hill and reputedly the highest pub in the south east at 850 feet above sea level. It is situated in good walking country, and perhaps with hikers in mind, the licensees were planning to offer overnight accommodation from late 1989. The family room, although well away from the bar, is furnished in the same style as the rest of the pub, so families do not feel socially ostracised. A menu of the usual children's favourites is available, or they may select dishes from the main list. No particular amusements are provided for youngsters, so bring something with you.

ENGLEFIELD GREEN
Sun

Tel. (0784) 32515
*Wick Lane, Bishopsgate (follow
signs to Savill Gardens)*

◎

🕭

✘ lunchtime and evening

🍺 **Courage Best Bitter, Directors,
John Smith Bitter**

FARNHAM
Bat & Ball

Tel. (025125) 4564
*Bat & Ball Lane, Boundstone
(near Wrecclesham)*
Open 11–11

◎

🕭

✘ lunchtime and evening

🛏

🍺 **Adnams Bitter; Brakspear
Bitter; Buckley Best Bitter;
Exmoor Gold; Fuller London
Pride, ESB; Shepherd Neame
Master Brew Bitter**

GODSTONE
Bell

Tel. (0883) 843133
128 High Street (B2236)
Open 11–2.30 (3 Sat); 6–11

◎

🕭

✘ lunchtime and evening (not
Sun eve)

🛏

🎭

🍺 **Friary Meux Best; Ind Coope
Burton Ale; Tetley Bitter**

This is a congenial, single bar pub which caters well for all its customers. The food is recommended; vegetarians as well as children are catered for – half portions being available on most meals. Snacks only are served on Sundays. The spacious family room can seat 25 people comfortably and is equipped with a television and books. There is a safe garden with an aviary and pets corner. More wildlife can be seen at Windsor Great Park which is close by.

Accessible only by unmade tracks or footpaths (OS grid ref. 834445), this pub is nevertheless well worth seeking out. It was once a tallyman's office where hop-pickers were paid in cash and beer. The original part of the bar, with its log fire, is dark and still full of character. The comfortable family room adjoins the main bar and thus maintains a proper pub atmosphere. It overlooks the large playhouse complex with a slide, situated in a sunny garden where barbecues are a regular feature at summer weekends. In inclement weather, children may eat from their own menu indoors. Local attractions include Birdworld bird gardens and aquarium, Frensham Ponds, Alice Holt Forest and Farnham Castle. Overnight accommodation at the pub includes a cot.

I have to admit to having doubts about including the Bell. After it appeared in the first edition, I received an unfavourable report by a reader about it being cold and unwelcoming. However, it has been recommended by local CAMRA members and as the facilities for families are good, I think it is fair to include it and let you form your own opinions. Dating from 1393, the Bell was a former coaching inn and is now a village pub, popular with the locals and families enjoying a day out in the country. The large family room is at the back and has video games, jukebox and pinball. Pub staff have video surveillance to check what is going on here (maybe it is the echoes of "1984" that put my reader off). The garden is also large, set back from the main road and has plenty of amusements, including slides, swings and old Mother Hubbard's shoe. The usual children's fare is offered at mealtimes. Godstone Farm nearby is open to the public and is a popular venue for families.

GREAT BOOKHAM
Old Crown

Tel. (0372) 58119
1 High Street (off A246)
Open 10.30–11

◎

🍴

✗ lunchtime (not Sun)

🍺 **Courage Best Bitter, Directors**

This pub is typical of many built by Hodgsons Brewery between the wars. A real "drinkers' pub" with a large, lively public bar where darts and pool are played, it does however, cater well for families too. The comfortable lounge has a window on to the family room which is well decorated and furnished with four large and two small tables – children could bring colouring books in here to amuse themselves. There is a good size garden with plenty of wooden bench tables, swings, a slide and climbing frames. The lunch menu includes special dishes for youngsters, or small portions of main meals can be ordered. The Old Crown sits at the crossroads in the centre of a village which has managed to retain its old character despite being surrounded by commuter belt development. The timber-spired church is worth a visit.

TRAVEL PURSUITS

As this is a pub-oriented book, why not try a pubby "I spy". The country is littered with pubs with the most weird and wonderful names, which provide ideal material for a long-running game of I spy. A single point could be awarded for spotting common names, increasing to a maximum for the rarest of all, and there are quite a few pubs dotted around the country that have unique names. A good resource for this game is "A Dictionary of Pub Names" by Leslie Dunkling and Gordon Wright, published by Routledge & Kegan Paul. This is available from CAMRA, or try your local library. To get you started though, the authors maintain that the twenty most common pub names are as follows:

Anchor	Nelson (Lord or Admiral)
Angel	New Inn
Bell	Plough
Bull	Railway
Coach & Horses	Red Lion (the most common of all)
Crown	Royal Oak
Duke of Wellington	Rose & Crown
George	Swan
George & Dragon	White Hart
King's Head	White Horse

KINGSTON-UPON-THAMES
Bricklayers Arms

Tel. (01) 549 7520
53 Hawks Road (quarter of a mile from town centre)
Open 11–3 (4 Fri, Sat); 5.30–11

ⓐ

🍴

✗ lunchtime (not Sun)

🍺

🍺 **Courage Best Bitter; John Smith Bitter**

A friendly, welcoming pub, which is handy for Kingston shopping centre and Fairfield Park. It has two bars and a separate children's room at the rear of the pub. This room is on the small side, but has plenty of seating. Crayons and paper can readily be provided for budding artists, or children (and adults) can tax their intelligence with the quiz machine. A warm family atmsophere is achieved here; reduced price soft drinks are served to children under 14. The garden is wonderful for imaginative play with a large purpose-built solid wood and metal cabin and a set of stocks. The Sunday lunchtime draw is also very popular. Facilities for feeding and changing babies can be provided – ask the staff.

Flamingo Brewery Company

Tel. (01) 541 3717
88 London Road (near bus station)
Open 11–3; 5.30–11 (all day Sat)

ⓐ

🍴

✗

🍺

🍺 **Flamingo Fairfield Bitter, Royal Charter, Coronation; Greene King Abbot Ale**

Originally one of the chain of brew-pubs built up by David Bruce, before he sold out in 1988, this continues to be a popular and pleasant place to eat and try the home-brewed beer. There is frequent live entertainment – jazz, pianists etc. and a quiz is held every Wednesday night. From a family point of view, the Flamingo's facilities are hard to beat. The separate children's room has tables and chairs, ball pits to play in and rope bridges. There is a Young Flamingo Club for children up to 11 years old, with a video every Friday night, when a childminder is employed, and a disco once a month on Saturday. The room can also be booked for children's parties (no hire charge and full buffet provided for £1.75 a head). Children's meals are normally good value too – no more than £1.50. There is a separate toilet for children and baby changing facilities. Nearly all of David Bruce's pubs were designed with families in mind, so it is well worth seeking them out; most are in or around London.

LOWER MORDEN
Beverley Tavern

Tel. (01) 337 3071
Lower Morden Lane (on B279, by busy roundabout south west of centre)
Open 11–3; 5.30–11 (all day Fri, Sat)

◎

🍴

✗ (lunchtime and evening)

🍺 **Ruddles Best Bitter, County; Webster's Yorkshire Bitter**

This is a large, two bar pub situated in an area regarded by CAMRA members as a beer desert and it is thus very popular with local drinkers of the real stuff. It has been nicely modernised; the spacious, open-plan conservatory with cane chairs and sofas serves as the family area. The toilets are conveniently placed here. A children's menu is served at lunchtime in the adjacent food bar. The large, enclosed garden is safe for youngsters to run around in and is equipped with slides, swings and other playthings. The pub is handy for Morden Park and swimming pool.

OXTED
Crown

Tel. (0883) 717853
53 High Street
Open 12–2.30; 6–11 (children Sat/Sun lunchtime only)

◎

🍴

✗ lunchtime and evening

🍺 **Adnams Bitter; Pilgrim Progress; Ruddles County; guest**

The pine-panelled upstairs bar at the Crown is closed on Saturday and Sunday lunchtime to allow families to use the pub. As these are probably the times (apart from holidays) when most parents are likely to want to take their children out to the pub, I thought it worthwhile including. In any case, the garden, which is enclosed and well away from the road is available at any time and has play equipment, including slides and swings. Families are also welcome at mealtimes in the separate restaurant which serves good food, including a traditional Sunday lunch (children's portions available on request). Whisky-lovers will wish to know that the pub has 60 different malts on sale. The pub is convenient for Godstone Farm, with its learning centre and very approachable animals, and is on the road to Chartwell.

THAMES DITTON
Crown

Tel. (01) 398 2376
Summer Road (off High Street)
Open 11–2.30; 5.30–11

✖ lunchtime and evening

🍺 **Ruddles Best Bitter, County;
Webster's Yorkshire Bitter**

Although no special amusements or entertainments are provided here, the Crown is included because the licensees and staff make a genuine effort to cater for families — even to the extent of providing nappies in real cases of emergency! Very much an eating establishment, food is available all day. An awesome menu is chalked up on a large blackboard in the bar; vegetarian and children's dishes are always listed. Highchairs are provided in the family dining area. In summer barbecues are held every night if weather permits. There has been a pub on this site for almost 300 years, although this one only dates from 1925.

BERWICK
Berwick Inn

Tel. (0323) 870002
By Berwick station, near Polegate
Open 10.30–2.30; 6–11 (all day summer)

✗ lunchtime and evening

🍺 **Courage Best Bitter; Hall & Woodhouse Badger Best Bitter, Tanglefoot; Harvey BB; John Smith Bitter**

The furnishings and decor in this pub could do with some sprucing up, but this hardly detracts from the warm, friendly atmosphere and terrific welcome given to families. The large bar has a food servery where your plate is filled to overflowing, although smaller portions and a children's menu are also available. Food may be taken into the pleasant garden room where families may sit (highchair provided). Here there are a couple of games machines and an aviary, while outside are some hutches with rabbits. The garden is a children's paradise with a wooden treehouse-cum-slide, climbing frame, swing and, just installed, a mini motorbike track for 20 pence a ride. There are plenty of tables and benches so parents can sit and watch their offspring play. In summer a hut in the garden sells crisps, ice cream and soft drinks. Berwick is a small village near the South Downs. Nearby attractions include Drusilla's children's zoo, Arlington Reservoir and Arlington Speedway.

BRIGHTLING
Jack Fuller's

Tel. (042 482) 212
Half a mile from Brightling towards Robertsbridge
Open 12–3; 7–11

✗ lunchtime and evening

🍺 **Brakspear PA; Gales HSB; Harvey BB; Marston Pedigree; Taylor Landlord; Theakston Old Peculier; Wadworth 6X**

The landlord takes full advantage of his pub being a free house and refuses to take any of the big brewers' beers. However, the place has not always had such a good reputation – it was a licensed brothel until 1798. It is set in a spectacular beauty spot, surrounded by follies built by Jack Fuller in the early nineteenth century. The restaurant is well regarded for its food and highchairs and children's portions are provided. There is no special play equipment for youngsters but they are welcome and catered for in the pub at any time. In good weather, the lovely garden is popular with families.

HORSEBRIDGE
Kings Head

Tel. (0323) 843712
Off A22 on Bexhill-Hastings road
Open 11–3; 5.30–11

◎

🍴

✘ lunchtime and evening

🛏

🍽

🍺 **Courage Best Bitter, Directors**

Situated six miles from Eastbourne, this large two-bar pub is also handy for other local attractions such as Drusilla's Zoo and Horam Farm. A complete range of food is available, from sandwiches for around £1 to à *la carte* meals at around £6, as well as a children's menu. The family room is a relatively new feature in a glass and brick conservatory with plenty of seating and a games machine. The garden has a good selection of playthings, viz. swings, climbing frames and wendy houses.

MILTON STREET
Sussex Ox

Tel. (0323) 870840
Half a mile off the A27 near Alfriston
Open 11–2.30; 6–11

◎

🍴

✘ lunchtime and evening

🍺 **Harvey BB, Armada**

In a beautiful downland setting, this rural free house is close to the picture postcard village of Alfriston, and Drusilla's Zoo, both of which get fairly busy in the tourist season. The pub has a spacious family room with a toy cupboard and television. Meals may be taken here and a children's menu is offered. The large garden also has much to keep little ones amused: a sandpit, tyre swings, climbing frame and slide.

NORMANS BAY
Star Inn

Tel. (0323) 762648
On minor road from Pevensey to Cooden Beach
Open 11–3; 6–11

◎

🍴

✘ lunchtime and evening

🍽

🍺 **Draught Bass; Charrington IPA; Harvey IPA; Tetley Bitter; Young Bitter; guest beer**

A feature of the Star is its very extensive menu which caters for all appetites – from children's to enormous. In fact some items are marked with a baby elephant to warn customers that only those with elephantine capacity should order them (however, doggy bags can be provided for those whose eyes are larger than their stomachs). Most of the items are freshly cooked to order. Highchairs are available in the dining area. If you are not tempted by the smells from the kitchen though, there is a separate, comfortable family room with video machines and other amusements. The garden has a large playground with swings, slides, a rope walk and climbing tower. A band plays on Sunday lunchtimes and there is generally a live jazz session on Tuesday evenings.

PEVENSEY BAY
Moorings

Tel. (0323) 761126
Seaville Drive (take coast road off A259, then first right)
Open 11–3; 6–11

◎

✕ lunchtime and evening

⊟ **Brakspear Special Bitter;
Harvey BB; Marston Pedigree;
Theakston Best Bitter**

This area is uncommonly well provided with free houses, this one being also great for families as it is situated right on the beach, with Pevensey Castle just half a mile away. The large, comfortable family room is next to the games room which has video games and other distractions. A good range of home-cooked meals is served either in the bar or restaurant and are, unusually, available all day on Sunday; the standard children's meals – beefburgers, fishfingers et al. are offered for around £1.50. In summer barbecues are an added attraction.

PUNNETTS TOWN
Three Cups Inn

Tel. (0435) 830252
On B2096, two miles from Heathfield towards Battle
Open 11–3.30; 6.30–11

◎

▩

✕ lunchtime and evening

⊟ **Courage Best Bitter, Directors;
John Smith Bitter**

Worth bearing in mind if you are touring, this pub has a Caravan Club approved site in its back field. Some 300 years old, this country hostelry abounds with oak beams and brass and has an inglenook fireplace. A family area is set aside in the restaurant where a highchair and children's menu are provided. Sandwiches and ploughman's are served if you just want a snack. A separate family room has a bar billiards table and other playthings. Chickens and ducks roam freely in the large garden.

Star Inn, ancient haunt of smugglers at Normans Bay

ROBERTSBRIDGE
George Inn

Tel. (0580) 880315
On A21, south of the village
Open 11–3; 6–11 (all day Sat)

⊚

🐕

✘ lunchtime and evening

🍴

🍺 **Flowers Original, Pompey Royal; Fremlins Bitter; Marston Pedigree**

The George aims for, and to a good degree achieves, a relaxed country house-style atmosphere, with comfortable furniture and magazines to browse through. Deceptively large, the building also houses an à *la carte* restaurant (children's menu available); although snacks and basket meals are also served. Families are made very welcome; the overnight accommodation includes cots and baby changing facilities are provided. The reasonably-sized children's room is in an extension off the main building, with blackboard walls (a very sensible idea), video machines, football game and pool table. A goat, rabbits, geese, chickens, ducks and pheasants inhabit a corner of the colourful garden, but most children make a beeline for the "Fort George" wooden play fort. Swings and rubber tyres to play in complete the picture.

RYE
Standard Inn

Tel. (0797) 223393
The Mint
Open 12 (11 Fri, Sat)-11

⊚

✘ lunchtime and evening

🍺 **Harvey BB; King & Barnes Draught Festive; Ruddles Best Bitter; Young Special; occasional guest beer**

Yet another free house – this time in the wonderful historic town of Rye, famous as a Cinque Port and for its connections with Henry James. There is a lot to see here, so the Standard comes as a welcome watering hole (the food is good value too). The pub was rebuilt in 1420 and is all bare brick and wood beams; somewhere a cannonball lies buried in the wall. The spacious family room has a pool table and lots of other games. This is a lively pub which always offers a warm welcome.

SEAFORD
Beachcomber

Tel. (0323) 892719
Dane Road (on seafront, west side of town)
Open 11–11 (10.30–3; 6–11 winter)

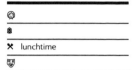

✕ lunchtime

🍺 **Draught Bass; Charrington IPA; Hall & Woodhouse Badger Best Bitter, Tanglefoot; Harvey BB**

A large pub, situated just across the road from the beach which underwent massive reconstruction (the beach that is) in 1988 to prevent the sea wall from being completely destroyed by the force of the sea. The Martello Tower museum is just along the seafront and Newhaven Fort is a few miles further round the coast. The pub has a large bar and smaller room for pool. A separate restaurant has highchairs and the menu caters for children. The family room at the back of the pub has some electronic games machines. Parents may sit outside this room if they prefer on hall benches; drinks can be ordered through a serving hatch. Outside, an enclosed play area offers scope for imaginative play with log climing frames and other equipment.

FELPHAM
Southdowns

Tel. (0243) 583916
*133 Felpham Way (three miles
along A259 from Bognor Regis to
Littlehampton)
Open 11–11*

☺

🏠

✗

🍺 Friary Meux Best; Ind Coope
Burton Ale; Tetley Bitter

This games-oriented pub has a large public bar with pool, darts, crib etc. The lounge bar has a raised area where families may sit and eat; a children's menu is served all day. There is a large enclosed play area in the garden with two swings, a slide, seesaw and good-sized climbing frame. Ideal for daytrippers, the pub is just two miles from South Coast World and not much further from Bognor Regis itself.

LANCING
Three
Horseshoes
Tavern

Tel. (0903) 753424
*182 South Street
By the mini roundabout on the
A259
Open 11–3; 6–11 (all day if busy)*

🏠

✗ lunchtime and evening

🍺 Ruddles County; Webster's
Yorkshire Bitter

Although it has no family room as such, this Chef and Brewer establishment is included because it does make a good effort to cater for families with occasional special attractions such as Punch and Judy acts or the addition of a bouncing castle to the garden. Children may eat in the restaurant and their menu comes very reasonably priced. The garden, one of the largest in the area, is only accessible via the bar and is completely safe. Here plenty of tables and seating make it a pleasant place for parents to sit while their offspring enjoy the adventure playground, tuckshop and domestic animal compound.

LAVANT
Earl of March

Tel. (0243) 774751
*Lavant Road (on A286, two miles
north of Chichester)
Open 11–2.30; 6–11*

☺

🏠

✗ lunchtime and evening

🍺 Ballards Best Bitter; Courage
Directors; Marston Pedigree,
Owd Rodger; Ringwood Old
Thumper; Ruddles Best Bitter,
County; Churchward Cider;
guest beers

Rather like the "Tardis", this seventeenth-century free house is larger than it appears from the outside. It may have not exactly have travelled in time, but its facilities are completely up to date and allow access to the disabled. It enjoys beautiful views of the South Downs and is convenient for Chichester, Goodwood and the Singleton Downland Open Air Museum. Children's portions are available for certain items on the very wide ranging menu which offers many home-made specials, including plenty of game dishes in season. An area at the back of this open-plan pub is set aside for families. This is comfortably furnished and has a selection of board games and a bar billiards table. There is direct access to the toilets and car park.

OFFHAM
Black Rabbit

Tel. (0903) 882828
*Mill Road, just out of Arundel
town centre
Open 11–11 (may close winter
afternoons)*

◎
&

✘ lunchtime and evening

🍺 **Hall & Woodhouse Badger
Best Bitter, Tanglefoot**

Idyllic for a summer's day, the Black Rabbit is situated on the river, surrounded by open fields, with splendid views of Arundel castle. There is a swing and plenty of seating outside; a safety fence keeps little ones from straying into the water. The family room becomes the restaurant in the evening (at lunchtime food is buffet style), so it does not have any particular amusements for children. It does however have plenty of windows and seating (including highchairs). Children's tastes are catered for on the menu and baby changing facilities should be available by the time you read this. Apart from the attractions of Arundel itself, other local tourist spots are the Wildfowl Trust, Fishbourne Roman Palace, the Bluebell Railway – a great favourite for families – and Parham House and Gardens.

SIDLESHAM
Anchor Inn

Tel. (02456) 373
*Selsey Road (B2145, midway
between Chichester and Selsey)
Open 11–2.30; 6–11 (11–11
summer Fri & Sat)*

◎
&

✘ lunchtime and evening

🍺 **Friary Meux Best; Ind Coope
Burton Ale**

A listed building, this pleasant, simple cottage pub is a popular village local. A good range of food is always available with lots of home-made specials: try the cockle and bacon pie. There is a children's menu for those with less sophisticated tastes. The family room is an integral part of the pub and is furnished as comfortably as the rest of the bar. The garden has a play area.

SOMPTING
Ball Tree Inn

Tel. (0903) 753090
*Busticle Lane, 400 yards off the
A27
Open 11–2.30; 6–11*

◎
&

✘ lunchtime and evening

♙

🍺 **Gales Butser Brew Bitter, HSB**

Billed as "Sompting's family local", this large two-bar pub is just a mile from the seafronts of Lancing and Worthing. The spacious family room leads out to the patio and garden which is safe for children and has a swing and climbing frame. Various snacks and meals are available from 85 pence but no special provision is made for children on the menu.

SOUTH HARTING
Coach & Horses

Tel. (0730) 825229
Near Petersfield, Hants.
Open 11–2.30; 6–11 (all day Sat)

⊚

🛏

✗ lunchtime and evening

🍺 **Gibbs Mew Bishop's Tipple;
Hall & Woodhouse
Badger Best Bitter, Tanglefoot;
Wadworth 6X; Whitbread
Castle Eden Ale**

Only just inside Sussex, and nestling at the foot of the South Downs, this free house benefits from its beautiful rural setting. If the wind blows in the right direction, hang gliders can be seen taking off and landing on the downs opposite the pub. The licensees here obviously know what appeals to children as their separate family room is well equipped with toys, but the real treat is being able to draw all over the chalk wall without fear of retribution. The pub's pets include a cat called Claude, a friendly red setter and two rabbits, normally found in the garden where there is a climbing frame and petanque pitch. The children's menu includes fishfingers, ham and chips and "lots of things that children enjoy".

White Hart Inn

Tel. (0730) 825355
High Street
Open 11–2.30; 6.30–11

⊚

🛏

✗

🍺 **Friary Meux Best; Ind Coope
Burton Ale**

No apologies for including two pubs in the same village as they are both excellent examples of what this guide is about. Would that every village had two such pubs – I would be out of a job. This sixteenth-century beamed inn is particularly welcoming in winter with its glowing open fires. In summer though, its particular attraction is its beautiful walled English country garden. Many licensees would worry that the presence of children might mar the serenity of such a place, but here they manage successfully to cater for all needs. The pub has three bars as well as a restaurant and a separate family room (open until 8) where a toybox is supplied. The garden is large enough to hold a pets corner with ducks, rabbits and guinea pigs, a fishpond and a play area with swings, slide and a climbing frame, without spoiling its charm.

STEYNING
Star Inn

Tel. (0903) 813078
130 High Street
Open 11–2.30 (3 Fri); 6–11 (all day Sat)

✕ lunchtime and evening (not Tue eve)

🍺 **Flowers Original; Fremlins Bitter, Pompey Royal**

Some years ago I used to visit the Star quite often when my in-laws lived in this delightful little country town. This was b.c. (before children) but I am reliably informed by local CAMRA folk that this is a must for the family guide – and very pleased too I am to hear it, because it is a smashing pub. Known affectionately as the "Bottom House", it is a traditionally arranged local which offers a warm welcome to all. The carpeted family room, which is integral to the rest of the pub, can hold about 20 people comfortably; it has a car game and toys for smaller children. There is direct access to the children's toilets and on to the garden. The garden is in fact divided into two: one part is safe for youngsters with a climbing frame; the other has a stream running through. Children are catered for on the menu which includes daily specials; prices range from 85 pence for sandwiches to around £6 for meals.

White Hart Inn, South Harting

STOUGHTON
Hare & Hounds

Tel. (0705) 631433
Off B2146, through Walderton
Open 11–3; 6–11 (all day Fri &
Sat summer)

✖ lunchtime and evening

🍺 **Boddingtons Bitter; Bunces**
Best Bitter; Fuller London
Pride; Greene King Abbot Ale;
Mansfield Old Baily; guest
beer

Recently returned to the free trade, this pretty flint pub was once a shop. Its location may be remote, set as it is in the South Downs, but the welcome is very warm. There are three small bars, the two lounges being divided by a brick fireplace; look out for the humorous posters advertising the guest beers. The family lounge is as comfortably decorated as the rest of the pub, and children are also welcome in the dining room where good home-cooked meals are served at reasonable prices – local seafood is often available. Highchairs are provided. Meals can also be taken in the garden.

WISBOROUGH GREEN
Three Crowns

Tel. (0403) 700207
On A272 Petworth-Billingshurst
road
Open 10.30–3; 5.30–11

✖ lunchtime and evening

🍺 **Friary Meux Best; Ind Coope**
Burton Ale

The Three Crowns opens half an hour earlier than most local pubs, but only coffee is served until 11 o'clock. It is a charming village inn dating back to the fifteenth century and situated in a beautiful village. Home prepared food, including enormous ploughman's, is served in the restaurant, bar, family room or garden. Children's appetites are catered for. The comfortable family room has Duplo to keep the very young amused and offers easy access to the loos. It opens out on to the patio and garden where there are swings, a pool table and pets corner. An adult must accompany children to visit the animals: ducks and Poppy, a giant lop-eared rabbit – with luck there may be some babies around.

WORTHING
Dolphin

Tel. (0903) 210582
Dominion Road
Open 11.30–3; 4.30–11 (all day Fri & Sat)

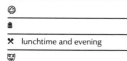

✖ lunchtime and evening

🍺 **Charrington IPA; Fuller ESB (winter)**

Situated on the corner of the busy Dominion Road and quieter Angola Road, the Dolphin is a popular local which also offers a warm welcome to visitors. It is a large pub with modern, but not unattractive decor. It boasts a "proper" public bar, and I am pleased to say a "proper" family room which is well furnished and offers some amusements for youngsters. The family room has its own toilet with facilities for nursing mothers and direct access to the enclosed garden (plans were afoot to obtain play equipment as we went to press). The food served equates good value with high quality; a children's menu is available.

JARROW
Western

Tel. (091) 489 6243
Western Road
Open 11–3; 6–11

◎

✗

⊿ **Cameron Traditional Bitter, Strongarm; Everards Old Original**

At present, the Western has limited facilties for families. They are simply, but warmly welcomed in the rear lounge which does not have a bar. However, plans are in hand to extend the pub to provide a kitchen, so that proper meals can be served to all customers, including children. A play area is also planned for what is at present just a back yard. Work should be finished by the time this book goes to press, but it may be as well to check by phone. The pub is a short walk from the metro station which means that both Newcastle and Gateshead are just 15 minutes away.

NORTH HYLTON
Shipwrights

Tel. (091) 549 5139
Feryboat Lane (off A1231)
Open 11–3; 7–11 (children until 9 pm)

◎

✗ lunchtime and evening (not Sun/Mon)

⊿ **Ward Sheffield Best Bitter; Vaux Samson, Double Maxim**

The Shipwrights is not really well equipped to cater for children, but if you do want to take your family out with you when you go to a pub in Tyneside, then there isn't much to choose from. At least here there is a room without a bar which families are welcome to use. The Shipwrights is a riverside pub, which has been much extended over the years. It has a carvery restaurant on the first floor (no concessions for children here, I'm afraid), which has excellent river views.

SOUTH SHIELDS
Marsden Rattler

Tel. (091) 455 6789
South Foreshore (A138)
Open 11–3; 6.30–11.30 (all day summer)

◎

✗ lunchtime and evening

⋈

⊿ **Ruddles County**

It is hardly surprising that the Marsden Rattler is popular with families with such a limited choice in the county (in fact we did not come up with any for the first edition), but this one has immediate appeal. Set right by the beach in converted railway carriages, the pub displays much memorabilia from the former coastal line. A huge conservatory is open to families with a ride machine for little children to enjoy. Highchairs are provided and a good value varied menu is served with special dishes for children. There is frequent live entertainment. The pub has chalet accommodation which can be booked for holidays. An added bonus is that the Rattler is accessible by metro, although a bit of a walk for very small children.

BAXTERLEY
Rose Inn

Tel. (0827) 713939
*Main Road (three-quarters mile
from A5 at Atherstone)*
Open 11–3; 6–11

✗ lunchtime and evening

🍺 **Draught Bass; M & B Mild,
Brew XI**

This picturesque pub sits on the village green with a duckpond and the licensees say very firmly that duck does not feature on the pub's menu – for fear of hurting their feelings I suppose! Children's meals however, are provided (for around £1.30), as well as small portions of adult dishes and are served either from the bar or in the separate restaurant. Highchairs are available as are amenities for feeding/changing babies. The restaurant is very popular with evening diners, so it is best to book ahead. There is a 20–seater family room which has plenty of toys. The open garden is deemed safe for children, and of course there is the green itself with the non-edible ducks.

BEDWORTH
Old Goose Inn

Tel. (0203) 313266
Orchard Street
Open 11.30–2.30; 7–11

🍺 **Ansells Mild, Bitter; Tetley
Bitter**

The Old Goose caters mostly for local trade, who obviously do not go there to eat, as no food is normally served. There is a fairly basic bar and a recently refurbished lounge. The children's room is on the small side and has no particular amusements; it does though have a fine view of the garden which attracts many local families in good weather as it is safe for children, a very pleasant place to sit out and equipped with swings, climbing frame and other playthings. Summer barbecues are held, weather permitting of course.

CORLEY
Horse & Jockey

Tel. (0203) 332643
Tamworth Road
Open 11–2.30; 6–11

✗ lunchtime and evening

🍺 **Ruddles Best Bitter, County;
Webster Yorkshire Bitter**

Although just outside Coventry, this really is a country pub with a very large garden backing on to fields. The medium-sized family room is decorated to appeal to children, and has a video machine. Meals, served daily can be reduced to children's portions, or a choice can be made from the children's menu. The garden is safe for children and has a rather exciting assault course, so some supervision maybe necessary for the younger ones The pub is just five minutes' walk from Corley Rocks.

HILLMORTON
Old Royal Oak

Tel. (0788) 61401
Crick Road (junction of A428 and Oxford canal)
Open 11–3; 5–11 (all day Thu-Sat and summer)

@

🛇

✗ until 8.30

🍺 **Courage Directors; guest beer**

An interesting canalside pub on the edge of the town, it has a large lounge bar which has been modernised and comfortably furnished. Children are alllowed in here to eat; there is an extensive menu with special dishes for younger tastes. The family room is rather bare with seating and a blackboard. If that reminds them too much of school, then children can explore the large garden which has a climbing frame and swings. The pub is very popular with families until early evening when it tends to become rather busy and noisy.

LEAMINGTON SPA
Newbold Comyn Arms

Tel. (0926) 338810
Newbold Terrace East (near park)
Open 11–3; 6–11 (all day Sat)

@

🛇

✗ lunchtime and evening

🍺 **Marston Burton Best Bitter, Pedigree, Merrie Monk**

This pub is actually set within Newbold Comyn Park and enjoys all the benefits that the municipal authority provides, ie pitch and putt, golf and a swimming-pool due to be completed in May 1990. The pub itself has a converted stables with a skittle alley and custom-built family room. There is also a restaurant. Alternatively, bar meals are available from around £1. Children are catered for on the menu and highchairs are provided. The beer garden has its own outdoor play area built on a soft surface for safety. The pub keeps an amazing selection of a hundred different whiskies and malts (and of course, good beer). For visiting families, Warwick Castle is roughly three miles away and Stratford on Avon just ten miles.

MARSTON JABBETT
Corner House Hotel

Tel. (0203) 383073
Nuneaton Road, Bulkington (on B4112, near canal)
Open 11–3; 5.30 = 11

@

🛇

🍺 **Marston Best Bitter, Pedigree, Owd Rodger**

This is a large pub with public bar and separate, spacious lounge. Facilities are a little bit limited, but then there is not a lot to choose from in this neck of the woods. The family room is also used as a games room which is fine if your offspring like pool, although there is a football table too (and even my four year-old enjoys playing on those). No meals are served, but snacks are available. The small garden has a nice lawn and tables and chairs, but again, no particular amusements for little ones. The motto round here is: travel well equipped.

NUNEATON
Hayrick

Tel. (0203) 348181
Meadowside, Whitestone
Open 12–2.30 (3.30 Sat); 6–11

✖ lunchtime

🍺 **Courage Best Bitter, Directors**

The Hayrick is probably the best of the family pubs in Warwickshire, a county not particularly well served by family hostelries. Things have changed since Shakespeare's day – we no longer see pubs as dens of iniquity from which innocent young babes should be protected. Many of them are quite respectable now and it would be nice if a few more opened their doors more readily to families and were prepared to treat children as proper customers. Well, here's one that does anyway. This is a large, modern, two-bar pub where adult entertainment includes a juke box and pool. For the younger customers the family room has a chocolate machine, video games, car ride, television and juke box – let's hope they are not all in action at the same time, in which case parents would most likely want to retreat to the patio. Chairs and umbrellas are provided out here and barbecues are sometimes held. At lunchtimes, children's meals can be had for £1.50; the grown-ups' food is good value too.

RUGBY
Saracen's Head

Tel. (0788) 77654
23 North Street
Open 11.30–2.30; 6–11

✖ lunchtime

🍺 **Ruddles Best Bitter, County**

This is an attractive town-centre pub close to the park, Rugby School and Gilbert's Rugby Museum. Families are welcome in the large L-shaped conservatory which is well furnished and maintains a good pub atmosphere. No amusements are provided, so youngsters should bring their own. Children's portions can be served from the lunch menu (ask at the food bar when ordering). There is a good garden surrounded by trees which is refreshing in a town-centre location.

Three Cranes

Overslade Lane (off A426, south Rugby)
Open 11–2.30; 6–11 (11–4; 7–11 Sat)

🍺 **Bass M & B Brew XI**

A large, modern estate pub on the south side of town, the Three Cranes sets out to cater for the whole family. The purpose-built family room is clean and tidy with a pool table and games machines and a soft drinks bar. No meals are served as such, but hot and cold snacks are available at both sessions (until 8.30). There is a large enclosed garden which is safe for children and has a climbing frame, slide and swings.

STRATFORD UPON AVON
Shakespeare Hotel

Tel. (0789) 294771
Chapel Street
Open 11–2.30; 5.45–11

---

⑧

✗ lunchtime

⌣

⌾ **Courage Directors; Donnington SBA; Hook Norton Best Bitter, Old Hookey; guest beers**

It is hard to find pubs in very busy tourist towns that cater well for families. This one is not ideal, but it does at least welcome children and what is more is the first in our listing for Warwickshire that actually sells ales from the smaller breweries. It is a smart Trust House Forte hotel, but attracts a mixed clientele including keen bar billiards players. Families may eat and drink in the Measure for Measure room, adjacent to the Froth and Elbow Bar whose entrance is directly on the street. Children can eat for half the adult price from the main menu. The hotel also offers family accommodation (cots available) and has a safe, enclosed garden.

STUDLEY
Old Washford Mill

Tel. (0527) 23068
Icknield Street Drive (A435 Birmingham-Evesham road, follow Redditch Hospital signs)
Open 11–2.30; 6–11 (all day bank holidays)

◎

---

⑧

✗

⌾ **Draught Bass; Courage Directors; Marston Pedigree; Wadworth 6X**

A free house that has its own vineyards and a wine bar offering over 30 wines that also caters for families. It can be done! The pub has in fact many unusual features: the Mill Bar, where real ales are served straight from the wood, has a water mill encased in glass in the centre of the bar. There is a choice of eating areas, either in the *à la carte* restaurant or in the bar serving snacks and pizzas; barbecues are held in fine weather. Children are well catered for on the menu. The family room is light and airy with a couple of machines for amusement and a video screen. The large gardens are situated between the mill race and the river Arrow, overlooking the vineyards; for children there is a boot slide and multi-activity unit (I don't think that's anything to do with the armed forces, even though it sounds like it).

BIRMINGHAM
Baldwin

Tel. (021) 744 3356
*Baldwins Lane, Hall Green (off
A34)*
Open 12–2.30; 6–11

☺

🛏

✗ lunchtime (not Sun)

🍴

🍺 **Courage Best Bitter, Directors;
John Smith Bitter**

Unfortunately, the West Midlands is poorly served by family pubs. There are very few indeed that have proper indoor rooms for children, although plenty have play equipment in the garden. This one, in a leafy 1930s suburb of Birmingham, is probably the best of the bunch. A large pub, it was restyled about three years ago, after a lengthy legal battle to provide family amenities (maybe this is the key to the lack of suitable family pubs in the county). Rather bizarrely, the pub was originally designed to represent half a ship; the other half is the Three Magpies on the same estate. The family room is a purpose-built canopied extension to the pub, with its own entrance. It is spacious, light and airy with seating for around 60 people. Some amusements are provided and a children's WC is adjacent to the room. Babies can be changed in the ladies, but more facilities for them have been promised. The usual children's meals are served for around £1.20. The family room opens on to the pub's triangular garden which has bench tables, rocking animals and a play area with bark surface. Barbecues are a feature. Next to the garden is the pub's own bowling green. Nearby is Swanshurst Park with a boating lake and other attractions and the centre of Birmingham is just five miles distant.

Burton Floater at the Bass Museum,
Burton on Trent (see over)

BRIERLEY HILL
Saltwells Inn

Tel. (0384) 69224
Off Saltwells Road at EPS factory
Open 11.30–11

🍴 all day (Sun lunch only)

🛏

🍺 Banks's Mild Ale, Bitter;
Hanson Mild Ale, Bitter

Situated half a mile off the main road, this inn is at the entrance to the Saltwells Nature Reserve – 100 acres of open land, run by the local council – so makes an ideal place to refresh yourselves after a country ramble. The 60–seater family room has a blackboard, video game and its own WC. Double doors open on to an enclosed garden which is floodlit at night, and offers an action tree, elephant slide and several swings. No particular children's menu is served, but the favourites of beefburgers, hotdogs and chips are very reasonably priced. It is necessary to book for Sunday lunch. The pub is approximately a mile from the Merry Hill Shopping Centre and not far from the Black Country Museum and Zoo at Dudley, which is much more appealing to youngsters I am sure.

COVENTRY
Biggin Hall
Hotel

Tel. (0203) 451046
214 Binley Road (main road to Rugby)
Open 11–2.30; 4–11 (11–11 Fri; 11–4, 6–11 Sat)

🍴 12–2 Mon-Sat

🍺 Marston Mercian Mild, Burton Best Bitter, Pedigree, Owd Rodger

According to the 1990 "Good Beer Guide", this pub (which is not in fact a hotel) serves the best Marstons in Coventry. It has a smart bar and a quiet, wood-panelled lounge, favoured by the locals. The family room is to the rear of the pub and doubles as a games room with a pool table and two video games for amusement. There are some tables and chairs in an enclosed area at the back of the pub. Smaller portions of the lunch dishes are served to children at reduced prices. Local attractions include a bowling alley just around the corner from the pub; Combe Abbey with its park, play area and boating lake is about one and a half miles away and it is the same distance to the centre of Coventry.

TETTENHALL WOOD
Royal Oak

Tel. (0902) 754396
7 School Road
Open 12–3 (4 Sat); 6–11

◎

🛏

✗ 12–2

🍴

🍺 M & B Brew XI; Highgate Mild; Springfield Bitter

This Bass house is a small, traditional pub, three-quarters of a mile from Tettenhall Green. Here again, the family room doubles as a pool/games room and is situated behind the pub. There is a bar here, but it is not normally open – just for special occasions – and children are always made welcome. The lunchtime bar food is all home cooked and with everything costing under £3 is very good value. Children may choose small portions of adult dishes or something from their own menu. The lovely beer garden is extremely well kept and has several swings for youngsters, but more play apparatus is also planned. Babies can be changed in the ladies, but otherwise there are no particular amenities for them.

BASS MUSEUM

Visitors to the Midlands can spend a fascinating day out at the Bass Museum of Brewing History in Burton on Trent. Opened in 1977 as part of the company's bicentenary celebrations, the museum site also includes the stables of the Bass shire horses.

The main museum is situated in what was originally the Bass joiner's shop and the restaurant is in the former wheelwright's workshop. The exhibits are all extremely good and show lifelike models, such as the cooper and his apprentice at work, and a brewery laboratory of the nineteenth century. The latest development is the Chairman's Gallery which displays how malting and brewing techniques have changed over the years and shows photographs of how Bass breweries operate today. Generally, guided tours are not provided, but audio-visual displays give additional information.

One of the most popular exhibits is the large railway model of Burton as it was in the early 1920s. At that time, Bass operated the largest private railway system in Europe and this model, which took four men two years to complete, is the largest accurately researched working model railway in Europe. Other exhibits for transport enthusiasts can be seen in the grounds of the museum, including a reconstructed railway ale-dock, old delivery wagons and, something I would have loved to have seen on the streets, a "bottle car" specially made for area sales managers of the twenties.

Four Bass shires are stabled at the museum, and although they are used for shows and displays, there are always two at home. They are highly prized animals, and prize-winning, as the many trophies on display attest. The grooms can often be seen at work cleaning and polishing their tack.

At the museum's Edwardian pub you can try your hand at some old pub games. The bar is open at lunchtime until 2.30 pm, and the restaurant from 10.30 am until 4 pm. The souvenir shop has books, postcards and memorabilia relating to Bass and Burton's brewing history. The museum is at Horninglow Street, Burton on Trent, Staffordshire, telephone (0283) 42031. It is open daily (apart from Christmas Day, Boxing Day and New Year's Day), 10 am -5 pm. Mon-Fri and 11 am-5 pm at the weekend (last admission 4.30 pm). Admission prices are £2 for adults and £1 for children and senior citizens.

BURTON
Plume of
Feathers

Tel. (045 421) 251
On B4039, two miles from Castle Combe
Open 11.30–2.30 (3 Sat); 6–11

◎

🍴

✗ lunchtime and evening

🛏

🍺 **Marston Pedigree; Usher Best Bitter**

The Feathers is a Grade II listed stone building, dating back some 400 years and set in the Wiltshire countryside on the outskirts of a small village. Just at the edge of the Cotswolds, it is ideally situated for exploring the many attractions of that scenic area, as well as being convenient for Bristol and Bath. Family facilities are somewhat limited here, there being no particular amusements for children, but they are welcome in the family room for a drink or to have a meal with their parents (children's portions available). According to Susan Nowak, author of CAMRA's "Good Pub Food" guide, Sunday lunchtime in winter is the best time to go when the licensees, who spent many years in the Far East, cook their speciality Indonesian meals.

CHISELDON
Patriots Arms

Tel. (0793) 740331
New Road (off M4 Jct 15; off A345, near Swindon)
Open 12–2.30; 6–11

◎

🍴

✗ lunchtime and evening

🍺 **Courage Best Bitter, Directors; John Smith Bitter**

Just a mile from the M4, this pub offers a convenient stopover for travellers, and families are made particularly welcome. It is a traditional pub: the public bar has pool and darts, there is a comfortable lounge and à la carte restaurant (closed Sunday evening), although bar snacks, with children's choices, are also available. Two highchairs are provided. The spacious family room is purpose built and has plenty of seating. Amusements include three video games, children's books and a Lego table. More play equipment is provided in the safe, enclosed garden. There is plenty to see and do in the area for families; local attractions include Barbury Castle, the Military Science Museum, Avebury Stones and Stonehenge.

DAUNTSEY
Peterborough
Arms

Tel. (0249) 890409
*At Dauntsey lock on the Swindon-
Chippenham road
Open 11.30–3; 6–11 (closed Mon
except Bank Holidays)*

Ⓒ

---

⑧

✘ lunchtime and evening

🍺 **Boddingtons Bitter;
Davenports Traditional Bitter;
Hook Norton Old Hookey;
Tetley Bitter; Wadworth 6X;
guest beer**

This well-appointed free house aims to suit all tastes, and certainly their beer range is fairly catholic. Food too, is excellent, specialising in home-cooked dishes which range in price from 80 pence snacks to main courses for around £3. Families are cordially welcomed and toys are provided in the two rooms (one large, one small) that are set aside for them. A children's menu is available as are facilities for nursing mothers. The large garden allows plenty of space for youngsters to let off steam and has a climbing frame, swings, slide and seesaws.

Plume of Feathers, Burton

FOVANT
Cross Keys

Tel. (072 270) 284
On A30, nine miles from Salisbury
Open 11–3; 5–11

ⓐ

🅱

✗ lunchtime and evening

🛏

🍺 Hook Norton Best Bitter;
Wadworth 6X; guest beer

The Cross Keys makes a good base for touring the area, situated a short drive from both Salisbury and Shaftesbury. It has a homely and welcoming atmosphere and the overnight accommodation includes a cot. This fascinating old coaching inn was built in 1485 of flint and stone, and is full of nooks and crannies. There are good views of the Fovant Emblems, chalk badges carved on the local hills. Children's portions are available on the reasonably priced menu, or special dishes can be prepared. There is a family room indoors and a play area in the enclosed garden.

HAMPTWORTH
Cuckoo Inn

Tel. (0794) 390302
Take B3079 Bramshaw road off
A36, turn right towards Redlynch
Open 11.30–2.30; 6–11
(11.30–11 Sat & Bank Holidays)

ⓐ

🅱

🍵

🍺 Bunces Best Bitter; Hall &
Woodhouse Badger Best
Bitter, Tanglefoot; Wadworth
IPA, 6X, Old Timer or Farmers
Glory; Wilkins Cider

A popular, but fairly basic, thatched pub in a quiet rural setting on the edge of the New Forest. The entrance opens onto the small garden bar where children are welcome, although a new room was planned as we went to press. There is a cosy lounge and public bar with darts and juke box, both of which are lit by real fires. Food is limited to snacks and ploughmans and are sometimes snapped up early in the session. The lawned front garden has picnic benches , swings and climbing frame and an aviary with a peacock and golden bantams. A new petanque pitch is an added attraction. Altogether this makes a delightful halt for visitors to the New Forest or walkers on the network of public footpaths that radiate from the pub.

HEDDINGTON
Ivy Inn

Tel. (0380) 850276
Two and a half miles south of the
A4 at Calne
Open 11–3; 6.30–11

ⓐ

🅱

🍺 Wadworth IPA, 6X, Old Timer

This 400 year-old idyllic village inn is set in beautiful, peaceful countryside. With its thatched roof, beams and stone floor it could not be more traditional, and the beer is all served from the wood behind the bar. The family room is separate from the bar, but is carpeted and comfortable. Here bar billiards is played and there are some electronic games, but these are thankfully silent. Cold snacks are available. The outside drinking area is a small orchard which offers some play equipment.

MALMESBURY
Red Bull

Tel. (0666) 822108
Sherston Road (B4040, west of town)
Open 11–2.30; 6–11 (children lunchtime & weekends)

☺

🛏

✗ lunchtime

🍺 **Draught Bass; Boddingtons Bitter; Wadworth 6X**

On the edge of the Cotswolds, and a mile away from Malmesbury, England's oldest borough, the Red Bull is a friendly, family establishment. The skittle alley acts as a spacious family room at lunchtimes and weekends; a toy cupboard offers a selection of games and playthings to amuse younger children. A special menu of sausages, fishfingers, and so forth is offered for youngsters at lunchtime. The garden has a pen with rabbits and guinea pigs, while a large play area is set aside with swings and slides of different sizes.

Smoking Dog

Tel. (0666) 822412
62 High Street
Open 11–3; 5.30–11 (all day Fri, Sat and Bank Holidays)

☺

🛏

✗ anytime

🛏

🍺 **range varies**

This free house offers up to nine real ales at any one time, mostly from local independent breweries such as Uley, Cotleigh and Wadworth. It is close to this ancient town's Norman abbey, and those wishing to tour the area could do worse than to book rooms here (a cot is available). Families with (well-behaved) children are welcome in an area at the rear of the pub, away from the bar where there are plenty of tables and chairs, as well as a highchair. Children's portions and milk can be provided on request. There is a safe, pleasant garden where boules may be played – ask at the bar for a set.

ASKRIGG
Kings Arms Hotel

Tel. (0969) 50258
Village centre, quarter of a mile off A684, Kendal-Leeming road
Open 11–4.30; 6.30–11

◎ _____

⊗ _____

✗ lunchtime and evening

⋈ _____

🍺 McEwan 80/-; Younger Scotch, No. 3

TV viewers may feel a certain familiarity about the Kings Arms – it featured as the "Drovers Arms" in the BBC series of "All Creatures Great and Small". It is set in an ancient conservation village at the heart of the Yorkshire Dales National Park, ideally situated for visiting Bolton Castle, the Hardraw and Aysgarth Falls, Stumps Cross Caverns and the Aysgarth Carriage Museum. The family room facilities are somewhat limited: highchairs and a children's menu are provided; outside the courtyard has some play equipment. There are changing facilities in the toilets. A good range of pub food is offered (from around £1) as well as morning coffee and afternoon teas.

CROPTON
New Inn

Tel. (07515) 330
Three miles from Pickering, off
A170 Thirsk road
Open 11–2.30; 5.30
(7 winter)–11

✕ lunchtime and evening

ℍ

🍺 **Cropton Two Pints, Special Strong Bitter; Tetley Bitter**

An imposing, stone-built pub in a quiet village at the foot of Rosedale, bordering the Cropton Forest and the Yorkshire Moors. The pub has operated its own brewery since 1984 (yes Cropton Two Pints is the name of its standard bitter!). The New Inn comprises a bar, restaurant, pool and family rooms. This latter is a recent addition with plenty of toys to choose from; french windows open on to the large garden. Children are catered for on the menu where home-made pizza is offered along with the more usual beefburgers and chips. Highchairs are provided. York, Scarborough and Whitby are all within easy reach.

EAST MARTON
Cross Keys Inn

Tel. (0282) 843485
On Leeds-Liverpool canal; on A59,
five miles west of Skipton
Open 11.30–3; 6–11

✕ lunchtime and evening

🍺 **Ruddles County; Webster's Yorkshire Bitter, Choice**

Situated right on the Leeds-Liverpool canal, this Chef and Brewer establishment makes an ideal lunchtime halt for families holidaying on the waterway. It is a traditional country inn – all dark beams and brasses. The small family room is next to the lounge which has a feature fireplace. Two highchairs are provided and a children's menu. After lunch take a trip to the delightful market town of Skipton; youngsters will love its castle.

EGTON BRIDGE
Horseshoe Hotel

Tel. (0947) 85245
On River Esk, seven miles west of
Whitby
Open 11–3.30; 6.30–11

✕ lunchtime and evening

ℍ

🍺 **Tetley Bitter; Theakston Best Bitter, XB, Old Peculier**

This large hotel is set in its own extensive grounds on the banks of the river Esk and is popular with walkers exploring the moors and the nearby coast, and salmon fishers (reserve tickets well in advance). The good value family accommodation includes cots. There is a small children's area to the right of the bar where highchairs and a special menu are provided. All the food served is excellent quality and value. Outside an area has been set aside with play equipment.

LINTON-IN-CRAVEN
Fountaine Inn

Tel. (0756) 752210
Open 11.30–3; 6.30–11

◎

✘ lunchtime and evening

🍺 **Theakston Best Bitter, XB, Old Peculier; Younger Bitter**

In an idyllic village of the Yorkshire Dales National Park, this traditional white-painted inn faces the green and stream. Linton must surely be one of the Dales prettiest villages and the seventeenth-century Fountaine Inn, with its beams, oak benches and vast fireplace looks absolutely in keeping with its surroundings. Families are welcome in a separate room, away from the main bar. No amusements are provided, so parents would be wise to bring something to keep little ones occupied. An extensive bar menu is served – last orders 1.45 and 9.30 – basket meals are available for children. The pub has no garden, but in fine weather much use is made of the delightful village green.

MALTON
Crown Hotel
(Suddaby's)

Tel. (0653) 692038
Wheelgate
*Open 11–3; 5.30–11; 11–11 Fri;
11–4;6.30–11 Sat*

◎

✘ lunchtime (not Sun)

🛏

🍺 **Malton Pale Ale, Double Chance, Pickwick's Porter, Owd Bob; guest beer**

A small Georgian-style hotel with a friendly unpretentious atmosphere, the Crown has been run by the Suddaby family for over a hundred years. The Malton Brewery Company is based in the stables and the pub has strong racing connections. The Double Chance Bitter is named after the 1925 Grand National Winner which was stabled there. A conservatory area for families has been created by covering the old courtyard whose walls are thick with climbing plants and shrubs. Highchairs and a limited children's menu or small portions of adult dishes are offered. Evening meals are only served to residents. The hotel has family accommodation, including cots. It is situated in the main shopping street of this historic market town, close to Castle Howard, Flamingoland and York.

RICHMOND
Black Lion Hotel

Tel. (0748) 3121
Finkle Street (off the market place)
Open 10.30–11

@

✗ lunchtime and evening

⋈

🍺

🍺 Cameron Strongarm;
Everards Original

Richmond is a popular tourist town, and rightly so, with its castle, colourful Saturday market and other attractions. The Black Lion is a 400 year-old coaching inn, offering family accommodation (including cots). You do not have to be a resident to make use of the comfortable "no-smoking" lounge where children are welcome. You can opt for a bar meal (from £1.80) or eat in the restaurant (£5 at lunchtime, £10 in the evening) where half portions and highchairs are provided.

SCARBOROUGH
Cask Inn

Tel. (0723) 500570
Cambridge Terrace (south end of Valley Bridge)
Open 11–3; 6–11

@

🍴

✗ lunchtime and evening

⋈

🍺 McEwan 80/-; Tetley Bitter;
Younger Scotch Bitter, IPA,
No. 3

This multi-roomed free house (with no less than five bars) is very popular with the locals, particularly the younger generation, who seem to enjoy the background juke box music. The room set aside for families has been refurnished recently. Here children may have a snack or meal; the menu is standard pub fare with special additions for children. Outside an enclosed patio and large beer garden features a free horse ride machine to keep youngsters amused while their parents sup. The inn offers family accommodation (cots provided).

Fountaine Inn, Linton-in-Craven

TUNSTALL
Bay Horse Inn

Tel. (0748) 818564
*Two miles off the A1, near
Richmond
Open 12–3 (2 winter); 7–11
(children welcome until 9)*

✕ lunchtime and evening

🍺 **Samuel Smith OBB**

This friendly, 200 year-old village pub was built as an alehouse and still serves the local community and visitors alike. The family lounge, to the right of the bar, has a wealth of exposed beams; traditional games such as bar skittles and shove-ha'penny are available on request. Darts and dominoes – and quoits in summer – are also played. This room opens directly onto the garden which is large and well maintained. Meals are served in a separate dining room; children's portions are available. The pub has its own campsite and makes a useful base for touring the Dales, Richmond with its Norman castle and Easby Abbey.

DUNFORD BRIDGE
Stanhope Arms

Tel. (0226) 763 104
Windle Edge Lane (on sharp bend off A628)
Open 11–3; 7–11

✕ lunchtime and evening

🍺 John Smith Bitter

Originally a shooting lodge, the Stanhope has several rooms interlinked with the bar and dining room. Licensee Edric Foster believes that children should be allowed to grow up in pub surroundings and learn to accept going to the pub as part of the family way of life, as they do on the continent. He therefore does not believe in making too many special concessions, but the pub is nonetheless very family oriented. There is a room without a bar for them to use and the garden has some play equipment. A varied menu (with children's portions) is served in the Wise Owl restaurant. The pub is set in dramatic scenery, next to a former railway station; Dunford Bridge itself has the entrance to the longest rail tunnel in Britain (now disused). The pub is the home of the Stanhope Mole Club and is popular with walkers. It lies on the Huddersfield-Holmfirth-Penistone bus route.

HAIGH
Old Post Office

Tel. (0226) 387619
Low Swithen, off A637 to Barnsley
Open 11.30–3; 5.30–11

✕ lunchtime and Tue-Fri
  evenings

🍺 Tetley Bitter; Marston
  Pedigree

This large stone pub is close the popular beauty spot of Woolley Edge and Bretton Country Park, and is a favourite watering hole for families on a day out from the nearby conurbations of Barnsley and Wakefield. It has a split-level lounge and a disco bar downstairs. Cartoon videos are shown in the family room and licensee Steve Butterfield will even arrange children's parties here. The bar meals are very popular, starting at £1.50, with a children's menu provided; you need to book for Sunday lunch. Outside the safe, enclosed garden has an adventure playground and some swings.

HATFIELD WOODHOUSE
Green Tree Inn

Tel. (0302) 840306
*Bearswood Green, at junction of
A18/A614
Open 11–3; 6–11*

⊗

✘ lunchtime and evening

🍺 **Vaux Best Bitter, Samson;
Ward Darley Thorne Best
Bitter**

The Green Tree Inn dates back to the eighteenth century, when it was a celebrated stopping place for coaches. Today it is equally popular, particularly for its food. Although no particular facilities are provided for families, children are made very welcome in the series of spacious interconnecting rooms and alcoves that make up this well-kept pub. Carpeted throughout, the premises have been well modernised and are comfortably furnished with leather seats and Windsor chairs. Outside the lovely, well maintained garden has bench tables and chairs.

HOLMSFIELD
Moorlands,
Owler Bar

Tel. (0742) 620189
*Six miles from Sheffield at
junction of A621/B6054/B6051
Open 11–11 (12–10.30 Sun)*

◎

⊗

✘ all day

🍺 **Marston Pedigree; Whitbread
Castle Eden Ale, Trophy**

"We unashamedley admit we set out when we opened in May 1989 to create a family-oriented pub". So say licensees, John and Brenda Uttley, and full marks for carrying out that promise. Their family room is an integral part of the pub with an indoor toddlers' play area offering Lego and other toys. The children's toilets also have facilities for changing babies. Highchairs are provided and a choice is given of small portions of the adult menu or dishes specially designed to appeal to youngsters. The safe, enclosed garden has a play area. Just in Yorkshire, at the border with Derbyshire, the pub is on the edge of the Peak National Park in a picturesque setting with superb moorland views. The local beauty spot, Cordwell Valley, is just a mile away, while Chatsworth House and Park and Haddon Hall are three miles distant. It sounds just perfect.

INGBIRCHWORTH
Fountain Inn

Tel. (0226) 763125
Wellthorne Lane (on A637 outside Penistone)
Open 11.30–3; 6.30–11

🍴 lunchtime and evening

🍺 **Tetley Bitter**

Another pub on the edge of the Peak District National Park which is popular with families on an outing from South Yorkshire's industrial areas. It can become rather crowded, but a warm welcome is always given, despite the crush. The pub has a traditional lounge bar, separate family room and restaurant. A children's menu is available. The garden is a great asset when the pub becomes overfull. It has a proper playground with slides, swings, climbing frame and even goal posts for football. There is a grassed area and seating for parents.

PENISTONE
Cubley Hall

Tel. (0226) 766086
Mortimer Road (on Stocksbridge road, three-quarters of a mile from town centre)
Open 11–3; 6–11

🍴 lunchtime and evening

🍺 **Ind Coope Burton Ale; Tetley Bitter; guest beer**

This former stately hall has been converted into a public house, but maintains its grand style: stained glass, mosaic tiled floors and fancy ceilings are just some of the fine features that have been retained. It is set in four acres of grounds and is extremely popular (so much so that, unfortunately, the staff cannot always keep up with demand). Two rooms are set aside for families. One is a small, characterful snug which seats around 20, the other is a conservatory, seating 40, which leads on to a well laid out garden, overlooking the play area. Here equipment includes a large adventure playhouse with two slides, climbing frames and a fireman's pole, as well as a seesaw. Along with all this, the pub manages to offer excellent food, including a children's menu.

SHEFFIELD
Royal Standard

Tel. (0742) 722883
156 St Marys Road (inner ring road)
Open 11–11 (11–3; 5.30–11 winter); family room open lunchtime only

✗ lunchtime

🍺 **Vaux Samson; Ward Darley Thorne Mild, Sheffield Best Bitter**

After being under threat of demolition to make way for a road widening scheme for no less than 12 years, the Royal Standard was finally reprieved in 1986 and given a new lease of life, which included renovation work. Popular with students and business people, it also has facilities for families, which is unusual for a pub so near the centre of Sheffield. The family room, however, is only open at lunchtime. This leads off the bar and is comfortably furnished in keeping with the rest of the building which also comprises a lounge and snug. Pool and darts are played upstairs. Children can be catered for on the lunchtime menu with small portions and are welcome in the attractive walled garden at any time the pub is open.

CROFTON
Cock & Crown

Tel. (0924) 862344
*570 Doncaster Road (A638, six
miles from Wakefield)*
Open all day

◎

⏣

✕ lunchtime and evening

⏴ **Whitbread Trophy**

There is an accent on food at this pub which is open all day, every day. In fact, meals are available from midday until 10 pm on both Saturday and Sunday. Children are catered for with their own menu and highchairs are provided. The pub has recently been attractively remodelled into a large split level lounge. The family room is quite plain and contains some electronic games. A pleasant enclosed garden features a terraced patio and climbing frames. Local places of interest include Nostell Priory and Park (towards Doncaster) and Wintersett Reservoir Water Park (ask for directions); both are within a couple of miles.

ECCUP
New Inn

Tel. (0532) 886335
*Eccup Lane (A660, Leeds to Otley
road, off A659)*
Open 11.30 - 3; 5.30-11

◎

⏣

✕ lunchtime and evening (not
Sun/Mon eve)

⏴ **Tetley Bitter**

This small, stone-built pub is set in open countryside and has a bar and pleasant, cosy lounge. Designated a "Family Inn" by the brewery, the room set aside for children is at the rear of the building overlooking the garden which has a slide, climbing frame, swings and playhouses. There is also an enclosed field for more energetic games such as football. Barbecues are held on summer weekends. Indoors, the family amenities include a play house, rides and video games; a children's menu (or small portions of adult dishes) and highchairs. A separate WC is provided with baby changing facilities.

TRAVEL PURSUITS

Most parents fervently hope that the motion of the car will quickly put young babies to sleep. Certainly there is nothing more distracting to a driver than a crying baby. However, if you have one that is less than obliging, then it is necessary to keep him amused in some way. Babies are always fascinated by mobiles, so as long as it does not interfere too much with the driver's vision try to hang something that will catch his eye. If you have a rear facing baby seat on the front seat, hang baby toys from the head rest or from the handle that most cars have above the door. To keep their hands occupied tie a few rattles or small soft toys to the safety harness. Babies are also often soothed by music, so put the radio on or a favourite tape, something soft might even induce sleep!

ELLAND
Barge & Barrel

Tel. (0422) 73623
*Park Road (A6025, north end of
Elland Bridge)*
Open 12 (11.30 Sat) - 11

◎

🐕

✗ all day (Sun lunchtime and
   evening)

🍺 **Marston Burton Best Bitter,
   Pedigree, Owd Rodger; Oak
   Best Bitter, West Riding Tyke,
   Old Oak Ale; Taylor
   Landlord; guest beers**

Located on the banks of the Calder and Hebble navigation where there is much activity during the summer months, this pub is also handy for visits to Halifax and the Calder Valley. In fine weather families enjoy the canalside beer garden, but youngsters do need supervision. Indoors, the large family room is well equipped with toys and books, a ball pool, slide and play area; video games and a juke box are available. Parents will be pleased to know that the furniture in this room is comfortable; the bar is furnished in plush Victorian style with polished wood and leaded glass. A separate WC is provided for children, along with baby changing facilities. Children may choose from their own special menu (a meal costs around £1) or small portions from the adult dishes. A traditional Sunday lunch is served from 12–2; cold snacks, tea and coffee are always available at this pub which opens all day except Sundays.

HORBURY
Old Halfway
House

Tel. (0924) 262090
*Westfield Road (B6128, one mile
from town centre towards Ossett)*
Open 11.30-11

◎

🐕

✗ lunchtime and evening (not
   Sun eve)

👕

🍺 **Ind Coope Burton Ale; Tetley
   Mild, Bitter**

The Old Halfway House is renowned locally for its variety of equipment to keep children amused while their parents engage in more adult pastimes within the comfortable surroundings of the family room. The licensees even take the trouble to provide live entertainment on alternate Fridays and a disco every Thursday evening; they will also cater for children's parties. Apart from the board games and machine rides indoors, a separate play area in the garden offers a sandpit, swings, slides and a bouncy castle. There is a children's toilet where babies can also be fed and watered. A child's lunch costs around £1.50 and highchairs are provided. This late nineteenth-century stone building is situated close to farmland and open fields.

HORSFORTH
Fox & Hounds

Tel. (0532) 678415
Tinshill Road, Cookridge (off ring road, near station)
Open 11–11

☺

☷

✗ all day until 7.30

ᗕ **Tetley Mild, Bitter**

A comfortable, convivial pub with distinctive windows, a traditional lounge and large tap room. A small snug behind the lounge bar serves as the family room where children are welcome until 7.30 in the evening. The food is standard pub fare and bar snacks which are reasonably priced; a children's menu is offered for around £1.50 - £2. Although there is no play equipment indoors, the beer garden has a playground with swings.

KIRKSTALL, LEEDS
Kirkstall Lites

Tel. (0532) 304062
On A65 Ilkley road at junction of Kirkstall Lane/Commercial Road, three miles from Leeds.
Open: 11 - 11

☺

☷

✗ lunchtime and evening

ᗕ **Courage Directors; John Smith Bitter, Magnet**

This split-level pub was only opened in 1987 and it is pleasing to find that the designers have taken account of the special needs of families and the disabled. On the upper level is a main lounge bar and games area offering pool, darts, dominoes and bar billiards. Downstairs there is another bar and the family room where amenities include a play area, video and football games and a satellite TV screen. The garden also offers play equipment: climbing frames and a bouncy castle. Snacks and meals (including a children's menu) are served at lunchtime and evening. Kirkstall Abbey and the Abbey House Museum are just half a mile away.

MIRFIELD
Dusty Miller

Tel. (0924) 492354
47 Dunbottle Lane (off A62 at Roberttown)
Open 11–11

☺

☷

✗ Mon - Sat lunchtime

ᗕ **Draught Bass, Light 5 Star; Stones Best Bitter**

This busy seventeenth-century village pub was originally supplied by its own brewery in the back yard. Now Bass-owned, the premises have been extensively refurbished with much wood panelling in evidence. An unusual conservatory style extension with cane furnishings serves as the family room. Play facilities here are limited to a video machine, but outdoors there is a well-equipped area with swings, climbing frames, see-saw and plastic drums for children to roll about in. Picnic benches are provided for summer days; the lunchtime menu caters for children.

NEW MILL
Crossroads Inn

Tel. (0484) 683567
*Penistone Road (A635 between
New Mill and Shepley)*
*Open 11–11, closed Mon except
Bank Holidays*

ⓒ

🍴

✗ lunchtime and evening

🍺 **Matthew Brown Mild;**
Theakston Bitter; Younger
Scotch, IPA

This is a food-oriented country inn which also caters for children. Set above New Mill, it offers splendid views of the surrounding hills and valley. The garden has benches, swings and a slide. There is a restaurant, but children are welcome to eat in the family room where one highchair and one booster seat are provided. An attractive feature of this room is the old black-leaded kitchen range. Small portions of all the items on the main menu are available, which gives a far greater choice than the sausage/chips/beans that seem to make up the majority of so-called "children's" menus.

OSSETT
Holme Leas
Hotel

Tel. (0924) 277851
*194–198 Dewsbury Road (off
A638 Wakefield-Dewsbury road,
near Kingsway roundabout)*
Open 11–2.30; 4.30–11

ⓒ

🍴

✗ lunchtime and evening

🛏

🏰

🍺 **John Smith Bitter; Stones Best**
Bitter; Younger Scotch

Converted from an old mill and cottages in a suburban area, with plain, but pleasant furnishings, this free house has a restaurant upstairs and an hotel in an adjacent building. The family area covers two rooms and includes a children's food and soft drinks bar, TV and pool table. The enclosed beer garden offers swings and a slide. Adult entertainment includes a weekly (Thursday) cabaret which is also grill night when a three-course meal is offered for £6.50

SOWERBY BRIDGE
Moorings Bar &
Restaurant

Tel. (0422) 833940
*No.1 Warehouse, Canal Basin
(opposite Ash Tree Restaurant on
Wharf Street)*
*Open 12–3; 5(6 Sat, 7 Mon) - 11
(children welcome until 8.30)*

ⓒ

✗ lunchtime and evening

🍺 **Moorhouses's Burnley Bitter;**
Younger Scotch, IPA, No. 3

A successful conversion from a 1790 canal warehouse to a distinctive free house/restaurant. Picture windows overlook the canal basin; as does the balconied family room where a toy box and children's menu are provided. There is canalside seating outdoors, but children have to be well supervised for safety. Apart from the attractions of the canal itself, other local places of interest include the Worth Valley and Halifax with its Piece Hall and Working Horse Museum.

STANLEY
Graziers Inn

Tel. (0924) 373709
116 Aberford Road (A642 to
Wakefield, two miles from M62
jct 30)
Open 11–4 (5 Sat); 7–11

◎
☷

✕ lunchtime and evening

🍺 **Bass Special Bitter; Stones
Best Bitter**

A small, friendly local where everyone is made truly welcome. It offers many rooms for drinkers to choose from and the homely family room is warm and cosy, although entertainment is limited to video games. Outside though, the garden has swings and rabbits. Meals (price range £2–£4) are served at lunchtime and in the evening and children may choose small portions of adult dishes or from their own menu.

STANLEY FERRY
Ferry Boat Inn

Tel. (0924) 290596
Ferry Lane (half a mile off A642,
two miles from M62 jct 30; no.
147 bus from Wakefield)
Open: flexible opening hours (no
children in main pub after 7)

◎
☷

✕ lunchtime and evening

😊

🍺 **Cameron Best Bitter, Strong
Arm Premium; Theakston Best
Bitter, XB, Old Peculier**

Stanley Ferry is in the process of being developed as a marina and a place of tourist interest with gardens and play areas. The Ferry Boat is a traditional canalside pub, actually in the marina. The family room is in fact a canal barge moored outside the front door! Facilities include highchairs, children's menu or small portions and baby changing/feeding facilities. There is a barbecue area in the garden and well-priced canal pleasure trips are also on offer. Nearby, the Ship Inn also offers good family amenities.

STOCKSMOOR
Clothiers Arms

Tel. (0484) 602752
Station Road (off A629, follow
signs to Thunderbridge/
Stocksmoor)
Open 11–3; 5.30–11 (11–11 Fri,
Sat)

◎
☷

✕ daily lunchtime and weekend
evenings

🍺 **Theakston Best Bitter, XB;
Younger IPA, No. 3**

This large, multi-roomed pub has a restaurant in an adjoining converted barn. At present, evening meals are only served at the weekend, but this may be extended, so check. A children's menu, from 75 pence is offered and highchairs are provided. Families are welcome in the sun lounge at the front of the pub and of course in the enclosed garden which has slides and swings in the shape of an elephant, shoe and cowboy. Parents can relax and enjoy the extensive views over the surrounding countryside.

UPPER HOPTON
Travellers Rest

Tel. (0924) 493898
252 Hopton Lane (Kirkheaton-Mirfield road)
Open 11.30–3.30 (not Mon); 5.30 (7 Sat) - 11

✕ lunchtimes

🍺 **Tetley Mild, Bitter**

A fine country pub, circa 1600, set in more than four acres of land with views of up to 20 miles over the Calder valley. Particular features of the pub are its huge collection of plates and Toby jugs and the fireplace covered in old pennies in the snug. Families are welcome in a large stone room, attractively decorated with pictures and signs. There is a large selection of books and games and a few toys for children, as well as a blackboard and highchair. It is a popular venue for birthday parties. Baby changing facilities are provided. The lunchtime menu of good, home-prepared food caters for small appetites (meals from £1.25). The beer garden is close enough to the enclosed children's outdoor play area for parents to be able to sit and talk while watching their offspring. A disco is held on Wednesday evening.

Moorings, Sowerby Bridge

BORDERS

AUCHENCROW
Craw Inn

Tel. (08907) 61253
Off B6437 (signed from A1)
Open 12–2.30; 6.30–11.30

⊚

☺

✘ lunchtime and evening

🍺 **Broughton Greenmantle Ale,**
Special Bitter; Tennent's 80/-

In a rather isolated, quiet village, this pub is perhaps more akin to the hostelries on the other side of the border than the traditional Scottish variety, for it has bar billiards in the bar which is most unusual for Scotland, and is probably the only Scottish pub with its own putting green. The latter is naturally much appreciated by families who can also enjoy the other play equipment provided in the large garden which is across the road from the pub. Children's amusements are restricted to those out of doors, although there is an indoor family room off the public bar and which has its own separate entrance; meals can be taken here or in the bistro-style restaurant. A children's menu of the usual fare – burgers, sausages, etc. is available or portions of adult meals may be ordered for them. Highchairs are on order for the 1990 summer season. Local tourist attractions include the fishing port of Eyemouth, an equestrian centre at Coldingham and a bird sanctuary at St Abbs Head beach which also has excellent facilities for sub-aqua diving.

COLDINGHAM
Spirit Level

Tel. (08907) 71387
School Road (A1107)
Open 11–2.30; 5–11 (11–11 Sat)

◎

🍺

✗ lunchtime and evening

🛏

🍺 **Smiles Bitter; guest beer**

Situated on Scotland's east coast scenic route in Berwickshire, the Spirit Level is within easy walking distance of the beach and the other attractions of this family resort, notably the sub-aqua faciles at St Abbs Head and the riding school. Family accommodation at the pub includes cots, and this is also a good area for campers, with many local sites. The pub has a well-deserved local reputation for its well-kept beer and good food (children's portions available) which ranges from simple toasties to very exotic dishes based on swordfish and alligator meat! The family room is to the right of the pub's entrance and a toy box is provided here at lunchtime. There is no play equipment in the pub's own enclosed garden, but at the rear of the building is a public playground.

COLDSTREAM
Newcastle Arms
Hotel

Tel. (0890) 2376
50 High Street (A697)
Open 11–midnight

◎

✗ all day

🛏

🎲

🍺 **Alloa Arrols 80/-**

A thriving, comfortable and friendly hotel, set just across the river Tweed from England. It considers itself a "fun" bar with pleasant staff who are always very helpful. There is a good display of miniature vintage cars, but otherwise not a lot to interest children, so take your own amusements. There is a family room, however, where highchairs are provided. The food, served all day, is of a high standard and a children's menu and small portions are offered. Cots are provided for overnight guests.

TRAVEL PURSUITS

Children who are just learning to read, are often very keen to learn, and to play games that allow them to practise new skills. Many parents (myself included) simply do not have much time at home to spend practising reading or other educational games with their offspring. A car journey can provide the ideal opportunity to enjoy such games together and can be a good indication of the extent of a child's understanding. Simple rhyming games can be good fun – you say a word, perhaps car, and the child has to think of a word to rhyme with it. When she runs out of steam, give clues so that she can find the word you are aiming at. Another simple one is an odd word out game. You say a list of several words which all have the same initial letter, except one, for instance, dog, duck, door, paper, desk, drink. The child has to tell you which is the odd one out. After a little while, older children should be able to test you in the same way.

INNERLEITHEN
Traquair Arms
Hotel

Tel. (0896) 830229
Traquair Road (near A72/B702 jct)
Open 11–11.59

◎

🏚

✕

🛏

🛡

🍺 **Broughton Greenmantle Ale,
Special Bitter; Traquair House
Bear Ale**

"Follow the bear" takes on a different meaning here – the draught Bear Ale comes from nearby Traquair House Brewery which has an interesting history. The house is an ancient fortified manor and is the oldest inhabited house in Scotland. Brewing started here back in the eighteenth century, but was revived in 1965 by the Laird of Traquair. Just 30 minutes from Edinburgh, this Victorian hotel is convenient for a weekend break (cots provided), with its own fishing, and riding and golf nearby. For casual visitors, amenities are again limited as far as amusements at the pub itself go; but there is a family room and provision for nursing mothers, as well as highchairs. Good home-cooked food from locally grown produce is served from noon until an hour before closing; children's portions can be provided. There is a safe, secluded garden to the rear of the pub and it is also close to Kailzie Gardens.

DUMFRIES AND GALLOWAY

GATEHOUSE OF
FLEET
Murray Arms
Hotel

Tel. (055 74) 207
Ann Street (off A75)
Open 11–11

🏚

✕

🛏

🍺 **Younger No. 3**

Gatehouse of Fleet is one of Scotland's designated Scenic Heritage areas and is rich in wild flowers, birdlife and historic remains. Threave, home of the National Trust's School of Gardening, Logan and many other beautiful gardens are a short drive away. The Murray Arms is another hotel which is more geared to families staying (cots provided), as it has no specific children's room. Youngsters are however, made welcome and can enjoy the half-acre garden in fine weather; a children's menu is provided too (food is served from midday until 9.45 pm). There are some lovely woodland walks in the locality and a superb safe, sandy beach within two miles. Robert Burns once patronised the Murray Arms and is said to have written "Scots Wha Hae" here.

FIFE

CARNOCK
Old Inn

Tel. (0383) 850381
On A803
Open 11–3; 5–11 (all day Fri/Sat)

🛈

✗ lunchtime and evening

🍺 **Maclay 60/-, 70/-, 80/-, Porter**

A cottage-style pub, the Old Inn is at the heart of the village and is a focus for village life. It has a functional bar with games area and a pleasant, comfortable lounge. As far as families are concerned, you really have to choose between the restaurant which caters well for children (highchairs provided) or the safe garden where there is a swing and seesaw. There is a separate toilet for the disabled.

GRAMPIAN

ABERDEEN
Carriages

Tel. (0224) 595440
Brentwood Hotel, 101 Crown Street
Open 11–2.30; 5–12

✗ lunchtime and evening

╨

🍺 **Flowers Original; Marston Pedigree; Wethered Bitter; Whitbread Castle Eden Ale; guest beer**

It seems that in Scotland, unfortunately, we are faced with listing pubs with minimal family facilities, or having no entries at all. Very few pubs seem to cater in any great way for children, except for meals. This bistro at the bottom of a smart hotel just away from the centre of Aberdeen is a case in point. Still, it is very hard to find anywhere in busy towns and cities that has proper family facilities. Carriages has friendly and helpful staff and provides a proper three-course menu for children for £1.85. Starters could be melon, home-made pate or soup, followed by haddock or barbecue chicken and chips, but the menu changes every month. The hotel itself provides family accommodation with cots.

BANCHORY
Tor-na-Coille
Hotel

Tel. (03302) 2242
Inchmarlo Road (A93 from Aberdeen)
Open 11–11

◎

🕭

✗ lunchtime and evening

🛏

🍺 **Theakston Best Bitter**

A country house hotel situated in Banchory, a small town which enjoys a beautiful location on Royal Deeside, and is just a short drive from Balmoral Castle. Families can come here without feeling obliged to have a meal as there is a separate family room with board games and children's toys. Bar snacks can be ordered at lunchtime or in the evening (children's menu provided) but the restaurant is open only in the evening. Baby feeding/changing amenities are available. Outside, the garden boasts a croquet lawn. The hotel is right opposite Banchory Golf Club and convenient for other outdoor pursuits such as fishing. Family accommodation includes cots.

ELGIN
Thunderton
House

Tel. (0343) 48767
Thunderton Place
Open 11–11 (11.45 Sat); 6.30–11 (children until 8.30)

◎

✗ lunchtime and evening

🍺 **Belhaven 80/-; Broughton Greenmantle Ale; Tennent's 80/-; Thunderton House Ale**

The Thunderton was an earlier venture of the enterprising Grahams, who have since moved on to the Boswell Hotel in Glasgow (see entry). It has recently changed hands again, but it still makes an ideal halt for anyone travelling up the west coast, since there is little else for families along this popular route.

The Grahams made a good job of restoring the decaying building which had in previous incarnations been a church, a masonic lodge, and a factory. In fact in his "Classic Town Pubs", Neil Hanson considered it one of the best pubs in Scotland. He mentions too, the many ghosts that haunt the place, including that of Bonnie Prince Charlie. With a history going back to the eleventh century, these spirits can seem all too believable. Now the pub has been brought right up to date (albeit in Victorian style), with proper facilities for families, and incidentally, disabled patrons too. The family room has its own entrance and is connected to the main bar by swing doors. The room is spacious with a central open area surrounded by wood and stained glass partitions. Most unusual of all though is the fact that the pub has a nappy changing area that can be used by both parents. Highchairs are provided for meals.

FINDHORN
Crown & Anchor

Tel. (0309) 30243
Open 11–11 (11.45 Sat); children until 9 pm

🍺

✗ until 9.45pm

🛏

🏆

🍺 **Brakspear Bitter; guest beer**

Once again, no children's room is provided here, but there is a good-sized family eating area with no less than three highchairs and half-price meals for children. As the most expensive main dish on the adult menu costs £2.80, it could well be worth indulging. The Crown boasts an excellent selection of bottled beers and often three guests on draught, but the main reason for coming here is its welcoming atmosphere and beautiful location. It stands right by the sea, within walking distance of a choice of beaches. In good weather, drinkers have a tendency to spill out on to the harbour area. The Yacht Club is nearby too.

FORRES
Royal Hotel

Tel. (0309)7261
Tyter Street (next to station)
Open 11–11 (11.45 Sat)

🍴

🍺

✗ 12–2; 5–8.30

🛏

🍺 **Younger No. 3**

This Victorian hotel has maintained intact many of its original features, one of the most magnificent of which is the Gents' loo (but I can't vouch for that!). Not far from Aviemore, the Royal is close to many local places of interest, such as the Falconer Museum, Brodie Castle, Nelson's Tower, Darnaway Farm and Dallas Dhu Distillery, both of which have visitor centres. The family room doubles as a games room (pool, darts and juke box). Children's portions are available, as are highchairs and baby changing/ feeding facilities. There is a large garden with play equipment.

STONEHAVEN
Marine Hotel

Tel. (0569) 62155
9–10 Shorehead
Open 11–midnight

McEwan 80/-; Taylor Landord

Overlooking the picturesque harbour, this popular pub gets very crowded in summer when customers go and sit on the harbour wall.

Families are welcome to join them here, or use the separate dining room where food, including high tea, is served all day. A children's menu and highchairs are provided, but that is the extent of family facilities, apart from cots for overnighters. If you go on a Sunday, watch out for the four o'clock swim; various other tourist events are organised every week.

Royal Hotel, Forres

HIGHLAND

AVIEMORE
Winking Owl

Tel. (0479) 810646
Grampian Road
Open 11–11 (children until 8.30)

---

⑧

✗ lunchtime and evening

⋈

⊕ **Alloa Arrols 80/-; Tetley Bitter**

Converted from farm buildings, this pub and restaurant stands in its own grounds near the centre of Scotland's most famous ski-ing village. Local attractions include the Cairngorms, a wildlife park, Landmark Centre and Aviemore leisure centre with its swimming-pools, ice rink and cinema. There is no family room in the pub, but families are made very welcome in the restaurant where highchairs are provided as well as a children's menu (main course £1.60) or portions. The open garden is quite safe for youngsters and has a climbing frame and swing, so summer visitors are not obliged to have a meal. Cots are available and the pub also has self-catering accommodation.

Old Inn, Gairloch

GAIRLOCH
Old Inn

Tel. (0445) 2006
Flowerdale (A832, near harbour)
Open 11–midnight (1 am Thu and
Fri, 11.30 Sat)

◎

⊗

✗ lunchtime and evening

⋈

🍺 Belhaven 80/-; Tennent's 80/-

Hooray, this pub has a proper family room! It is off the lounge bar and overlooks the riverside and old footbridge. Highchairs are provided and babies' needs are catered for too (including cots for overnight stays and a baby listening facility). Children are welcome at mealtimes and in the afternoons. There is a good variety of bar meals with smaller portions available. This is a popular, family-run hotel with a lively traditional Scottish atmosphere. It enjoys a picturesque setting of loch and mountains on Scotland's most spectacular coastline. There is a safe, sandy beach nearby for children to enjoy; the pub also has a garden where there is no formal play equipment, but a great tree rope swing.

LOTHIAN

EDINBURGH
Dell Inn

Tel. (031) 443 9991
27 Lanark Road, Leith (A70, three
miles from centre)
Open 11–11 (midnight Fri & Sat;
children until 8pm)

◎

⊗

✗

🍺 Alloa Arrol's 80/-

A large modern pub and restaurant on the banks of the Water of Leith. The garden, overlooking the start of the Water of Leith Walkway, has fine views of the nearby canal and railway viaducts. There are plenty of seats in the family room which is well equipped with a snack bar serving sweets, soft drinks and ices, as well as various amusements including table football and board games. Food is served all day and children's portions are available; they have their own WC.

Malt Shovel Inn

Tel. (031) 225 6843
11–15 Cockburn Street (100
yards from Waverly Station)
Open 12–12 (children until 8 pm)

✗ 12–8 (12.30–2.15 Sun)

🎓

🍺 range varies

A busy city-centre bar catering primarily for the business community and tourists, the Malt Shovel appeals particularly to beer drinkers because of its good and constantly changing range of ales which mostly come from small independent breweries. The food is good too, the extensive menu catering for vegetarians, and most dishes can be served in children's portions.

It is in the food area where children are permitted, as there is no other room set aside for families, and they are welcome at any time up until 8 pm. Baby food can be heated by the staff on request. No amusements are provided, so take something to keep the youngsters occupied.

Malt Shovel On The Shore

Tel. (031) 554 8784
10 Burgess Street, Leith
Open 12–12 (children until 10 pm)

✘ 12–10 pm

🍺 **range varies**

Overlooking the Water of Leith, this pub is another which caters for children during the period that food is served, although they are not obliged to have a meal. The front lounge area is set aside for families, but no playthings are provided. Used by the business community during the week, the pub particularly welcomes children at the weekends. If you do want to eat, then the food comes highly recommended, especially the seven-inch Yorkshire puddings, which are a complete meal. In common with the other Malt Shovel above, this pub too features a changing range of guest beers, not all of them Scottish.

Southsider

Tel. (031) 667 2003
3–7 West Richmond Street
Open 11–12

✘ lunchtime (not Sun)

🍺 **Maclay 70/-, 80/-; guest beer**

Like so many city-centre pubs, this one has limited amenities for children, but at least they are made welcome and the Southsider is very conveniently situated for visitors to the city, just south of Princes Street, off "the Bridges". Being close to the university too, it is popular with students. Families may use the large room off the lounge bar. No concessions are made for children on the menu but as lunch dishes start at 50 pence, they can be fed quite reasonably.

SOUTH QUEENSFERRY
Hawes Inn

Tel. (031) 331 1990
Newhalls Road (under rail bridge)
Open 11 (12.30 Sun-11 (children until 8pm)

○
⌾
✕

🍺 **Alloa Arrol's 80/-; Ind Coope Burton Ale**

A 350 year-old coaching inn which serves good food both in the bar and separate restaurant. A children's menu and half portions from the main menu are served. If you do not wish to eat, then the family lounge, situated off the main lounge bar, is open until 8pm. Early closing of family rooms is one thing that niggles some parents – having to keep looking at your watch instead of relaxing with the family. As long as children are not being noisy, or a nuisance and provided, of course they are in their own room, and not near the bar, I really do not see why publicans should be the guardians of our children's bedtimes. If there is any chance of the little ones being corrupted by what is going on in the adjoining bars, I am sure most parents would be swift in removing them. Well, enough of a grouse, at least this pub *does* have a family room, which is rare in these parts. It has a garden, too, with a play area.

BRODICK
Ormidale Hotel

Tel. (0770) 2293
On Isle of Arran
Open 12-2.30 (closed Mon-Thu winter); 4.30-12

⌾

✕ lunchtime (Fri- Sun only winter)

🍺 **McEwan 70/-**

STRATHCLYDE

Very much a pub for a summer's day if the family is in tow, as indoor facilities are minimal, but the Ormidale is worth a visit for its large garden and breathtaking view. While you drink in the surroundings along with your pint, the children can enjoy the playground. If it does get a little chilly, then you can retreat to the spacious sunlounge. Lunches are served every day in the summer season; children may order from their own menu or small portions of adult dishes. The pub is convenient for the ferry and overlooks the golf course.

CATACOL
Catacol Bay
Hotel

Tel. (0770 83) 231
On Isle of Arran (on A841)
Open 11–1 am (children until 8 pm)

🕿

✗   until 10 pm

⊨

♖

🍺   Tennent's 80/-

This is another sunny day pub, unless you are staying (cots are provided). It is a small, family-run hotel overlooking Kilbrannan Sound and Kintyre. Set in the hills in a picturesque spot at the northern end of the island, it is an ideal base for outdoor pursuits, including sailing, riding, golf and birdwatching. A children's menu and highchairs are provided; bar snacks and meals start at just 50 pence. There is an enclosed garden which is safe for children, but no particular amusements are provided.

GLASGOW
Boswell Hotel

Tel. (041) 632 9812
27 Mansion House Road, Langside
Open 11–11 (children until 8.30 pm)

◉

🕿

✗

⊨

♖

🍺   Belhaven 60/-, 80/-, Tennent's
60/-; guest beer

Somehow Glasgow does not seem to be the place where you would find one of the best family rooms in the country. And you won't – well, not yet, because it is not finished; but when it is you can be sure that it will provide everything a family pub should have. How do I know that? Well simply because the Boswell Hotel has been taken over by Robin and Gay Graham who wrote an article for our first edition, saying exactly how good family facilities should be organised, based on their own experience at the hugely successful Thunderton House in Elgin (see entry). At the time of writing, their new venture is a splendid Victorian edifice in need of restoration, but even while the current family room is still somewhat basic, it is well used, probably because of the Grahams' attitude; children are treated as apprentice people and not as a sub-species of the human race. Definitely one to watch.

LOCHRANZA
Lochranza Hotel

Tel. (0770 83) 223
On Isle of Arran
Open 11–1am

☎

☺

✕ lunchtime and evening

🛏

🍺 McEwan 80/-

A pleasant place to stay awhile, this quiet, homely seafront hotel has views across the loch to Argyll and is popular with yachtsmen. Local amenities include golf, tennis, fishing and boating; sights include Ossian's Cave and Lochranza Castle. Children are welcome in the dining room where a junior menu is offered. There are baby changing/feeding facilities and the family accommodation includes a cot. The enclosed garden is safe for youngsters to play in.

CLWYD

ACREFAIR
Duke of Wellington

Tel. (0978) 820169
Llangollen Road (off A539)
*Open 11.30–5; 6–11 (all day Fri
& Sat)*

☺

🛏

✗ (lunchtime and evening)

🍺 **Marston Border Mild, Border
Bitter, Pedigree**

This is a very well run and popular pub with a tiny bar and singing dog! It is right next to Pontcysyllte aqueduct and is a mooring point for the Llangollen canal, so offers a warm and cheerful stopover for narrowboaters. Meals, which are served seven days a week, are of high quality and generous proportions, but small appetites are also catered for. The family room doubles as a games room and the pub's regulars are keen supporters of the local darts, dominoes and football leagues. If you find this offputting, then visit on a warm day and you will be delighted with the two elegant beer gardens. Here children are properly provided for with an old tractor to play on as well as a large bank slide, swings and other attractions. Barbecues are often held. Campers are welcome to pitch their tents in the garden (ask the landlord). The pub is very convenient for the Llangollen steam railway (a must for children) and Plas Madoc Leisure centre.

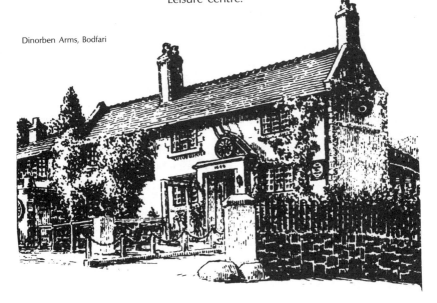

Dinorben Arms, Bodfari

BODFARI
Dinorben Arms Hotel

Tel. (0745 75) 309
Take Tremeirchion turn off A541
Mold-Denbigh road
Open 12–3.30; 6–11

◎

⊞

✘ lunchtime and evening

⊟ **Thwaites Bitter**

The award-winning terraces and gardens alone make a visit to this free house worth while. More importantly, the owners go out of their way to make families feel welcome. Parents of fractious children will doubtless be interested in Deifar's Well which was uncovered during rebuilding works at the pub. Deifar was a Christian hermit who settled by the well at Bodfari and had a reputation for great wisdom. Later Deifar's Well was thought to have magical properties and local mothers dipped their babies in the well believing that they would never cry at night. Some people will try anything: I know I would have been tempted with my youngest! The Well Bar is just one of the charming rooms in this rambling hostelry which has no less than three dining areas, one of which is a serve yourself carvery. Daily specials are prepared and children have their own menu. Highchairs and baby changing/feeding facilities are provided. Children are welcome in the garden room and terraces or in the garden itself which has a play area with swings, seesaw, sandpit and climbing hats.

BURTON GREEN
Golden Groves

Tel. (0244) 570445
Two miles west of Rossett village
(OS 354487)
Open 11.30–11

⊞

✘

⊟ **Webster's Yorkshire Bitter;**
   Wilson's Original Bitter

A black and white timbered inn set in rural surroundings with low ceilings, open fires and old furniture, this is really, as far as families are concerned, a fairweather pub – and a jolly good one too. Children *are* allowed in the pub, and it does have a restaurant, but there is no specific family room as such. However, it does have lots of tables and seating outside and barbecue facilities. There is also a particularly good aventure playground in the safe garden. Mike Dunn, author of CAMRA's "Best Pubs in North Wales", tells me that there is some dispute as to whether the pub's name is Golden Grove or

Groves. It has no inn sign to prove it either way. However, it is an unmistakeable, large black and white building which it needs to be, otherwise potential customers could miss it, set as it is in a remote spot, a little way from Burton Green itself.

HANMER
Hanmer Arms

Tel. (094874) 532
Just off A539, six miles west of Whitchurch
Open 11–11

☺

☎

✗ lunchtime and evening

🛏

🍺 **Ansells Mild; Ind Coope Burton Ale; Tetley Bitter**

Families have long been welcome at the Hanmer Arms, but as we went to press, the owners were planning proper facilities for children which should be ready now. There is certainly much to attract families to this pub set in a peaceful, undulant landscape. The village stands by Hanmer Mere, which is popular for fishing, while other leisure pursuits include good walks and golf. The games room is one of the areas where families are currently welcome, amusements include pool and darts. There is a restaurant or bar meals (including a children's menu) can be ordered. Vegetarians are catered for, but the pub makes a special feature of its meat dishes, using local produce where possible. There is a play area in the garden.

LLANDULAS
Valentine Inn

Tel. (0492) 518189
Mill Street (off A55)
Open 12–3 (flexible); 5.30–11

☺

☎

✗ (until 7.30)

🍺 **Draught Bass, M & B Mild**

This small village inn, situated in its traditional place opposite the church, has been tastefully renovated; a comfortable, beamed lounge with open fire complements the tiny public bar. There is a separate family room with a selection of toys, card games, dominoes and other amusements. This opens directly on to the landscaped garden with its lawns and wooden tables and benches. Meals finish at 7.30, but snacks are available at any time; a children's menu is available. The pub gets very popular in summer with visitors to the area. It is just one mile from Gwrych castle and beach and there are many good country and coastal walks in the locality.

LLANFAIR TALHAIRN
Swan Inn

Tel. (074584) 233
Swan Square (over bridge off A548)

@

&

✗ lunchtime and evening

⋈

◁ **Marston Mercian Mild, Burton Bitter, Pedigree**

A pub that is traditional in many ways except two – it caters both for children and the disabled. I do not mean to imply any connection here, but it is salutary to think that even ten years ago, breweries and indeed licensees tended to look no further than the other side of the bar for their customers and would not have troubled to provide any extra amenities for anyone that could not stand on their own two feet and see over the top. The Swan has a cosy lounge at the front, the bar and a reasonably sized family room at the rear. This opens on to the garden which has a safe play area. Food is of the traditional pub variety, but children, and that other growing minority, vegetarians, are catered for on the menu.

LLANGOLLEN
Wynnstay Arms Hotel

Tel. (0978) 860 710
Open 12–4; 7–11

@

&

✗ lunchtime and evening

⋈

◁ **Ansells Mild; Ind Coope Burton Ale; Tetley Bitter**

A multi-roomed pub where children are welcome in any of the small bar-less rooms and the restaurant. Dating back some 400 years, this old world hostelry has been little altered over the centuries and is decorated in a style befitting its age and history. The pub is equally welcoming to locals and visitors, of which there are many as this is a popular area for holidaymakers. Local attractions include the canal museum, horse-drawn barge trips, a traditional weaving mill and riverside walks with a multitude of ducks for the youngsters to feed. The licensees are happy to try and accommodate particular tastes in their restaurant, vegetarian and children's dishes are produced as a matter of course; for anything more unusual, ask and it may be given. Highchairs and baby changing/feeding facilites are available.

MINERA
City Arms

Tel. (0978) 758890
Wern Road
Open 11.30–3.30; 6.30–11

@

&

✗ evening

🍺 **Ind Coope Burton Ale; Tetley Bitter**

Standing in the lee of the Minera Mountain, this popular family pub is close to the Worlds End beauty spot. Also nearby are some old lead mine workings which are due to be landscaped for a picnic area. The Minera Brewery operated from the pub until it was sadly closed down early in 1989. Now the only beers on offer are Allied's national brands. Even so, the pub does still warrant an entry in CAMRA's "Good Beer Guide", so it must be OK. The family area which seats around 25 people, is at the front of the pub. Children's meals are good value, and for grown-ups, the home-made steak pie is recommended; only snacks are served at lunchtime. The garden play area has a large "play boot" and some swings. A feature of the pub is its collection of over a hundred Toby Jugs.

Sun Inn, Rhewl

RHEWL
Sun Inn

Tel. (0978) 861043
Two miles off A5
Open 12–4; 6–11

@

🍴

✗ lunchtime and evening

🍺 **Felinfoel Best Bitter**

On a picturesque road, just off the Horseshoe Pass and two miles from the Horseshoe Falls, this lovely old drovers inn makes a delightful halt for hikers, hillwalkers and motorists. Some 500 years old, it is a pub of immense character with a wealth of dark beams, stone floors, oak settles and open fire. It has many small rooms: the walls of the bar are adorned with coalmining mementoes; the family/games room has a pool table, dartboard and jukebox. Not the ideal amusements for small children, but there is a lovely garden too and of course the scenery all around of the Dee Valley is breathtaking. When the offspring become restive, tempt them with a trip on a horse-drawn barge or a visit to the Llangollen railway, but don't let them spoil your enjoyment of this delightful spot. Maybe the best thing is to feed them – small portions and a children's menu are offered, as well as regular barbecues.

DYFED

AMMANFORD
Wernoleu Hotel

Tel. (0269) 2598
31 Pontaman Road (A474)
Open 12–2; 6–11

@

🍴

✗ evening

🛏

🍺 **Draught Bass; Buckley Best Bitter; Felinfoel Double Dragon; Wadworth 6X; Younger IPA; guest beer**

Formerly the home of an industrial magnate, this mansion has been transformed into an attractive hotel, set in six acres of gardens. Although it may sound rather formidable, you can just go there for a drink if you wish. If you find it hard to drag yourself away, then the overnight accommodation is reasonably priced and cots are available. Families are welcome in a pleasant, comfortably furnished lounge which has a supply of books and easy access to both the bar and the garden. There are some swings in the grounds, but a rather more unusual feature is the full-sized croquet lawn. Those who know about these things, will also notice that there are many interesting species of tree in the grounds too. Full meals are only served in the evenings, and booking is necessary. Bar snacks are available all day though and there is a children's menu. Highchairs and baby facilities can be provided on request. Visitors to the area will find plenty to see and do, including four castles to visit, Roman gold mines, fishing and golf.

BRYNHOFFNANT
Brynhoffnant Inn

Tel. (0239) 78413
On A487, midway between Cardigan and Newquay
Open 11–3; 6–11

⚲

🍽

✗ lunchtime and evening

🍺 **Buckley Best Bitter**

Enjoying a commanding view of the sea, the Brynhoffnant Inn is on the main coastal road, within easy reach of many attractive family beaches, such as Penbryn, Tresaith, Aberporth and Llangranog. Externally, the pub is virtually unchanged since it was built in 1860. Inside, one room has been created with a two-way fireplace. The sixteenth-century stables have been converted to provide a room where children can play video games or use the pens and paper available to amuse themselves. There is also a safe, lawned garden. A children's menu is offered in the dining room where hearty portions are the order of the day.

Wernoleu Hotel, Ammanford

DREENHILL
Denant Mill Inn

Tel. (0437) 766569
*Dale Road (B4327, from
Haverfordwest)*
Open 11–3; 6–11

◎

⊞

✕ lunchtime and evening

ᴻ

⊟ range varies

No regular real ales are kept here, but a merry-go-round of weird and wonderful brews from all parts of the country which makes it almost a place of pilgrimage for dedicated beer buffs. This is altogether an unusual pub. It started life as a cornmill in the sixteenth century and the last surviving inside water wheel is preserved in the lounge, making a spectacular feature. It is in this lounge, where there is a television, that families are welcome (although children are not encouraged to stay late in the evening). There is an informal restaurant where children's portions are available as well as vegetarian dishes. The open garden is fairly safe, but youngsters do need some supervision here; some play equipment is provided. Overnight accommodation (including cots) means that the Denant Mill can be used as a base by families touring the area. It is a paradise for birdwatchers; Pembroke Castle and the vast beaches at Broad Haven and Newgale and many picturesqe coves are all within easy reach.

LLANDYBIE
Red Lion

Tel. (0269) 851202
6 Llandeilo Road
Open 11.30–3; 6–11

◎

⊞

✕ lunchtime and evening (not
Sun eve)

ᴻ

⊟ **Flowers Original; Marston
Pedigree; guest beer**

A listed building, standing near an historic church, the interior of the Red Lion has been sympathetically restored and decorated in local style. The restoration work uncovered beautiful stone fireplaces and there is also an interesting collection of mirrors. The family room has its own exit to the large lawned garden and play area which offers a scramble net, slide and climbing frame. Children should bring their own amusements for indoors though. There are four highchairs available, so you do not have to cope with a wriggling toddler when the only one provided is taken up, as is often the case. All the food is freshly prepared on the premises and small portions can be ordered of anything on the menu, but fishfingers etc. can be given to less adventurous youngsters.

MILFORD HAVEN
Priory Inn

Tel. (06462) 5231
*Lower Priory (one mile north of
town centre)*
Open 11–11

✖ lunchtime and evening

🍺 **Draught Bass; Felinfoel
Double Dragon**

Steeped in history, the inn is a protected monument with a low bar, reminiscent of an old priory cellar. The small family room has some very interesting historical features, but it is used as a restaurant in the evening, so visit during the day if you wish to take advantage of this facility. Outside there are extensive grounds, with a stream running nearby, a play area for children and a bowling green. The menu represents excellent value for money and includes seasonal specials; a children's menu and vegetarian dishes are also available.

The Denant Mill Waterwheel

MILTON
Milton Brewery Inn

Tel. (0646) 651202
Off A477 in village
Open 11–11

🍽 lunchtime and evening

🍺 **Draught Bass; Welsh Brewers BB**

No longer a brewery, but an extremely attractive creeper-clad inn, this pub claims to be the most photographed in Pembrokeshire. Inside it oozes character too, with stone walls, beamed ceilings and log fires. Only the family room is not so "old world", but benefits from being lighter and airy. It is pleasantly furnished and can seat 32 adults and children (highchairs are provided). No amusements are provided in the pub, but the family room leads directly on to the garden which is next to the village playground with all the usual equipment, as well as plenty of space for ball games. The children's menu offers standard "kiddifodder", but in ample amounts; small portions of adult meals can also be ordered. Babies can be dealt with in the ladies' toilet. The village stands in the Pembrokeshire National Park where two very popular family attractions are Folly Farm, a working dairy farm and the Oakwood Adventure and Leisure Park.

NEWCASTLE EMLYN
Bunch of Grapes

Tel. (0239) 71185
Bridge Street
Open 11.20–11

@

🍴

✗ lunchtime

🍷

🍺 **Courage Best Bitter, Directors;
guest beer**

The licensees were still in the process of installing family facilities at this pub as we went to press – they should be finished by now, but it would be wise to check before making a special trip. It is a sixteenth-century pub of stone walls and oak beams, which has now been opened out into a single bar area, with pine floors and furniture. Reasonably priced lunches are served (12.30–2.30) and a children's menu is offered.

TALYBONT
White Lion

Tel. (097086) 245
On village green (A487)
*Open 11–11 (11–3; 5.30–11
winter); closed Sunday*

🍴

✗ lunchtime and evening

🛏

🍺 **Banks's Mild, Bitter**

Although the White Lion does not have a family room as such, it is included because it does allow children into the pool room and dining room and the overnight accommodation includes cots. The other reason it is listed is because it lies just three miles from the long, sandy beach at Borth, so the beer garden would make a change from sandy sandwiches for lunch on a fine summer's day. The usual children's menu is provided and there are facilities for feeding and changing babies. Other local attractions are the narrow gauge railway and eighteen-hole golf course.

WOLF'S CASTLE
Wolf Inn

Tel. (0437 87) 662
*On A40, Havorfordwest-
Fishguard road*
Open 11–11

@

🍴

✗

🛏

🍺 **Draught Bass; Charrington
IPA; Felinfoel Double Dragon**

Another pub where children's facilities are limited, but is worth including as they are at least welcome and catered for on the food menu. Here too, cots are available for overnight stays. It is a sixteenth-century building of considerable charm, with easy access to the Pembrokeshire coast. A separate family room is available for meals (highchairs are provided) and you can eat at any time. With the all day opening, this gives the oppportunity to have a late lunch, which many pubs do not offer. The children's menu costs £1.95

GLAMORGAN

CARDIFF
Radyr Arms

Tel. (0222) 843185
Station Road (off B4262), Radyr
(S. Glam.)
Open 12–2.30 (3.30 Sat); 5.30–11

◉

⌧

✕ lunchtime and evening (not
   Sun)

🍺 **Brain Dark, Bitter, SA**

A former mansion, the Radyr Arms is now a large, wood-panelled lounge bar and bistro, useful for visitors to the capital, but a little away from the centre. Families are welcome in the comfortably furnished conservatory area adjoining the lounge. This gives a good view of the safe, enclosed garden where there is a play area for children. The Garth Bistro is very popular and aims to cater for all ages and tastes – children's included – at a reasonable price.

Ty Mawr Arms

Tel. (0222) 754456
Graig Road, Lisvane
Open 12–3; 6–11

⌧

✕ lunchtime and evening

🍺 **range varies**

Sympathetically restored after a fire all but destroyed the bar, the Ty Mawr Arms was a recent winner of the local CAMRA branch's Pub of the Year award. Real ale fans are pleased to be able to try different brews on a regular basis, up to six are available here at any one time. The pub has limited amenities for families, but is popular on Sunday lunchtimes when children's videos are shown in the function room. The restaurant also caters for them with a children's menu or small portions and highchairs. The garden has a play area and domestic animals which keep youngsters amused, but keep your sandwiches away from the peacocks!

EAST ABERTHAW
Blue Anchor

Tel. (0446) 750329
Off B4265 (S. Glam.)
Open 11–11 (children until 8 pm)

◉

⌧

✕ 12–2 (not Sun)

🍺 **Brain Dark, SA; Buckley Best
   Bitter; Flowers IPA; Marston
   Pedigree; Theakston Old
   Peculier; Wadworth 6X**

This fourteenth-century thatched inn is reputed to have been a smugglers' haunt and has a long history connected with wrecking and piracy. The building has not changed much over the years, although hopefully the customers have less evil intentions. Six, low-ceilinged interconnecting rooms are set around the central bar. One of these, which seats around 45 people is nominally the family room, although children are allowed in any of the areas without a bar (until 8 pm). There is a play area in the garden for supervised children. Children are catered for on the lunchtime menu. Being right on the coast, the pub is often very busy; it is also handy for Cardiff airport.

KENFIG
Prince of Wales

Tel. (0656) 740356
Ton Kenfig, off B4283 (Mid Glam.)
Open 11.30–4; 6–11

◎

🕮

🍺 **Draught Bass; Eldridge Pope Royal Oak; Felinfoel Double Dragon; Marston Pedigree; Robinson Old Tom; Wadworth 6X**

Local history is worth delving into here, if you have the time as this old pub is linked with historic Kenfig, supposedly buried under the sand dunes. Natural historians will find much of interest too as there is a nature reserve opposite the pub. There is a large main bar with exposed stone walls and two smaller rooms, one of which is used by families. No meals are served, but bar snacks are available. The safe garden has a play area.

Fox and Hounds, Llancarfan

LLANCARFAN
Fox & Hounds

Tel. (04468) 297
Off A48 from Cardiff (S. Glam.)
Open 11–3.30; 6.30–11 (all day Sat)

◎

🕏

✖ lunchtime and evening

🍺 **Brain Dark, Bitter; Felinfoel Double Dragon; Wadworth 6X; guest beer**

Llancarfan is one of the prettiest villages in the Vale of Glamorgan and this sixteenth-century inn is one of its main attractions. There are plenty of other local tourist spots including St Fagan's Welsh Folk Museum, Dyffryn Gardens, Barry Island beach and pleasure park and Cardiff Castle. The family room, seating 25 leads off the bar, but also has its own entrance. Children's meals are available, and on Sunday, roast beef is something of a speciality here; a child's portion costs £1.50. The pub's garden leads down to the river, well more of a stream really, but children do need some supervision. Unfortunately, no playthings are supplied, but this still is a useful halt if you are touring the area.

LLANGYNWYD
Old House (Yr Hen Dy)

Tel. (0656) 733310
Off A4003 (Mid Glam.)
Open 11–11

◎

🕏

✖ lunchtime and evening

🍺 **Flowers IPA, Original**

This picturesque thatched pub is one of the oldest in Wales and is full of atmosphere. It is set in a small village where the church is even more ancient, dating back to the sixth century. Families are welcome in the pub's recently completed extension. A good selection of reasonably priced food is served daily – try the gammon. There is also a children's menu. The safe garden has a play area with swings, climbing ropes, slides and springy animals.

MWYNDY
Barn

Tel. (0443) 222333
Off A4119, near Llantrisant (Mid Glam.)
Open 11–11

◎

🕏

✖ lunchtime and evening

🍺 **Felinfoel Double Dragon; Marston Pedigree; Wadworth 6X; Welsh Brewers HB; guest beer**

As its name suggests, this is in fact a barn, converted into a two-bar pub, set in an acre of ground, surrounded by woodland and opposite a lake. It has been nicely done out, with exposed beams, stone walls and much rural bric-a-brac. The upstairs restaurant is open in the evenings; at lunchtime bar meals are served. A children's menu and highchairs are provided. There is a small family room at the rear of the building which leads on to the patio and beer garden which is enclosed and safe for youngsters. Parents need to come equipped, however, as no playthings are provided. It is a shame, that when care has been taken to make the rest of the pub so nice, that the family room is so dull.

NEWTON
Globe Inn

Tel. (0656 71) 3535
Off A4106, Bridgend to Porthcawl road (Mid Glam.)
Open 11.30–11 (11.30–3.30; 5.30–11 winter)

🛇

✖ lunchtime and evening

🍺 **Draught Bass; Welsh Brewers HB (summer)**

Situated at the edge of the seaside resort of Porthcawl, the Globe has a very seasonal trade: full to bursting in the summer, but quiet in autumn and winter. Porthcawl offers a choice of beaches, funfair and other distractions; also in the vicinity are Margam Country Park, Afan Argoed Country Park and Miners Museum. This is a welcoming pub, where families are particularly taken care of. The large family room has pool table, darts, two ride machines and space invader games. There is a children's bar serving sweets, drinks, snacks and basket meals. This room opens on to the patio (bench tables) and car park, but a separate beer garden is enclosed by a wooden fence to provide a safe, well-equipped area for children to play in.

PONTLLIW
Glamorgan Arms

Tel. (0792) 882409
Bryntirion Road, near M4 Jct 47 (W. Glam.)
Open 11.30–4; 6–11

🛇

✖

🛡

🍺 **Ruddles County, Best Bitter; Webster's Yorkshire Bitter**

I could not put my hand on my heart and describe this place as a pub, but it does sell real ale and it is a children's play paradise, so that fulfills two of the criteria necessary for entry in this guide. Originally a farmhouse, it now consists of two function rooms, a lounge bar and restaurant, aimed heavily at the coach trip/ tourist market. Outside is a vast play park with over 30 rides, slides, roundabouts, swingboats, and tractors. It is illuminated during the evenings so it can be used from 11 until 11 (although bars keep to the hours above). A shop selling junk food, an outdoor music system and amusement machines complete the picture. Four sets of toilets have been installed which include facilities for the disabled and for nursing mothers. There is wheelchair access to all parts of the complex – no, I can't bring myself to call it a pub.

GWENT

BLACKROCK
Rock & Fountain Inn

Tel. (0873) 830393
Old Black Rock Road, Clydach (just off A465)
Open 12–4 ; 7–11

✗ lunchtime and evening

🍺 **Ruddles Best Bitter, County ; Webster's Yorkshire Bitter ; guest beer**

Recently refurbished as an open-plan pub, the Rock and Fountain is situated just inside the Brecon Beacons National Park in the Clydach Gorge. This area is famous for its eighteenth-century iron work, while the history of the local mining industry can also be discovered at the Big Pit Mining Museum. Another local attraction is the Brecon Canal. The pub has a separate bistro, where children are able to eat (highchairs and junior menu provided). Families are also welcome in the small Welsh parlour. No play equipment is provided however, and outdoors there is only a patio, no garden. Facilities for dealing with babies' needs can be made available on request. A different guest beer is offered every week.

LLANTILIO CROSSENNY
Hostry Inn

Tel. (060 085) 278
On B4233, Monmouth-Abergavenny road
Open 11–3 ; 6.30–11

✗ lunchtime and evening

🍺 **Smiles Best Bitter, Exhibition ; occasional guest beer**

The beer here should bring a smile to the face of enthusiasts as it is unusual to find these brews regularly on tap in Wales. But this is a free house, so not obliged to take the national brands. The Hostry is an unspoilt, fifteenth-century village pub, set right by Offa's Dyke footpath. It is popular with walkers and the accommodation includes a bunkhouse which sleeps eight at a reasonable rate (bring your own sleeping bag). The food is good and vegetarians are catered for. There is a quiet lounge, public bar and separate family room; long alley skittles are played and can keep children amused for quite some time, in fine weather they can also play out in the large, enclosed garden.

PANTYGASSEG
Mountain View

Tel. (04955) 57763
Two miles from Pontypool, off
A4043 (OS 255001)
Open 12–11 (may close Mon–Fri
lunchtime in winter)

ⓒ

⑧

✗ (until 10pm)

🍺 **Hall & Woodhouse Badger Best Bitter; Samuel Smith OBB; Wadworth 6X; regular guest beer**

Families who make the effort to find this remote village pub will be amply rewarded, both with the fine mountain views and the excellent provision made for children. This is another free house, with a good choice of ales and food always available. A restaurant is due to be completed in Spring 1990. Children's portions or their own menu are offered. The family room has video games and junior fruit machines, and a children's toilet. There is a mini-zoo in a delightful enclosed area which is home to guinea pigs, rabbits and even snakes, as well as a well-stocked aviary. An open area outside has swings, a slide and climbing frame.

Hostry Inn

ST. BRIDES WENTLOOGE
Church House Inn

Tel. (0633) 680807
On B4239
Open 11–3; 6–11

@

🏠

✗ lunchtime and evening (not winter Sun)

🍺 **Brain Dark, Bitter, SA**

This is an old country pub in a low-lying area close to the Severn estuary. The family room, housed in a modern extension, offers a selection of toys and a tuck bar. Small portions of the adult dishes and a children's menu are available at both sessions. More play equipment in the form of a slide and swings are provided out in the large, enclosed garden.

SHIRENEWTON
Carpenters Arms

Tel. (02917) 231
On B4235, Usk to Chepstow road
Open 11–3; 6–11

@

✗ lunchtime and evening

🍺 **Archers ASB; Courage Best Bitter; Hook Norton Best Bitter; Marston Pedigree; Theakston Old Peculier; Wadworth 6X**

Set on the outskirts of the village, this traditional, old country inn has remained largely unspoilt. It has several small rooms, one of which is set aside for families to use, although no particular games or amusements are provided. The food is good and the large range of ales is supplemented even further by regular guest beers. The pub is convenient for anglers on the rivers Usk and Wye.

GWYNEDD

ABERGWYNGREGYN
Aber Country Inn

Tel. (0248) 680664
Station Road (off A55 towards sea)
Open 11.30–3; 6–11

@

🏠

✗ lunchtime and evening

🎭

🍺 **Thomas Greenall's Original Bitter**

The weekly entertainment is popular at this hotel where they say people come from miles around to hear the local choir and organist on a Saturday night. If choral singing is not your scene, then this pub has plenty of other amenities; there is a games room, Poachers Den restaurant and a large children's room with toys and videos to watch. Bar meals and snacks are available as an alternative to the restaurant; highchairs and a children's menu as well as baby feeding/changing facilities are provided. An enclosed garden is safe for children to stretch their legs in. The pub is well situated for visitors to the Snowdonia National Park and the seaside resorts on the north-west coast.

CHWILOG
Madryn Arms

Tel. (0766) 810250
On main Porthmadog to Nevin Road
Open 12–3; 5.30–11 (11–11 Sat)

☺

🍴

✕ lunchtime and evening

🍺 **Burtonwood Mild, Bitter**

Holidaymakers going AWOL from the Butlins camp a mile away at Pwllheli will find this a convenient watering hole. It is the only pub in a quiet country village, a quarter of a mile from the popular beauty spot of Ln Goed, and enjoys a good local trade, with an influx of tourists during the holiday season. The family room is outside the main pub and has video games, fruit machines and a juke box. It may not be as convenient for parents as an integral room, but I guess the noise level could get quite high if all the machines are in action at once, so at least the other customers are not disturbed. Food is served at both sessions and all day Saturday; the children's menu comprises the usual beefburgers and fishfingers, but also steak and kidney pie for the more adventurous! The pub itself is fairly basic, but it has a good garden with benches and a super children's playground with big wooden equipment.

DEGANWY
Farmers Arms

Tel. (0492) 83197
Towyn Hill (just off the Conwy road)
Open 11–11

☺

🍴

✕ lunchtime and evening

🍺 **Ansells Mild, Bitter, Ind Coope Burton Ale, Tetley Bitter**

Situated in a residential area, this busy pub is popular with both locals and visitors; office-workers make a bee-line there too for bar lunches, which are very good value (children's portions can be ordered). There is an attractive array of old farm implements in the spacious bar. The cheerful family lounge is roomy too, but it appears it is the garden which appeals to youngsters, as a reader wrote in response to our first edition: "I must say how much we enjoyed this pub. They only have a small yard at the back, but it is a children's paradise. I loved the giant banana balloons and the fruit decorating the swings and slide.... the staff were wonderful, nothing was too much trouble. We couldn't persuade the five year-old to go anywhere else." That must be the ultimate seal of approval.

FAIRBOURNE
Fairbourne
Hotel

Tel. (0341) 250203
Open 11–3; 6–11

@

🏠

✖ lunchtime and evening

🛏

🍺 McEwan 70/-; Younger IPA

A seaside hotel situated on the road between Dolgellau and Tywyn, the Fairbourne is ideal for lovers of all outdoor pursuits with the coastal resorts as well as fishing, pony trekking and golf course close at hand. Cots are available for families staying at the hotel. For casual visitors there is a play room with a pool table and other games, and a large garden with bowls green. Children's meals cost around £1.75, adults can expect to pay around £3.45.

GLYNGARTH
Gazelle

Tel. (0248) 713364
On the A545
Open 11–11 (may close afternoons if quiet)

@

🏠

✖ lunchtime and evening

🛏

🍺 Robinson Best Bitter, Old Tom (winter)

Situated on the shores of the Menai Strait, the Gazelle benefits from some breathtaking views of Snowdon and, in the foreground, the less natural, but no less awe-inspiring Menai Bridge. A good place to stay awhile (particularly in August, during the Straits Regatta), the pub also offers good facilities for passing tourists. Children are welcome in any of the bar-less rooms which are all equally attractive and comfortable, as well as the restaurant, where they are catered for on the extensive menu. The garden, of course, is also open to families.

LLANBEDROG
Glyn-y-Weddw
Arms

Tel. (0758) 740212
Open 11–11 (11–3; 6–11 winter)

@

🏠

✖

🍺 Robinson Best Mild, Best Bitter

This old-fashioned family pub lies just 400 yards from the beach, on the main road between Pwllheli and Abersoch. The beach is popular with families as it is safe for children and is often used for canoeing and boating. Food is served at the pub at any time during opening hours; the children's menu costs around £1.50. The family room has no amusements for youngsters, but there is some play equipment in the safe garden outside.

Ship Inn

Tel. (0758) 740270
*Open 11–11 (closed winter
afternoons)*

◎

⊗

✕ lunchtime and evening

🍺 **Burtonwood Dark Mild, Best
Bitter**

The Ship has recently been renovated and extended and the new play area is not due to be completed until August 1990, so it may be worth checking the facilities before you visit. Children are welcome in the family room at any time and a full range of suitable dishes is offered, including smaller portions of parent's meals. Highchairs and baby changing amenities are provided. Surrounded by countryside, with many good walks, the pub is half a mile from the beach. Also nearby is an art gallery housed in a Victorian mansion. The Ship has won awards for its floral displays, and although the garden is open, it is deemed safe for children.

LLANDUDNO
London Hotel

Tel. (0492) 76740
*131 Mostyn Street
Open 11.30–4 ; 7–11*

◎

✕ lunchtime and evening

🛏

🍺 **Burtonwood Mild, Bitter**

Sporting an unusual theme, for a North Walian pub, the London's inn sign shows Dick Whittington. The capital connection is continued inside this somewhat quirky pub, where there is an old red telephone box. I am sure it has great appeal for children who are welcome in the terrific family room at the back of the pub. In the evenings though, this room is used as a piano bar. Centrally situated and thus very popular, especially at lunchtime, the London is close to the pier and promenade as well as the shops on Mostyn Street itself.

MARIANGLAS,
ANGLESEY
Parciau Arms

Tel. (0248) 853766
*On B5110 Moelfre to Llangefni
road
Open 11–11*

◎

⊗

✕ all day

🍺 **Banks's Bitter ; Ind Coope
Burton Ale ; guest beer**

A cosy, welcoming pub with an "old world" atmosphere, the Parciau enjoys good views over Red Wharf Bay and beyond to Snowdonia. It is just half a mile to some fine beaches which are popular for sailing and water ski-ing. In summer, families tend to use the sheltered patio, while children enjoy the large, safe garden with its action tree, swing, slide and play tractor. A "Children's Kabin" has a kiosk selling soft drinks, sweets, crisps etc. All other food is ordered at the bar. Families with children can eat in the dining room before 8.30. There is a good selection of children's food: apart from the old favourites with chips and beans, they can also choose jacket potatoes with various fillings, or half portions of steak and kidney pie, shepherds pie, lasagne, small steaks and junior selection of vegetables and salads. It is not surprising that the pub merits an entry in CAMRA's "Good Pub Food" guide. The dining room opens for breakfast and also serves afternoon teas.

PWLLHELI
Penlan Fawr Inn

Tel. (0758) 612486
3 Penlan Street
Open 11–11 (closed Sun)

Ind Coope Burton Ale; Tetley Bitter

The oldest pub in Pwllheli, and indeed the oldest building in the town, the Penlan dates back to 1600. The family room is not that old. This is a rather unusual feature of an "indoor garden" built at the back of the pub, so that families can be accommodated in all weathers. Children are also allowed in the games room which has two pool tables and various video games. If hungry, there is a choice for youngsters from their own menu or portions of adult dishes. The pub also has the more usual type of beer garden outside which is large enough to hold a hundred or more people.

Ship Inn, Red Wharf Bay

RED WHARF BAY, ANGLESEY
Ship Inn

Tel. (0248) 852568
Off A5025, seven miles from Menai Bridge
Open 11–11 (12–3.30; 7–11 winter)

☺

🛏

✗ lunchtime and evening

🍺 Banks's Bitter; Sam Powell BB; Tetley Mild

Set right by the beach, this classic Welsh country pub is quite unspoilt and offers a cosy atmosphere with coal fires in both bars. The two main bars have a nautical theme. There is a separate games room with a pool table and darts, and the family room off the bar seats 36. The Ship has a good reputation for food; freshly prepared dishes might include game pie in season or smoked fillet of trout. A special menu is offered for youngsters. The garden has a play area.

POWYS

ARDDLEEN
(Arddlîn)
Horseshoe Inn

Tel. (093875) 318
On A458, midway between Welshpool and Oswestry
Open 12–3; 5.30–11 (11–11 Sat)

☺

🛏

✗ lunchtime and evening

🍺 Draught Bass; Marston Pedigree; Westons Cider

This well-restored old pub is set off the main road, on Offa's Dyke and the canal. Other local places of interest include a bird garden, leisure complex and a rare breeds farm. The family room, which adjoins the bar, can seat 40. For the summer months a further family room is available in an outbuilding, where games machines and a pool table are provided. There is also a large outdoor area with an adventure playground. A children's menu or small portions of adult meals can be ordered until an hour before closing time.

GLASBURY-ON-WYE
Harp Inn

Tel. (04974) 373
On B4350, just off A438
Open 11–3 (4 summer Sat); 6–11

🛏

✗ lunchtime and evening

🍺 Flowers Original, IPA; Robinson Best Bitter

According to the Post Office, this pub is in the county of Hereford and Worcster, although it is actually miles within the Welsh border. It is situated six miles from Hay-on-Wye, that now famous haunt of bibliophiles, on the bank of the river Wye. The Black Mountains nearby attract pony trekkers and other outdoor enthusiasts who are drawn to this former cider house because of its brilliant cooking. Families are very welcome but facilities are rather limited because of the lack of a suitable room. The games room has plenty of amusements, including chess, Connect Four, cards and dominoes, but it is best to go in summer when you can enjoy the fresh, well-prepared food (children's portions offered) out in the riverside garden.

LLANDRINDOD WELLS
Llanerch Inn

Tel. (0597) 2086
Waterloo Road (by station)
Open 11.30–2.30; 6–11

ⓒ
___
⑧
___
✗ lunchtime and evening
___
ⱨ
___
☺
___
🍺 **Draught Bass; Welsh Brewers HB; Robinson Best Bitter; guest beer**

Although Powys is somewhat lacking in family pubs, they do at least offer good food – this is the second that is also listed in CAMRA's "Good Pub Food" guide. The Llanerch is a sixteenth-century inn set in its own grounds. It has low beamed ceilings, a large stone hearth and many other original features. The family room has a pool table and outside terrace which leads on to the children's play area in the garden. Highchairs are provided for bar meals which are excellent, and include a children's menu if preferred. Baby changing/feeding facilities are also available. An annual ale tasting week is held at the pub at the end of August. Llandrindod Wells is, as its names implies, a spa town – the spa has been renovated in a rock pool and is just five minutes' walk from the pub.

LLANGADFAN
Cann Office Hotel

Tel. (0983) 88202
Adjacent to A458
Open hours vary according to season

ⓒ
___
⑧
___
✗
___
ⱨ
___
🍺 **Marston Burton Best Bitter; Pedigree (summer)**

Set deep in the heart of mid Wales, this pub has a very seasonal trade and caters for visitors who come to enjoy the fishing, walking, pony-trekking and other rural pursuits. Very sensibly, the pub has two rooms allocated to families, one for eating and one with amusements, including a pool table and video machine. The open garden is deemed safe for children. Meals are generally available, with a children's menu or smaller portions served for little ones.

PONT ROBERT
Royal Oak

Tel. (093 884) 474
Off A495, south of Meifod
Open 12–3; 5–11

◎

⊞

✗

⋈

🍺 **Marston Pedigree**

All your children's favourite super-heroes are to be found at the Royal Oak - on the menu! The list of eats, featuring such delights as the He-Man burger and Batwoman jumbo fish finger, is illustrated with puzzles, dot-to-dot pictures, mazes and so on to occupy the little ones while they wait for their food. Then of course they can take their efforts home with them when they leave. Families are welcome in the large front lounge and the overnight accommodation includes a cot and baby listening service. Facilities are also provided for nursing mothers. Above the pub is a very large grassy area with tyre swings and a climbing frame and lots of space for children to run around and play. This is an ideal base for an outdoor holiday; fishing is available by arrangement.

TALYBONT-ON-USK
Travellers' Rest

Tel. (0874) 87233
On B4558, off A40
Open 11–3; 7–11 (all day summer)

◎

⊞

✗

🍺 **range varies**

The garden at the Travellers' Rest backs on to the Monmouthshire and Brecon canal, so you can watch the waterways activity while you sup. This pub has a friendly atmosphere and children are made very welcome. The conservatory which enjoys lovely scenic views is used as a family room and highchairs and toys are available. The disabled WC also has baby changing facilities. The Travellers has two bars and a separate restaurant.

Traveller's Rest

THE MAPS

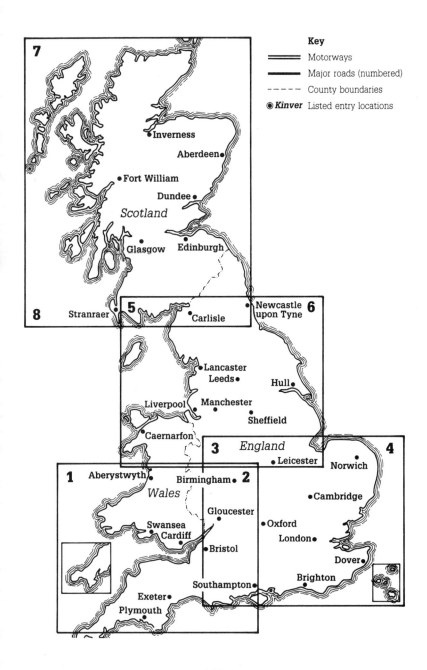

Key

═══ Motorways
▬▬▬ Major roads (numbered)
– – – – County boundaries
◉ *Kinver* Listed entry locations

7

Inverness
Aberdeen
Fort William
Dundee
Scotland
Glasgow Edinburgh

8 Stranraer 5 Carlisle Newcastle upon Tyne 6

Lancaster
Leeds
Hull
Liverpool Manchester
Sheffield
Caernarfon

3 *England* 4
Leicester Norwich

1 Aberystwyth Birmingham 2
Wales
Gloucester
Swansea Cambridge
Cardiff Oxford
Bristol London
Dover
Southampton Brighton
Exeter Plymouth

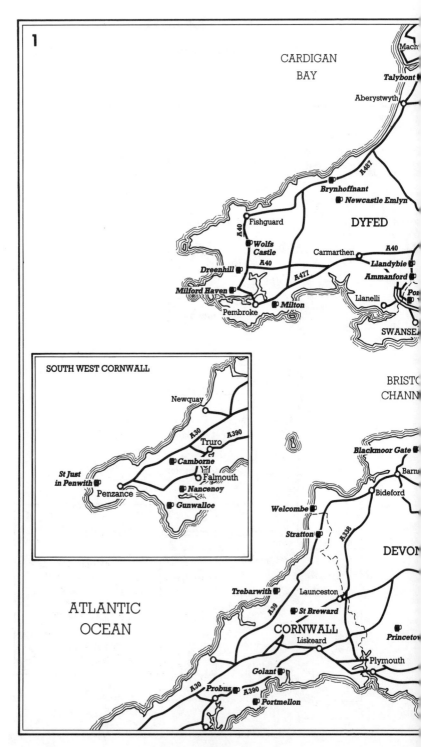

1

CARDIGAN
BAY

Mach

Talybont

Aberystwyth

Brynhoffnant

A487

Newcastle Emlyn

Fishguard

A40

DYFED

Wolfs Castle

Carmarthen

A40

Llandybie

A40

Dreenhill

A477

Ammanford

Milford Haven

Milton

Llanelli

Por

Pembroke

SWANSE

SOUTH WEST CORNWALL

BRISTO
CHANN

Newquay

A30

A390

Truro

Blackmoor Gate

Camborne

Barn

St Just in Penwith

Falmouth

Bideford

Penzance

Nancenoy

Welcombe

Gunwalloe

A338

Stratton

DEVON

ATLANTIC
OCEAN

Trebarwith

Launceston

A39

St Breward

CORNWALL

Princeto

Liskeard

Plymouth

Golant

A30

Probus

A390

Portmellon

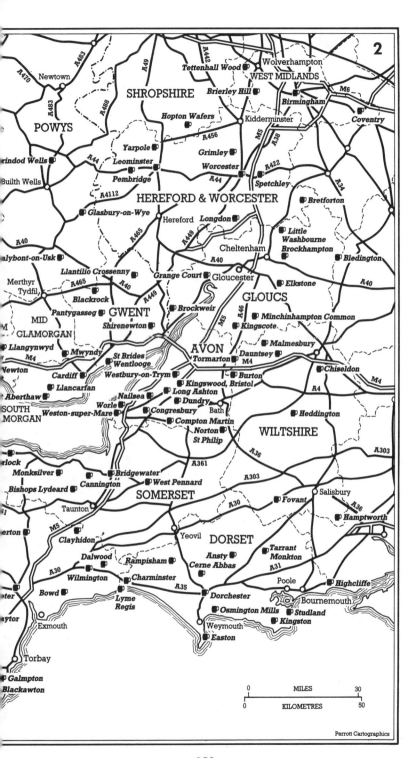

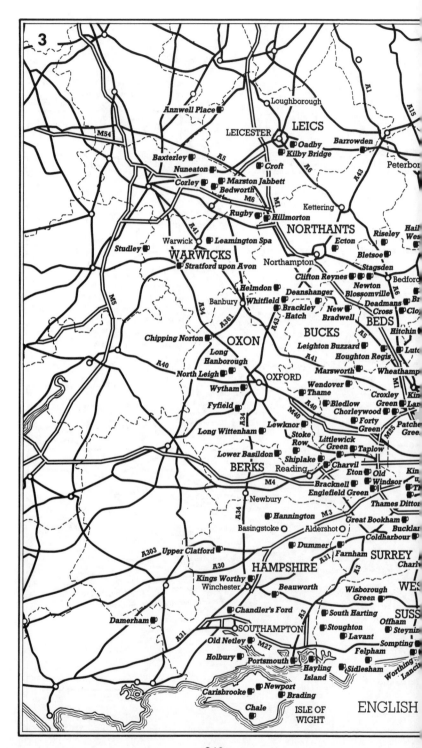

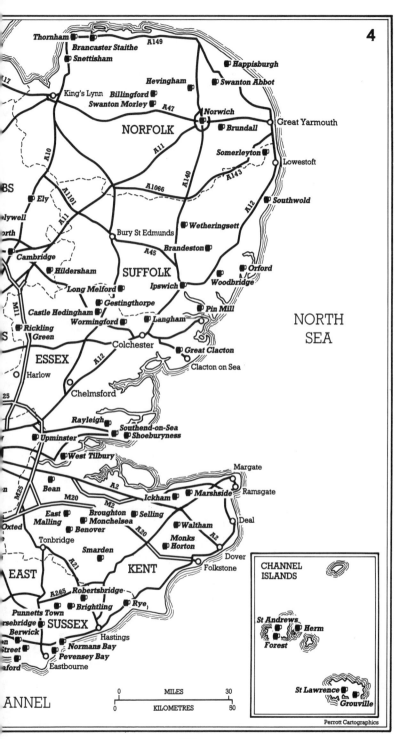

Thornham
Brancaster Staithe
Snettisham
Happisburgh
Hevingham
Swanton Abbot
King's Lynn
Billingford
Swanton Morley
A47
Norwich
NORFOLK
Brundall
Great Yarmouth
A11
A140
Somerleyton
Lowestoft
A10
A1066
A143
A12
A101
Ely
A11
Southwold
A11
Bury St Edmunds
Wetheringsett
Cambridge
A45
Brandeston
Hildersham
SUFFOLK
Orford
Long Melford
Ipswich
Woodbridge
Gestingthorpe
Castle Hedingham
Pin Mill
Wormingford
Langham
Rickling
Green
Colchester
NORTH
SEA
ESSEX
A12
Great Clacton
Harlow
Clacton on Sea
Chelmsford
Rayleigh
Southend-on-Sea
Upminster
Shoeburyness
West Tilbury
Margate
Bean
A2
Ramsgate
M20
Ickham
Marshside
M25
M2
East
Broughton
Selling
Deal
Malling
Monchelsea
Oxted
Benover
A20
Waltham
A2
Tonbridge
Monks
Horton
Smarden
KENT
Dover
EAST
A21
Folkstone
A265
Robertsbridge
Punnetts Town
Brightling
Rye
rsebridge
SUSSEX
Berwick
Hastings
treet
Normans Bay
aford
Pevensey Bay
Eastbourne

CHANNEL
ISLANDS

St Andrews
Herm
Forest

St Lawrence
Grouville

MILES   30
0
KILOMETRES   50
0

ANNEL

Perrott Cartographics

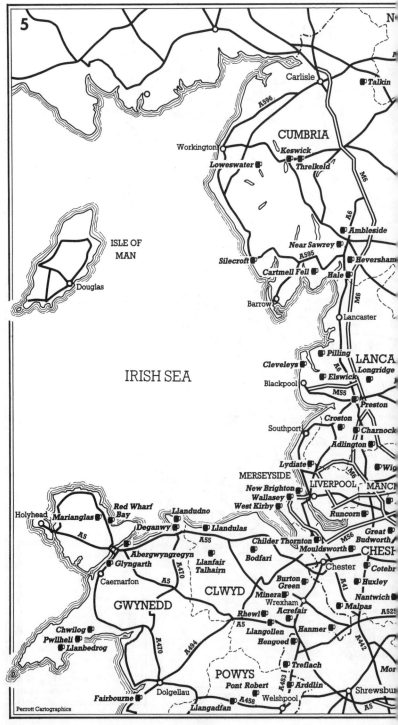

N

Carlisle

Talkin

A596

CUMBRIA

Workington

Keswick

Loweswater

Threlkeld

M6

A6

Ambleside

Near Sawrey

ISLE OF
MAN

Silecroft

A595

Heversham

Cartmell Fell

Hale

Douglas

M6

Barrow

Lancaster

IRISH SEA

Pilling

LANCA

Cleveleys

Longridge

A6

Blackpool

Elswick

M55

Preston

Croston

Southport

Charnock

Adlington

Lydiate

Wig

MERSEYSIDE

M6

New Brighton

LIVERPOOL

MANC

Holyhead

Marianglas

Red Wharf
Bay

Llandudno

Wallasey

West Kirby

Runcorn

Great
Budworth

Deganwy

Llandulas

A55

Childer Thornton

M56

Abergwyngregyn

Mouldsworth

CHES

Glyngarth

Llanfair
Talhairn

Bodfari

Chester

Cotebr

A5

A470

Caernarfon

A5

Burton
Green

Huxley

A41

Minera

Nantwich

GWYNEDD

CLWYD

Wrexham

Malpas

Chwilog

Rhewl

Acrefair

A525

Pwllheli

A5

A442

Llanbedrog

Llangollen

Hanmer

A470

A494

Hengoed

Treflach

POWYS

A483

Arddlin

Mor

Fairbourne

Dolgellau

Pont Robert

Shrewsbu

A458

Welshpool

A5

Llangadfan

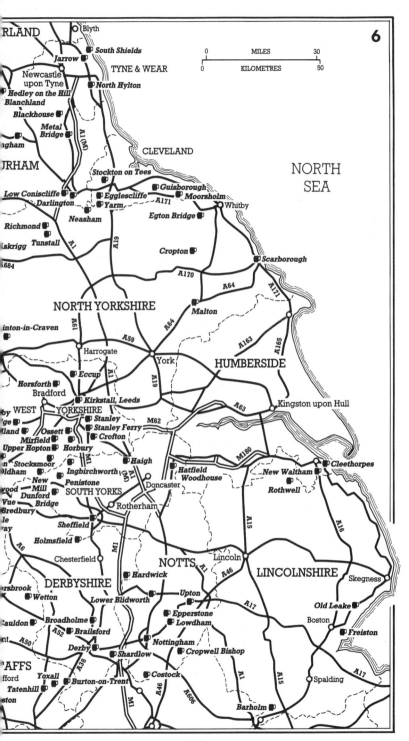

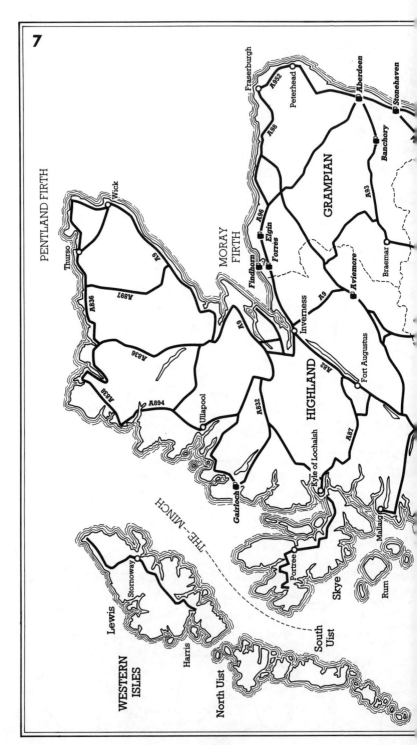

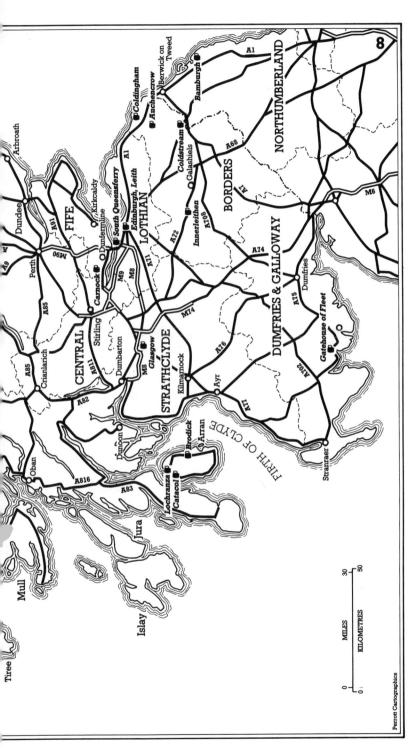

Perrot Cartographics

ALMA BOOKS

Alma Books Ltd is the publishing company set up by CAMRA (the Campaign for Real Ale) to produce titles of interest to pub-lovers, beer-drinkers, tourists and travellers.

For more information about Alma Books and to obtain the books listed below (which are also available at all good bookshops), write to Alma Books Ltd., 34 Alma Road, St Albans, Herts. AL1 3BW.

Available now:

The Best Pubs in Yorkshire	**£4.95**
The Best Pubs in East Anglia	**£4.95**
The Best Pubs in Lakeland	**£3.95**
The Best Pubs in North Wales	**£4.95**
The Best Pubs in London	**£4.95**
The Best Pubs in Devon and Cornwall	**£4.95**

A series of regional guides offering the reader detailed descriptions of the finest pubs in the area.

Good Pub Food	**£5.95**

Over four hundred pubs around the country where good food is as much a priority as good beer and you may find some of the best examples of traditional British cooking, using the finest local produce.

Forthcoming attractions:
A Bedside Book of Beer
The Great British Pub

Join CAMRA

If you like good beer and good pubs you could be helping in the fight to preserve, protect and promote them. CAMRA was set up in the early seventies to fight against the mass description of a part of Britain's heritage.

The giant brewers are still pushing through takeovers, mergers and closures of their smaller regional rivals. They are still reducing the availability and diluting the quality of a magnificent and uniquely British product - real ale. They are still trying to impose national brands of beer and lager on their customers whether they like it or not, and they are still closing down town and village local pubs or converting them into grotesque 'theme' pubs.

CAMRA wants to see genuine free competition in the brewing industry, fair prices, civilised licensing laws, and, above all, a top quality product brewed by local breweries in accordance with local tastes, and served in pubs that maintain the best features of a tradition that goes back centuries.

If you are in sympathy with these aims you could be expressing that sympathy in a positive way, by joining CAMRA. We have well over 20,000 members and that's not including our three fully paid-up dogs and two cats! Yet we're pitting ourselves against the power and financial muscle of a multi-million pound, multi-national industry. We desperately need active campaigning members, but we are also grateful for the support of people whose only involvement may be to pay their membership subscription once a year. It's only £9, but each additional subscription helps us to campaign that bit more effectively across the whole spectrum of pub issues on behalf of *all* pub-users.

If you leave it to others, you may wake up one day to find *your* local pub shut, *your* local brewery closed down, *your* favourite beer no longer being brewed. So join CAMRA and help us to prove that the most important person in the brewing industry isn't the megalomaniac chairman of some brewing giant, but that most vital, and under-valued person - the pub customer.

Full membership £9 Joint husband/wife membership £9 Life membership £90 I/We wish to become members of CAMRA Ltd. I/We agree to abide by the memorandum and articles of association of the company. I/We enclose a cheque/p.o. for £9/£90.

Name(s) _____

_____

Address _____

_____

_____

_____

Signature(s) _____

_____

CORRECTIONS AND AMENDMENTS

Every year sees hundreds pubs change hands. A new licensee can bring improvements or disaster to even the finest establishment. While most details were checked shortly before going to press, errors will inevitably occur and changes come thick and fast.

If you come upon listed pubs which have been ruined or if you find an undiscovered gem on your travels, let me know and I will investigate for the next edition.

Complete the form below or write to: Jill Adam, Alma Books, 34 Alma Road, St. Albans, Hertfordshire, AL1 3BW.

County _____

Town or village _____

Name of pub _____

Address _____

Location (A or B road) _____

Tel no. _____ Name of licensee _____

Description of pub (including bars, food, family room and any special facilities)

_____

_____

_____

_____

_____

Beers _____

_____

Food _____

_____

_____

Reasons for recommendation for inclusion in/deletion from the guide

_____

_____

_____

_____

Your name and address _____

_____

_____

Postcode _____

County _____

Town or village _____

Name of pub _____

Address _____

Location (A or B road)_____

Tel no. _____ Name of licensee _____

Description of pub (including bars, food, family room and any special facilities)

_____

_____

_____

_____

_____

Beers _____

_____

Food _____

_____

Reasons for recommendation for inclusion in/deletion from the guide

_____

_____

_____

_____

Your name and address_____

_____

_____

Postcode_____

County _____

Town or village _____

Name of pub _____

Address _____

Location (A or B road)_____

Tel no. _____ Name of licensee _____

Description of pub (including bars, food, family room and any special facilities)

_____

_____
_____
_____
_____

Beers _____

_____
Food _____

_____

Reasons for recommendation for inclusion in/deletion from the guide

_____

_____
_____
_____

Your name and address_____

_____
_____
Postcode _____

County _____

Town or village _____

Name of pub _____

Address _____

Location (A or B road) _____

Tel no. _____ Name of licensee _____

Description of pub (including bars, food, family room and any special facilities)

_____

_____

_____

_____

_____

Beers _____

_____

Food _____

_____

Reasons for recommendation for inclusion in/deletion from the guide

_____

_____

_____

_____

Your name and address _____

_____

_____

Postcode _____